ONE MAN'S MOUNTAINS

Born in 1932, Tom Patey grew up in Ellon, just north of Aberdeen. He was educated at Ellon Academy and Robert Gordon's College, going on to become a medical student at Aberdeen University. His long series of epic first ascents commenced when Patey was only eighteen (on Lochnagar, above Balmoral Castle) and he quickly became the mainspring of the Aberdeen climbing world of the 1950s. He achieved outstanding successes in the Scottish hills, the Alps and the Himalayas and was well known to non-climbers for his appearances in the television climbing spectaculars of the 1960s, notably on the Old Man of Hoy. A regular contributor to a number of climbing journals, Tom Patey was a G.P. in Ullapool at the time of his death in 1970.

ONE MAN'S MOUNTAINS

Essays and Verses

TOM PATEY

With an Introduction by
CHRIS BONINGTON

THE
MOUNTAINEERS

 Published by
The Mountaineers
1001 SW Klickitat Way, Suite 201
Seattle, WA 98134

First published in Great Britain 1971
by Victor Gollancz Ltd

This edition first published in Great Britain in 1997 by
Canongate Books Ltd, 14 High Street, Edinburgh EH1 1TE

ACKNOWLEDGEMENTS

I would like to thank the following for kind assistance
in the illustration of this book: Aandalsnes Foto, Mike
Banks, John Cleare, John Hartog, Hamish MacInnes, J.
R. Marshall and Douglas Scott; and the editors of the
following journals for assistance in the preperation of the
text: *The Alpine Journal*, *The Climbers' Club Journal*,
The Etchachan Club Journal, *Mountain*, *The Scottish
Mountaineering Club Journal* and the *Scots Magazine*.
E. P.

Library of Congress Cataloging-in-Publication Data
A catalog record for this book is available at the Library of Congress
ISBN 0-89886-542-5 (North America)

Printed in Finland by Werner Söderström Oy

For Tom

PUBLISHER'S NOTE

At the time of Tom Patey's death, he had already signified his intention of preparing his writings for publication. Had he lived, he would doubtless have linked and edited the pieces that appear in this book, and would have pruned from them the very few passages that must inevitably (in a collection of this nature) repeat information already given. Under the circumstances, they have been printed unedited, as they originally appeared.

The two pieces "The Art of Climbing Down Gracefully" and "The Shape of Things to Come" were originally written to be published in *Mountain*; publication in that journal was, however, held over until the autumn of 1971.

CONTENTS

PART IV   VERSE

LIST OF ILLUSTRATIONS

INTRODUCTION

GOING CLIMBING with Tom Patey was a delight. A day in the hills became a magical mystery tour full of surprises. It could start with a trip to a secret crag which he had recorded in his big black book, the repository of all his potential new routes. We'd set out late – he was never an early riser – get to the foot of the crag and start climbing unroped. He'd be in front, I'd have the rope, and it all too often became a race in which I was trying to catch him, to persuade him to put on the rope before we reached the top of the climb. There were drives across Scotland to attend a ceilidh, or songs by the camp fire accompanied by his squeeze box. He was the most unpredictable, sheer-fun-to-be-with, richest character I have ever come across in my climbing career and yet at the same time there was a very real depth to him, both in terms of the prolific number of new routes he achieved, and the range and quality of his writing. He had that rare gift of being able to write satire without being hurtful to the butt of his humour. His articles for *Mountain Magazine* and his verse, sung to the accompaniment of his accordion, were unique.

He was born in 1932 and went to school at Gordon's College, Aberdeen. From a young age he was taken walking in the Scottish hills by his father but his inspiration to climb came, as to so many other of his generation including myself, from W. H. Murray's *Mountaineering in Scotland*. He went to Aberdeen University to study medicine and served his climbing apprenticeship in the Cairngorms, rapidly moving on from repeating the comparatively few routes in existence at that time, to pioneering new ones. He had a superb eye for a line and rapidly developed a bold technique. He was a superb all-round mountaineer, with a solo climbing standard at just about the same level as when leading. He was not overly concerned about protection or the technicalities of climbing and he put up some of his finest climbs before the development of the drop pick for ice tools or the array of camming devices used today.

His outdoor clothing, worn even in the wildest, windy conditions, consisted of a torn old sweater, a pair of worn knee breeches, some woollen mitts, a few slings around his neck, and neither a crash hat nor even a woolly hat, no matter how bad the weather. He seemed impervious to the cold, and anyway believed in keeping moving to stay warm.

His list of new routes are legion – certainly one of the most prolific of anyone in the story of British climbing. He was never interested in repeating routes and was always searching for something new. He was at the forefront of opening up the Cairngorms in the Fifties, at a time when hardly anything had been climbed. He made the first ascent of Zero Gully with Hamish MacInnes, the first traverse of Creag Meaghaidh, and the first continuous winter traverse of the Cuillins.

He went to the Himalaya at an early stage in his climbing career. Bill Murray had recommended him for Everest in 1953, but he was turned down as being too young. He joined Joe Brown, Ian McNaught Davis and John Hartog on the Muztagh Tower in the Karakoram in 1956 and then climbed Rakaposhi in 1958. He was a brilliant high altitude climber, but his work as General Practitioner in Ullapool and his enjoyment of climbing in the Highlands, with snatched trips to Norway and the Alps, fulfilled his appetite for adventure. In the next few years Tom made first ascents of nearly all the sea stacks around the coast of the Northern Highlands. In the Sixties he put up a series of new routes in the Chamonix region, picking good but subtle lines that others had overlooked, climbing mainly with Joe Brown.

I invited him to come with us in 1970, to the South Face of Annapurna, but he decided against it, partly because he was wary of a comparatively large, structured expedition and also because of the time commitment involved. He lost his life while we were away on the mountain, just a few days before

Ian Clough, a good mutual friend, was killed on our expedition. Tom died after making a first ascent on the Maidens, off Whitten Head on the Sutherland coast. He was abseiling down when somehow the gate of his karabiner opened and he fell to his death. He left a wife, Betty, and three children.

I had, with Tom, some of the best and most enjoyable climbing I have ever experienced, some of it recorded in this collection. 'Over the Sea to Skye' tells the story of a wonderful summer's holiday in 1960 when we climbed around fifteen new routes in as many days. Then there is 'Climbing the Old Man of Hoy', with Rusty Baillie playing the part of the ape-like technical climber and me as photojournalist for the Sunday Telegraph – which made me the butt of Tom's humour. He went on to inspire Chris Brasher, who was then a senior executive in the BBC, with the idea of televising the climb as a live broadcast – probably one of the most successful and memorable ever completed. But the piece that I enjoyed the most from this period was 'A Short Walk with Whillans'. It is funny, it captures Don's personality and is a delight to read.

We sorely miss all our friends whose lives were prematurely ended in the hills. There is always that sense of lost potential, the deprivation of shared enjoyment, but Tom's loss left a particularly painful void. He had crammed so much into his thirty-eight years and has left a fine memorial reflected in the contents of this book, but there is still the nagging question of how much else he was capable of, whether he would have embarked on a full-length book, of how his multi-faceted skills might have developed. I miss those shared adventures and days on the hills with Magical Mystery Tours that only he could create.

Chris Bonington
February, 1997

PART I

Scotland

PARALLEL GULLY "B", LOCHNAGAR

From The Scottish Mountaineering Club Journal, 1953

PRIOR TO 1951 all the principal gullies and buttresses in Loch-nagar's NE. Corrie had been climbed, several in the preceding few years. There remained, however, one major problem—the ascent of the 700-foot Parallel Gully "B". It had been inspected by parties on various occasions and yet, although it seemed as if there might be a route somewhere, very few determined attempts had been made.

The term "gully" is perhaps misleading. In its lower part a well-defined chimney, and above expanding into a shallow depression on an open face, it nevertheless follows one continuous fault throughout, separating the slender, tapering, Parallel Buttress on the left from the grosser flank of the Tough–Brown Ridge on the right. The climb may be roughly subdivided into three huge pitches separated by two grassy scoops. The lower scoop was crossed by Tough and Brown in 1895 in their early attempt on the ridge now bearing their name; but the upper one had never been reached, though apparently fairly easy of access from the normal Parallel Buttress route.

It will, therefore, be apparent that, by following the Tough–Brown Traverse, an attempt could be made on the more promising second pitch of the climb, avoiding the formidable 250-foot start. This was actually done a few weeks prior to our attempt by I. Brooker and A. Lyall, who succeeded in forcing their way up the top section by a route which they described as very severe.

This exploit immediately stimulated our interest in the gully, and several of us discussed the possibility of forcing the forbidding first pitch and thereby accomplishing a complete ascent of the gully as soon as conditions were favourable. The opportunity offered itself at a meet of the Aberdeen University Club on a brilliant Sunday in June 1952. Interest in the route was now so general that no fewer than eight assembled at the foot of the crags.

While the party debated over the dubious honour of the lead, Mike Taylor and I slipped off quietly and set to work on the lower rocks.

The first of the three great pitches forming the gully is probably about 250 feet in height, but its general contour gives an impression of greater height. Starting as a 50-foot slimy crack, holdless and nearly vertical, it leans back for a short distance at a more moderate angle, then soars up straight in a narrow 120-foot chimney, cleaving a succession of smooth, incredibly steep slabs.

Unroped, we climbed speedily up the good rocks on the left side of the crack, gaining a good stance 50 feet up. This was an excellent site from which to discharge some well-aimed divots on our companions below, just to advise them that the climb was under way.

Here the first difficulty immediately confronted us; we had reached the foot of a vertical wall, and further progress was only possible to the right, where a smooth, sloping ledge traversed back to the top of the initial crack. At the extreme end it would obviously be necessary to achieve a long stride over the top of the crack to a good ledge on the far side.

A few minutes' indecision at the start allowed the other six to catch us up. Eventually, more to relieve the congestion than from eagerness to start, I was edged out on to the traverse under the disturbing scrutiny of a large and expectant audience. One humorist even did his best to improve the leader's morale with a running commentary. The tiny rounded wrinkles on the slab afforded small purchase for tricounis, and, although the problem was merely one of balance, the handholds were few and not reassuring. Eventually I found myself poised on small holds over the steep gap which terminated the ledge. In rubbers this pitch would have been much simplified, but we had agreed to retain nails as long as possible. The final stride over the gulf was only the work of an instant, but very delicate, and I was glad to establish myself on a comfortable block and prepare to watch the discomfort of the others.

At this juncture, much to my chagrin, a cine-camera was produced on the platform, and Taylor came nonchalantly across, his every movement a conscious exhibition of style, and passed on to the steep rocks above me. Here he was lost to view for a considerable time, and I became so absorbed in Brooker's antics on the traverse that I had to be recalled to reality by an imperious tug on the rope from above, signalling me to come on.

At first there was no sign of my companion, until eventually the rope led me towards a small dark hole in the rock in which he could be observed, crouched in ill-concealed discomfort. The 6 feet immediately below the cave were very dirty and wet, even under the dry conditions at the time, and I was thankful for a slight tension on the rope above. We had now almost attained the foot of the long chimney, but the way was barred by the short overhang above the cave. From the edge of this a short coping slab ascended steeply into the commencement of the chimney. This was the point at which a previous attempt on the climb had failed. Even from a foothold on the left wall on a level with the overhang it was still extremely difficult to gain lodgment on the slab above; two cracks, a yard or so apart, limited the slab on either side, but a widening at the foot seemed to provide doubtful friction for a jammed boot. A tiny chockstone jammed in the nearer crack provided a vital hold for the necessary jerk upwards. Even so, it took some time to pluck up enough courage for an attempt, though exhorted by sundry cheerful comments from the invisible troglodyte.

The advent of the second party ultimately provided the incentive. Although the primary move was executed according to the textbook, the next few feet degenerated into an undignified scrabble, hastened by the absence of any positive holds. From a secure stance at the back of the chimney I summoned Mike from his cave, with the encouraging information that the pitch was very severe. However, he made disappointingly short work of it and led through into the enticing upper reaches of the chimney.

By now everyone was engaged on the climb, and the corrie re-echoed to the instructions confidently supplied by those who had successfully completed the pitches; in contrasting tones were the protestations of those who had still to surmount the difficulties. The fact that three of the party answered to a call of "Mike" did nothing to simplify matters. Morrison alone could be identified with any certainty, his clear ringing tones revealing a fiendish joy in being at large in this abode of the mountain demons.

I was soon joined by Mike Dixon, whose head and shoulders compensated for any lack of footholds in the next few feet. Thence the going was easier for a brief space as the chimney deepened, though I felt sure that some sterner test lay ahead. I joined Taylor 60 feet below the top. It was obvious we were in no position for premature celebration. For 40 feet the chimney steepened to vertical with a dark recessed slit at its back, and finally jutted out in a slight overhang—a last gesture of defiance.

For a short distance I squirmed up the inner cleft, becoming extremely wet in the process. Then came the agreeable discovery that the main chimney was now narrow enough to allow backing up. Progress was immediately easier to a jammed block platform below the final overhang. Cavilling at the use of a piton, we had to exercise patience to manufacture a small thread belay to safeguard further progress. Mike first reconnoitred the initial few feet, cleaning several of the holds, and then invited me to go ahead. Simple back and foot technique took me almost to the top. Here, unfortunately, the walls diverged the merest fraction until equilibrium could be maintained only by exerting considerable pressure with the tip of the large toe. At this critical juncture I had a horrible suspicion of the onset of cramp, but averted the danger by the discovery of a vital handhold on the back wall of the chimney, only sufficient to swing inwards and proceed straight up the overhang. I had just extended one groping arm over the top when Brooker, from below, volunteered the information that he had heard that there were no holds above for the last move. Not deigning to acknowledge this refreshing piece of news, I struggled breathlessly over the lip, and gave tongue to an exuberant yell. The response was somewhat discouraging; the others evinced but mild surprise, and the answering cheer came instead from some climbers on Shadow Buttress, who seemingly thought I was hailing them.

The arrival of Taylor was heralded by the dislodgment of a large boulder which luckily fell outside the chimney to impact on the screes in one giant bound. No harm done, the whole party assembled below the second main pitch, with the conquest of Parallel Gully "B" practically an accomplished fact. Here four of the party called it a day and departed to the Tough–Brown Ridge, but the rest of us were anxious to complete the climb by following our predecessors' route to the plateau.

Taylor led off like a bloodhound on the leash, following a trail of tiny scratches and scars on the slabs and progressing steadily towards some particularly repulsive overhangs on the Tough–Brown flank of the gully. The first confirmation of the route was the discovery of a small belay piton in a slab. The giant holdless groove above looked the essence of impregnability. We had almost decided to retreat when a second piton was spotted, 15 feet up on the wall to the left of the groove. The challenge was accepted, and progress made up the groove by vigorous contortion— entertaining to watch but painful to perform. The ensuing traverse leftwards to the top of the second pitch was severe all the way and ended in a remarkable hand traverse which almost exacted the last reserves of energy from everyone concerned.

The familiar Lochnagar drizzle had now set in and, as a result, nobody seemed keen on following up the gully to its bitter end—a huge pitch of easy angle, yet abominably loose and wet. We agreed on aesthetic grounds that it would be a travesty to conclude such a fine route in this way. This may have been mere rationalisation, however; for by this time the call of the inner man had become more pressing. By mutual consent we unroped and sped up to the plateau by the easier rocks on Tough–Brown Ridge.

So ended one of the most enjoyable climbs we have had on Lochnagar. With sound rock, continuous difficulties and pitches following one another with sparkling variety, it was all that a Lochnagar gully usually is not. Above all, the unorthodox tactics we were obliged to adopt at times added spice to the climb. It was indeed one of those days which are not easily forgotten, and the memory of which is rekindled anew in camp-fire reminiscence.

APPOINTMENT WITH SCORPION

From The Etchachan Club Journal, 1956

The Scorpion was the first route, summer or winter, on the 700-foot face of Càrn Etchachan above the Shelter Stone.

MIKE TAYLOR AND I had long been fascinated by this face, the more so after a meeting with Mac Smith, that redoubtable bloodhound of a climber, who had stuck his nose into most of the odd spots of the Cairngorms, in an endless quest for new routes. In answer to our question, he assured us that there was nothing there worth the walk from Derry—it was all rotten and loose and were it otherwise would have been climbed long ago. Knowing Mac as we did, it was immediately obvious that he was only waiting an opportunity to return. We could delay no longer.

One frosty evening in December 1952, four of us sat round the stove at Derry Lodge conversing in hushed whispers. A few hundred yards away at Luibeg, replete after his evening in the Fife Arms, Mac Smith slept "the sleep of the just" unaware of the conspiracy against his intended route. Mike and I had been joined by Graeme Nicol and Kenny Grassick, two whose names are now associated with many a hard-fought battle on Cairngorm crag and gully—upright and venerable men. Yet it is perhaps not generally known that in those days Kenny and Graeme belonged to an organisation known as the Boor Boys. The Boor Boys, or the Corrour Club, to give them their more domesticated title, were a motley collection of ex-grammar school boys, "brigands of the bothy", who enforced a regular reign of terror on a community where misanthropes and ornithologists were rife. Their boisterous high spirits and uninhibited wit, always well to the fore on a University Club Meet, gave many headaches to the conscientious club secretary.

I had done a route with them the previous week-end, and by dint of climbing well beyond my limits of safety and using more than a little "climbsmanship", had managed to earn their temporary respect. Whether we could maintain this relationship was less certain.

The evening was well on before the conference came to an end. Mike and I, to preserve our respectability, were residing at the Lodge, but the others preferred the plebian atmosphere of Luibeg. In any case they could keep an eye on Smith's movements.

The snow had come early to the hills that year, and already the climbs were in excellent condition for winter climbing. We left shortly after dawn in thick mist which cut visibility down to a few yards. The crackle of crisp snow underfoot, music to a hill lover's ears, was offset by the jingling of many pitons and karabiners—a recent assignment from the factories of Kincorth!

From the start the pace was terrific. Nicol had been practising for the ordeal for several weeks, by performing the statutory number of pull-ups on his bedroom door, and was now in the peak of condition. Mike and I stumbled along behind him as best we could, trying hard to conceal our laboured breathing; Grassick brought up the rear.

Four hours later we stopped for the first time and looked up at our prospective route. The mists had cleared revealing a magnificent pointed crag split by a multitude of cracks and chimneys all plastered with snow and ice. We had never seen the cliff at close quarters before and estimated that there were at least twenty routes there for the taking. So much for Smith!

At this point, the two senior members of the party proposed a halt for eats. Some time later, having recovered their breath, they both arose suddenly, acting on a preconceived plan, and reached the foot of the climb a few seconds in advance of the other pair.

I led off immediately up a holdless groove starting 100 feet below the entrance to Castlegates Gully. Nicol seemed determined to give his leader every assistance by advising him exactly where to place his feet. It wasn't long before these backseat-driver tactics had their desired result. I had only gained 12 feet when a hold crumpled away and I landed at my second's feet.

Before I could regain my footing, Nicol had sprung into the breach. At first he gained height quite rapidly, then more slowly.

After watching his progress for a few minutes with mixed emotions, Mike and I spotted an easier way up at the side and left Grassick sitting at the foot, half-heartedly minding the rope. To our delight we met with no major difficulties. "No real need for the rope here," I shouted down to Grassick. He took me at my word and started off on his own, leaving Graeme to seek his own salvation.

A quarter of an hour later we were all four of us "stuck" at different points on the face between 50 and 100 feet from the ground. Nicol who was in the worst position, was very much incensed at finding his rope had been left unattended. Luckily I had a spare rope to hand and was able to establish contact with Mike. The two of us eventually reached a stance. The others were still well out of our reach to the right, and the way ahead was barred by a blank wall. Or so we thought, for I had only advanced a few feet when the thin drapery of snow collapsed in front of me revealing a deep crack going straight into the rock. It was very dark inside but there appeared to be an opening at the top, blocked by snow. I squirmed up inside the rock for 20 feet, feeling like one of the little chimney-sweeps who were sent up chimneys in Victorian days to clean out the soot. Any elbow movement was severely restricted; so I had to break an exit through the snow crust with my head. From the short ledge above the end of the tunnel we could look down on Graeme's white mop of hair, and before long both he and Grassick had been drawn up to safety.

The next pitch was slightly overhanging and all the holds were hidden under the snow. I was an hour on the first 30 feet and above that the climbing was no easier. Though now out of sight of those below, I was still very much aware of their presence. They were engaged on a lusty rendering of bar-room ballads, punctuated by spells of hammering as they secured themselves against the leader's possible downfall. It reminded me of an absurd version of Verdi's "Anvil Chorus".

Mike came up and joined me, with a message from the end of the rope to get a ruddy move on; we had already been three hours on the climb and were not yet half-way up. Indeed the face was offering much more formidable opposition than we had anticipated. Our progress, measured against the wall of the Shelter Stone Crag opposite, seemed pitifully slow.

I had forgotten to bring gloves and my fingers had turned white with cold. Despite the inconvenience it causes, I am secretly rather proud of this peculiarity, which is known to the layman as "dead fingers" but in a medical textbook, rejoices in the title of "Reynaud's Phenomenon". Furthermore, it is always a valid excuse for shirking a disagreeable lead, and this was just such an occasion. Mike took over the lead up a vile-looking wall, leaving me sharing a belay with Nicol who was steadily working himself into a Teutonic frenzy at the prospect of a bivouac on the face— a distinction he had long coveted. He insisted that I take his only pair of gloves, saying that mine was the greater need. Hadn't Hermann Buhl walked round Innsbruck with a ball of ice clenched in his fists to harden himself for grade VI climbing?

The pitches were gradually easing off, and at last we seemed to be getting somewhere. This gave me the opportunity to produce the camera and secure the necessary evidence of our route. (Climbers who make a first winter ascent in the Cairngorms nowadays must supply well-authenticated photos to prove validity of their claims, otherwise nobody, least of all the guide-book editor, will believe them. It is recommended practice always to point the camera down the climb, to ensure that the maximum amount of snow will be visible. If this is done properly and the climb is within the "safe" period of December to March, you will then stand a fair chance of having your route accepted as a "first winter ascent": it helps, of course, if you have a few frostbitten fingers and toes to show as additional proof.)

Presently we came on to a stretch of broken ground below a 250-foot vertical rampart—the final obstacle. There was not a hope of taking this direct in the existing conditions, but on the right a steep rocky gully curved round a corner out of sight. "There is the route," I assured them. "Once round the corner, it'll just be a dawdle to the top. . . ."

With only an hour of daylight remaining, we stared dumb-founded at the termination of our gully. This was the sting in the tail of the "Scorpion". Two tiers of overhangs, smooth and shining with verglas, blocked the gully, and there was no way out to right or left. With a bit of luck we might force the first overhang before pitch darkness, but a bivouac above this seemed a certainty.

The overhang was the worst pitch I'd seen for many a long day. If only the ice had been thick enough to cut a notch, instead of this thin glaze everywhere! It was no time for niceties of technique and I struggled up anyhow, using the adhesion of my gloves to the verglas as the principal support if my boots slithered off the sloping holds. Just below the top there was a cramped little hole where I could jam myself for an instant with my head bent double under the ice roof and take the strain off my arms. Leaning out on an icicle to support one hand, I tried to cut a hold for the final swing up. No dice! The ice was still too thin and there wasn't even a crack for a piton. Descent was impossible and I only had enough energy to hang on for a few more seconds. Nicol shouted, "Do you want me to come up and give you a hand?" At that moment I spotted a tiny finger hold away out on the right which would allow me to swing clear of the overhang. It was now or never. . . . At full stretch I got my fingers just over the top of the hold and swung out on the one arm. Simultaneously the left hand grabbed some frozen turf just two feet higher. One final convulsive heave and I was up.

Nicol came next using a fixed nylon cord as a handrail. It was now dusk, but there was just a chance we might still pull it off, so the two of us pressed on up a long holdless groove, towards the top overhang.

The best climbs keep their surprises to the end. At the last minute a horizontal, foot-wide ledge appeared, traversing the vertical right-hand wall of the gully. Our escape was assured. I shouted down the glad news to Mike, but before he could reply there was a dramatic reversal of fortunes.

Grassick had been heaving himself up the fixed rope to the accompaniment of much grunting and hoarse cackles of laughter. Now for the first time we could see his face, distorted with a horrible fixed grin, appearing over the lip of the overhang like some strange monster from the deep. At that moment, with a long drawn out howl he dropped from our sight. The rope to Mike went taut, and simultaneously the snow stance he was occupying disintegrated, leaving him dangling from his belay. I glanced at Nicol in dismay. "It's all right," he assured me, "We're not tied on to them anyway."

As he spoke, the rope spinning through Mike's hands stopped abruptly. There was a long silence. Then a stream of profanities rent the air—Grassick was safe. He had fallen only 30 feet and plummeted into some deep soft snow which effectively broke his fall.

Nicol and I edged across the wall following the tiny ledge. At 50 feet we reached a small rock tower projecting from the plateau rim. The icy sepulchre was behind us and the moonlight revealed an easy snow slope leading to the top.

On the other hand our fellow prisoners still had a long way to go. Grassick's efforts had at last been rewarded and Mike was leading up the groove, his head-lamp bobbing about in the darkness like a gigantic glow-worm. He was singing sadly to himself in a sonorous baritone "There was Mary Beaton and Mary Seaton and Mary Carmichael and me". The old Scots air seemed to gain additional pathos from the melancholy surroundings.

Our offer of a rope was accepted reluctantly and the last man reached the top at 5.30 p.m.—seven hours after leaving the screes.

A few hours later we sat once more round the fire at Derry. Nicol broke the silence—"You know, Tom, you boys are quite reasonable climbers, and Kenny and I are quite agreeable to you climbing with us in future." We grunted our appreciation. The bond was sealed.

THE ZERO GULLY AFFAIR

From The Scottish Mountaineering Club Journal, 1958

"STILL PLENTY TIME to get up before dark," observed Graeme Nicol. It was two o'clock on a February afternoon, and he was gazing wistfully at the 1,000 feet of vertical ice which constitutes Point Five Gully on Ben Nevis.

On such occasions there is nothing for it but to humour my fellow Aberdonian's enthusiasm. These brain storms only occur periodically. A well-thumbed copy of Anderl Heckmair's *Derniers Problèmes des Alpes* is ever on his bedside table, and on the night before a hard climb he is accustomed to search for inspiration in selected readings from the text.

An hour later the argument was renewed. I had climbed the first 100 feet of 70-degree snow-ice and been swamped by several powder snow avalanches before taking advantage of a sheltering bulge of green ice to insert a peg and rope down. As a consolation I diverted him round the foot of Observatory Ridge for a brief inspection of Zero Gully, also unclimbed, vertical, and bulging with overhanging ice. It formed the perfect counterpart to Point Five.

Between them these two gullies had aroused more interest among post-war climbers on both sides of the Border than any other ice climb. Zero had always seemed the more likely of the two to go, if only because Point Five was so seldom in climbable condition. A mere sprinkling of fresh powder in the upper *couloir* of Point Five would fill the vertical lower cleft with choking clouds of spindrift—the latter a virtually uninterrupted ice-pitch of 500 feet. We had visited Ben Nevis six times in recent winters with intentions on Point Five but had not succeeded in leaving the ground. Always there was the threat of avalanche. The only serious attempt had been made by a Rock and Ice party, and this had ended in a spectacular exodus from the gully when the leading pair were held at full stretch by the last man on the rope.

Zero Gully, on the other hand, had survived several attempts, although the upper 500 feet had often been climbed by parties engaged on the winter ascent of Observatory Ridge. The real problem is the direct ascent of the lower ice-fall, and on the most successful attempt by Bell and Allan in 1936 this had been avoided by an excursion towards Slav Route on the left. A further *tour de force* by an O.U.M.C. party in 1950 ended in disaster. They were near the top of the difficult section when the leader fell, ripping out several ice-pitons and dislodging the second. By a miracle they both survived the 400-foot fall. Subsequently Zero Gully became linked with the name of Hamish MacInnes, of whom more anon. The climb had now withstood several MacInnes blitzkriegs: numerous ice-pitons and an ice-axe marked the site of the battle. Perhaps inspired by Hamish, the Creag Dhu entered the lists in 1956 with summer ascents of both Zero and Point Five gullies. They found neither gully a satisfactory summer climb. There was far too much unreliable rock, but no one doubted that in winter conditions they would provide ice routes of unique length and difficulty.

"Sans compétition pas de sport", wrote Alain de Chatellus. Perhaps that explains why no less than a dozen climbers from Aberdeen and Glasgow were due to congregate at the Clark Hut that week-end in quest of Zero and Point Five gullies. There had been a mutual agreement among all the interested parties. Nicol and I had inadvertently broken faith by arriving one day in advance, thanks to an impromptu lift in a cement lorry. We had therefore to await the main body with patience despite all Nicol's protestations. His argument that the premature bagging of Point Five would leave us all free to concentrate on Zero was hardly adequate.

Len Lovat was the first on the scene next morning—quite out of breath after a furious chase up the Allt a' Mhuilinn. We had written to him to say we might be a day late, but his jubilation had turned to dismay on finding fresh tracks in the snow. There followed at a more leisurely pace a succession of the Glasgow "faithful"—Malcolm Slesser, Donald Bennet, Douglas Scott, and Norman Tennent.

The cast was complete, but the stage was not yet set. Ben Nevis is notoriously temperamental on important occasions, and a strong south-west wind was already whipping the spindrift off the Observatory and drenching the north-east face in dense white clouds. A gully climb was out of the question—today at any rate. Len joined forces with Nicol and myself, while the other four set off towards North-East Buttress. We watched them proceed smoothly up Slingsby's Chimney to the First Platform, and then transferred our attention to the left-hand flank of the Buttress which fronts Corrie Leis. Bill Murray had drawn our attention some time before to the possibilities of this fine 1,000-foot face. Although a rock climber's midden in summer, like many similar faces it seemed to offer glorious winter climbing—a miniature Scottish Brenva, in fact. We picked the easiest route, a central line up a long snow *couloir*. This ended about 600 feet up, below some overhanging ice, where a long traverse rightwards involving a 120-foot lead-out provided the highlight of the climb. All the party were in good fettle, and we reached the top in three hours from the corrie floor. The Cresta Climb seemed to be an apt name for the new route, in view of the Alpine nature of its environment. During the descent we observed that another and more exacting line existed between our *couloir* and the edge of North-East Buttress. It could provide one of the longest ice routes in Britain.

Back in the hut we had visitors—two climbers, whose characteristic patois, coupled with a distinct air of authority, stamped them as members of the Creag Dhu Club. They were, in fact, Johnny Cunningham and Mick Noon. They mentioned casually that they expected to climb Zero Gully on the morrow, without apparently noticing the disquieting effect this had on the rest of the company.

We remarked upon the absence of Hamish MacInnes. "He doesnae ken we're here, and furthermore we're no tellin' him," said Cunningham. However, he had apparently underestimated Hamish. Scarcely were the words out of his mouth when the door crashed open and the self-appointed guardian of Zero Gully stood before us in a state of wild disorder.

The news of our arrival had reached him at Steill Hut, where he was acting as instructor on a Mountaineering Association course. He had set off immediately across the Carn Mor Dearg Arête, delaying not even to collect provisions for the trip. (Hamish makes a habit of travelling "light".)

It was impossible to remain indifferent towards such a man: his appearance alone invited controversy. A great rent extending the whole length of one trouser leg had been repaired unsuccessfully with string. In his hand was the famous all-steel hammer-pick, named affectionately by the club "The Message".

Cunningham challenged him gruffly, "Just where do you think you're going?"

"Zero Gully, of course."

"Solo?"

"I suppose I might allow you two along as well."

"That's very generous considerin' we're going anyway."

So the composition of the party was settled to the chagrin of the rest of the company, who had not allowed for such formidable competition. We reflected sulkily that there was always Point Five.

Around midnight some conscientious person drew attention to the fact that the North-East Buttress party were "rather late back". With some grumbling a search party was organised, but before we could leave the four absentees staggered in, mumbling excuses about "Two feet of ice on the Man Trap". It was easy to commiserate with them on their misfortune, as they would now be unable to rise from their beds before noon, certainly too late for serious climbing.

Nicol and I were up at crack of dawn, but only in time to witness the departure of the Creag Dhu who had already breakfasted. "It's a great day for avalanches," Hamish declared enthusiastically as he opened the door to a full-scale Ben Nevis blizzard.

At other times I would have returned to sleep with an easy conscience, but Graeme Nicol was bursting with impatience and would brook no delay. The distant roar of avalanches was a sufficient contra-indication to an attempt on Point Five, and we left without any fixed intentions. A momentary clearing in the mist revealed our rivals at the foot of Zero Gully, where a minor altercation seemed to be in progress. The tall figure of Hamish kept pointing insistently skywards.

I don't know why we finally selected Comb Gully. It would seem in retrospect to have been a most inappropriate choice. Not only did it enjoy a considerable reputation for difficulty, but we had just witnessed a fair-sized powder avalanche issue from the gully. However, Graeme inclined to the view that all the unstable snow now must be swept clear, and we scuttled up the first three pitches with great abandon. Despite the blizzard and a steady stream of spindrift we could not complain about the quality of the snow. It was ideally suited to step cutting, with a fine hard crust as a legacy of the recent avalanche.

Along came the crux, a 30-foot vertical ice-pitch, above which the angle appeared to relent. It was not a pitch to linger over, as the streaming drift found its way into our windproofs, rapidly numbing wrists and fingers. I crouched for a minute's respite in the lee of the top overhang and knocked in two ice-pitons for security. The next few feet were the worst. At this point the falling spindrift met a violent up blast of wind going straight up the gully, and the result was a regular maelstrom. Eyes crusted over, and holds refilled as fast as they were cut. I fought for breath, almost choking with the snow going into my mouth. There was little finesse in the climbing, and I was extremely thankful to get out of the place without literally suffocating. Above this there were no further difficulties as the cornice had come away in the avalanche, and we reached the top in little over an hour after starting the climb.

We cut our way down North Gully of Creag Coire na Ciste, feeling very pleased with ourselves at disposing of Comb Gully in such a short time, and returned to the hut in time for a second breakfast. We were soon followed by the Creag Dhu who had turned back with reluctance in the face of several avalanches. The weather had now deteriorated further so Cunningham and Noon decided to return to Glasgow on the motor bike that evening. Before he left Johnny asked us about our plans for tomorrow. We had been offered a lift back to Banff by Norman

Tennent and it seemed too good an opportunity to miss. "But what about Point Five?"

"It'll wait," I replied.

"It'll no' wait for ever," he countered with a grin.

"Neither will Zero, come to that," rejoined Nicol.

Hamish suddenly came to life. "Are you guys interested in Zero tomorrow?"

Fate was obviously taking a hand, and I recalled that the best climbs usually arrive unexpectedly. Leaving Aberdeen that weekend we had spoken little about Zero Gully; our hopes were all for Point Five. I thought for a moment of Norman's cosy van and yielded. "O.K. It's on." In vain did Johnny remonstrate with Hamish to keep it in the club. Hamish was unyielding. It was *his* climb, he pointed out; and it was *his* gear that was on it. Indeed, few men would dispute his ownership. He had earned it, if only by reason of a recent solo winter ascent of Observatory Ridge, undertaken merely to inspect Zero Gully! We parted with good wishes on both sides, but it was satisfying to deduce from the heat of the argument that the climb must be in excellent condition. The other five were remaining an extra day, and Len Lovat was undecided whether to join us; but the prospect of a possible benightment and the absolute necessity of returning to Glasgow for the following afternoon tempered his enthusiasm.

Next morning we rose at 6 a.m. to find a clear sky and hard frost. Over breakfast Hamish disposed of the climb as if conducting a business transaction. "You can lead the first four hundred feet and above that it's just a steady slog. I've led it once, so I'm satisfied. It took six and a half hours," he added as an afterthought.

"Then why didn't you get up?" I inquired.

"There was a wee avalanche."

Probably quite a large one, I thought, if they had decided to retreat so high up.

We ploughed up to the foot of the cliffs through 3 feet of new snow. Our luck was in. The recent powder had failed to adhere to the almost vertical snow-ice of the gully and conditions were ideal. It was Zero hour.

Whoever christened it a gully was an optimist. For 400 feet it is no more than a vertical corner bulging with overhangs, but Hamish's eye of faith could detect a route. The first pitch was obvious. A shallow trough ran up the centre of the 85-degree wall for 100 feet to peter out below a fair-sized overhang. By cutting handholds on the side wall of the trough it would be possible to climb in balance despite the extreme angle. A line of steps terminated abruptly at 20 feet. I looked at Hamish inquiringly.

"That's where Long John got hit on the head with some ice," he answered. "It's a pity because he was going fine."

My fears that I might emulate Cunningham were unfounded. For once Ben Nevis was tolerant of Hamish's presence and no debris fell. It was a model ice-pitch and the security astonishingly good despite the exposure. I straddled the side walls of the trough, unable to resist a morbid satisfaction in noting that the rope hung absolutely free from my waist to the two at the bottom. They seemed strangely remote and not very interested in my progress, though Hamish would occasionally stir himself to shout "Straight on up" whenever I stopped for a rest.

I halted below the overhang with 120 feet of rope run out and still no stance worthy of attention. "There's a bit of nylon cord sticking out of the snow here," I yelled.

Hamish was delighted. "It's attached to Hope's ice-axe," he roared. "That's your first belay."

I ventured to say that it was "quite steep up here".

"Don't worry about that. You've done the worst bit and it's just a doddle now."

Leaning backwards on the frozen cord to inspect the overhang I came to the conclusion that Hamish was either a superlatively good climber or a fanatic. Watching him climb neatly up the first pitch I decided that he was probably a bit of both. Nicol, not to be outdone, came up with equal nonchalance, but spoiled it all by dropping his axe at the top. It plummeted down without striking the face and impaled itself in the snow at the bottom. Fortunately for him we now had a spare axe. This had been left by Hamish and Bob Hope when they ran out of ice-pitons during the disastrous retreat of the previous month. On that occasion

Hamish had made the dramatic entry in the hut log book—"This climb is not possible in one day."

I started on the overhang with some misgivings, convinced that the best route lay to the right, hard in by the corner; but Hamish assured me that he had tried this himself and the overhang was the only way through. Fortunately the ice was deep enough to take pitons, and for 20 feet I was very glad of their assistance. The technique is to take tension through an ice-piton placed as high as possible above the climber until the next few handholds have been cut. Then, hanging on with one hand, a higher piton is inserted and the one below removed for further use. This is all very delicate work, as any outward pull on the piton will have the maximum result. The other two inclined to the view that I would profit from a couple of *étriers*, but I assured them without any real conviction that I was quite happy.

Half an hour later I crouched in another miserably cramped stance above the overhang. I couldn't find Hamish's ice-piton which was buried somewhere in the vicinity, but had hammered an ice-axe well in, using the "Message" for the purpose. Its owner now had nothing to assist his progress. He dispenses with an axe on ice climbs and only uses the hammer-pick. At last a shout came from below. "Keep the rope tight and I'll come up on the *Prusiks*."* At another time I would have enjoyed the joke, but I was beginning to realise the range of this man's enthusiasm.

"Stop!" I roared, as he prepared to launch out into space. There followed a short pause and the rope started hesitantly to come in.

Hamish appeared to be rather disgruntled. He claimed we had lost a full three minutes. Personally, I couldn't see the importance of this as we had already put 300 feet behind us in one and a half hours, and this section had taken four hours on the earlier attempt.

Now the route went rightwards towards the corner, at the point where it bends out of view as seen from the foot of the gully. The traverse led along a narrow strip of high-angled snow between two overhangs, with some quite superb exposure.

* Prusik knot technique for climbing up a fixed rope, held from above, used in Alps for rescue from crevasse, etc.

For the first time we could progress without the constant support of a handhold or ice-piton.

At the end of the traverse I stepped on to an easy snow slope running back at 50 degrees into the face. This was the limit of the MacInnes–Hope *tentative*. It was difficult to conceive how they had considered themselves above all difficulties, even allowing for the prevailing snow-storm and limited visibility. For the next 80 feet the route had some of the characteristics of a gully climb, hemmed in by smooth ice walls. Then a gigantic ice-patch soared up vertically for 100 feet seeming to seal off all access to the upper gully.

From round the corner came the familiar shout, "He's up— no bother at all now."

I smiled sardonically. This joker must be held to his promise. "Hamish, it's your lead—there's still a wee pitch left."

Nicol and I belayed at the foot of the wall to two ice-axes and three ice-pitons. On the right an easy snow shelf led on to Observatory Ridge, but since any avoidance of the direct line would amount to sacrilege, nobody dared draw attention to it. In went the first ice-piton, and with a violent heave Hamish got a crampon level with where his nose had been. The only indication of his passage was a large bucket hold every 6 feet. The urgency of his climbing indicated that this pitch was to be a vindication of the use of crampons for the benefit of the tricouni-favouring Aberdonians. However, we were satisfied to observe that his initial impetuosity soon waned, and presently the rope came to a dead stop. All that was now visible of Hamish was the soles of his boots outlined against the sky—an apparent contradiction of the laws of gravity, until you realised that his weight was supported by the angled spikes on the front of his crampons.

"Let's sing him a song to cheer him up," suggested Nicol. He broke into the traditional New Orleans funeral march, "Oh, didn't he ramble". I joined in on the chorus, which ends triumphantly with the line, "Yes, he rambled till the Butchers cut him down."

Hamish, whose preference is for chamber music, was rather nettled. "There's a lot of loose stuff up here and some of it's going to come down."

Nicol failed to heed the warning and jerked his head back in time to catch the full force of the avalanche. When the debris cleared he was bleeding from a cut above the eyebrow, but otherwise intact as his spirited rejoinder demonstrated.

More and more snow came down as the minutes ticked past. Hamish was now out of sight, and we wondered if he was tunnelling the overhang. Every now and then we heard a gasp, "Thank God for a piton," but that was all. Two hours elapsed before the signal came to follow on.

I won't attempt to estimate the difficulty of the pitch, as I did most of it on a tight rope, and the steps seemed designed for a Yeti. Suffice to say that it was quite up to anything else on the climb, which indeed had seldom varied below Very Severe. Hamish was satisfied with his "shift" and prepared now to rest on his laurels. "It's the interesting stuff that gets me, I'm afraid. I'm not much of a hand at the step bashing," he said, indicating the rest of the gully with a lordly gesture.

It was true. We had at last penetrated the forest of ice overhangs, and the way was clear to the top cornice. All the pent-up energy of the last two hours exploded in a frenzy of activity. We moved together, the pace of the party (contrary to the textbook) dictated by the fastest member. Nicol was the most exhausted; he carried the pitons. The slope eased off all the time, and the few minor pitches passed almost unnoticed. Fifty minutes later and five hours from the start of the climb we emerged into the warm sunlight of the summit plateau.

Nicol's yell of ecstasy was intercepted by Tennent and Slesser, who were completing the second ascent of the Cresta Climb. They shouted their congratulations, and the knowledge that a lift home was still in the offing completed our jubilation. We wished Len Lovat had been with us, but he too had enjoyed an excellent first winter ascent of No. 5 Gully Buttress in company with Donald Bennet. It was one of those rare days on Ben Nevis. Everyone satisfied, perfect climbing conditions and an unlimited vista as far as Sutherland and the Western Isles.

"A great climb!" Hamish declared. "Up to Ravens Gully standard."

"In fact, it might even hold its own on Lochnagar," added Graeme with patriotic fervour. They were still arguing as we reached the hut.

The sequel to that eventful week-end merits a full article.

How Cunningham and Noon, thirsting for revenge, attacked Point Five Gully in appalling thaw conditions and almost carried the day against all odds till the collapse of 20 feet of waterlogged ice enforced retreat. How Hamish returned alone to the Ben, dragging 600 feet of Alpine line which he attached to an ice-axe at the top and descended the gully till the rope gave out, dangling like a yo-yo over the abyss. His climb back to the top, unaided by the rope, left much less virgin snow for future pioneers.

But these are stories that will be better told by Hamish or John Cunningham when they finally succeed in their campaign, as I have little doubt they will.

POST-WAR WINTER MOUNTAINEERING
IN SCOTLAND

From The Alpine Journal, 1960

"A CLIMBER WHO is strong and sure of himself, should . . . prefer winter ascents because these more than any others give him a chance of measuring his strength against mountains in severe conditions. They force him to battle without respite, completely on his own, day after day, and with no possibility of reprovisioning."(!) So wrote the mighty Gervasutti (others might have expressed it less literally). His conception of winter mountaineering finds a faint echo in recent deeds north of the Border.

Winter mountaineering as currently defined in Scotland, only began as late as the 'thirties. With the exception of the three classic ridges of Ben Nevis, routes made by the early pioneers were almost entirely of the gully variety. The highlight of the gully climb was the Ice Pitch, followed by some good old-fashioned fun at the cornice. Such a climb was remarkably lacking in variety.

Broadly speaking the tendency was to regard the Scottish winter cliffs as a training ground for Alpine mountaineering. Consequently the early climbers employed a technique that had been perfected in the Alps—a technique that envisaged so-called "ideal conditions" of hard compact snow or Alpine *névé*, admirable conditions for step cutting and belaying. Except in the gullies which soon accumulate consolidated snow, these conditions occur perhaps once or twice in the course of a Scottish winter. Thus the annual pilgrimage to Nevis, like the Quest for the Holy Grail, was apt to be frustrating.

The renaissance of the 'thirties was mainly the work of an enthusiastic group of Glasgow J.M.C.S. climbers, W. H. Murray, W. M. Mackenzie and others. Independent parties led by Macphee and Bell shared in the new developments. Concentrating particularly on Glencoe, they worked out a series of fine new winter routes, unique in their conception and fulfilment. Buttresses, ridges, and faces offered more open, varied and interesting lines than the conventional gully climbs. Accurate route finding, based on a shrewd assessment of prevailing conditions, was an all-important factor on these climbs. All snow conditions were regarded as climbing conditions. It merely became a question of adapting the technique to meet the prevailing conditions— *névé*, powder snow, verglassed rocks, frozen vegetation, etc.

Scottish winter climbing is unique in many ways. Above all, it moulds for itself a technique which is as different from that employed on an average Alpine snow climb as chalk is from cheese. The present-day formula that any summer rock climb (providing it is suitably plastered in ice) makes a good winter climb, speaks for itself. It has been responsible for routes of the calibre of the Orion Face on Ben Nevis—a climb involving a greater degree of difficulty and technical skill than could be contemplated in the Alps, where the overall scale of a route and its potential objective danger are the more important factors.

The salient features of this new vigorous technique may bear repetition. Few climbers now pin much faith on the ice-axe belay—one-time symbol of impregnability. One could quote many incidents in the past when the axe has been uprooted or splintered under the impact of a falling leader, even when the correct waist belay technique was employed by the second. On a face route, where in any case there is seldom adequate snow for an axe belay, it is always worth the trouble to excavate a natural rock belay, or at the worst a crack for a piton belay. Pitons are now standard equipment for winter climbing, although artificial technique in itself has had only a minor part to play in recent developments.

Most recent ice routes involve long periods of one-armed cutting, where a handhold is consistently required for balance. In those circumstances the ordinary Alpine axe is as cumbersome as a sledge hammer. The leader usually wields a short hand-axe (shaft length 20–25 inches) or, occasionally, a modified slater's pick. A few, like Hamish MacInnes dispense altogether with an axe, and use a *marteau-piolet*. Hamish's own implement is known, appropriately, as "The Message".

Along with the advances in technique and the vast amount of activity in recent years, has gone a noticeable improvement in the speed and competence of the average winter party. I cannot recall off-hand a single serious incident in the last ten years befalling an experienced Scottish party on a Scottish winter climb.

Pre-war classics, such as the Tower Ridge, where climbers of Alpine repute have been benighted, are now frequently accounted for in remarkably fast time. Recently Len Lovat and Tom Weir, starting out without record-breaking ambitions, disposed of the three Nevis ridges in the course of a single winter's day—up Observatory Ridge, down Tower Ridge and finally up the North-East Buttress. To spend a season away from the front is to find oneself automatically relegated to the ranks of the "dead-beats".

I shall pick up the threads of the story in the late 'forties. The earlier instalments are so well described in Bill Murray's two books on Scottish mountaineering as to render further comment superfluous. Suffice it to recall that those early routes inspired everything that followed; Garrick's shelf on the Crowberry Ridge is the prototype of the modern ice climb.

The immediate post-war revival was dominated by two separate schools of climbing, in Aberdeen and Glasgow, who deployed their forces on Lochnagar and Glencoe respectively. Neither adhered to any orthodox faith. Few of the contemporary tigers were versed in Alpine technique, and they adapted their technique to meet the needs of the situation.

Glencoe

Glasgow were represented by two factions—the Creag Dhu Club and a further heterogeneous group comprising members of S.M.C., Glasgow J.M.C.S. and G.U.M. Club.

In the Ravens Gully campaign, which extended over several seasons, the major contestants were the Creag Dhu. Ravens Gully, the dark rift alongside the North Buttress of the Buachaille was a formidable adversary. Although a mere 350 feet, it carries six to eight major ice pitches and positively bristles with severity.

On one occasion MacInnes got to within striking distance of the cornice when his rope froze through a succession of karabiners, condemning him to a miserable night *"en face nord"*—literally hoist with his own petard. His "rescue" by some well-meaning onlookers deprived him of the first ascent.

This was only delayed however, for in 1953 Hamish and Chris Bonington won through after a six-hour tussle. On this occasion, to quote the scanty information available, "the chockstone on Pitch 5 was lassoed thereby allowing pendulum action and saving hours of effort."

Ravens was not repeated until last winter when John Cunningham, one of the original protagonists, and Jimmy Marshall completed the climb in three hours "without hurrying".

The Crowberry Ridge by Abraham's Direct route, and Agag's Groove also yielded to MacInnes. Crampons had been demonstrated effectively on exposed iced rock, although MacInnes had been forced to remove his boots on the Crowberry crux. Clachaig Gully was later added to the Creag Dhu collection, although they were fortunate in finding genuine winter conditions in such a low-lying gully. Deep Gash Gully on Aonach Dubh (1957) was the only subsequent climb to rival the 1951 routes for sheer technical brilliance. The gulf between the Creag Dhu and the S.M.C. has narrowed appreciably. The S.M.C., benefiting from an infusion of young blood, is again one of the most active clubs in the country. It has achieved this without sacrificing its traditional principles of a sound preliminary grounding in conventional snow technique. In contradistinction, the transient ebullience of the Creag Dhu "gnomies" has given way to a more serious calculating approach.

The first post-war sorties by the S.M.C. produced two fine ice routes in Twisting Gully and the Red Gully of Sgor nan Ulaidh: Bill Murray and Douglas Scott respectively carrying on the traditions of the 'thirties. With the arrival of Len Lovat and later Jimmy Marshall the remaining major problems capitulated in rapid succession. Scabbard Chimney on Stob Coire nan Lochan, led by Lovat, is reputedly as hard an ice climb as any in Glencoe. These parties carried their investigations further afield to Stob

Coire nam Berth and Stob Coire nan Lochan—crags that generally carry more snow than the Buachaille and offer more natural winter lines.

Glencoe was the birthplace of modern Scottish ice climbing and as such is unlikely to suffer neglect. Nevertheless the recent spate of activity has proved that its virtues as a winter playground are inferior to those of Ben Nevis, Lochnagar, and Creag Meaghaidh. Snow conditions in Glencoe are very variable and it is not unusual to find the Buachaille stripped of snow in mid-February.

Lochnagar and the Cairngorms

The climbs in the North-East Corrie of Lochnagar set the tempo for Scottish winter climbing throughout the period 1950–6. Initially there was but one solitary winter climb and the rock climbing possibilities were by no means fully explored. Now, every major ridge, gully and buttress has been climbed in winter, a total of thirty routes, each 600–700 feet in height. On all these climbs the unrelenting angle and considerable exposure merit deep respect. Local parties were largely responsible for the pioneering. A hard core of ice addicts from Aberdeen took up residence in the Corrie from November to May. Often the winter ascent followed within months of the first summer ascent and in a few cases actually preceded it. Unlike the Creag Dhu the Aberdonians favoured tricouni-nailed boots for all-round mountaineering (the tricounis v. crampons controversy still persists in Scottish climbing circles: dependent on conditions, both have their merits and demerits).

In 1950 "Goggs" Leslie and I selected the Douglas Gully of Lochnagar as the scene for our first encounter with steep ice. It proved to be a most unsuitable choice: the Gully was in excellent shape, but we were not. In fact, the last 200 feet of 70-degree snow-ice took us seven hours and we finished in darkness by tunnelling the cornice; the only apparent solution, as the edge projected far out over the gully.

The Douglas Gully as events proved scarcely deserved the notoriety our ascent earned for it. On subsequent winter ascents of Eagle Ridge and Parallel Buttress we encountered more sustained difficulty, but were better equipped to deal with it, having served our apprenticeship.

Bill Brooker, Jerry Smith, and Mike Taylor, all local Aberdeen climbers, led the way in winter exploration. Indeed, the Aberdeen group held a monopoly in the North-East Corrie till 1957, when Jimmy Marshall and a raiding Edinburgh party scored a notable triumph on Parallel Gully "B". On the first summer ascent of this route our party had encountered at least three V.S. pitches and its winter aspect is far from encouraging.

As the North-Eastern Corrie neared saturation point, the search for new routes widened to include every corrie in the Cairngorms area. Access to these remote corries was a problem on a winter week-end and skis often proved an invaluable asset.

Upwards of sixty new winter routes were discovered in the course of a few years and exploration is still continuing. It is hoped that the forthcoming *S.M.C. Climbing Guide* for the Cairngorms area will clarify the situation.

The 900-foot Labyrinth of Creag an Dubh Loch is among the finest Scottish ice routes, and its first ascent by Ronnie Sellars and Jerry Smith in 1959 followed several unsuccessful attempts. Further afield the remote Mitre Ridge of Beinn a' Bhùird gave Bill Brooker and myself a rousing tussle with deep powder snow on as late a date as 12 May.

Unfortunately Braemar, the poor man's Courmayeur, is a difficult place to reach in mid-winter. The direct route from the south via the Devil's Elbow is often closed by deep snow for several months and the local Tigers still lack competition.

Creag Meaghaidh

The full potentialities of Corrie Ardair as a winter climbing ground have yet to be realised.

The Centre Post excited a lot of attention in the 'thirties and Bell's route skirting the main ice-fall at mid-height has yet to be bettered. For some obscure reason, the other two Posts and the 1,200-foot Pinnacle Buttress attracted no custom. When Tennent and Slesser climbed the great *couloir* of the South Post in 1956 there was no record of a previous attempt.

Yet Creag Meaghaidh is no more inaccessible from Edinburgh than Ben Nevis, and the Loch Laggan road is seldom blocked. It will be surprising if this winter's activities do not finally dispel the aura of mystery from Corrie Ardair.

The opening salvoes of what may prove to be a long campaign were fired last winter by the Edinburgh musketeers. The Pinnacle Buttress gave Marshall, Stenhouse, and Haston a route typical of all that is best in Scottish winter mountaineering—complicated route-finding, magnificent situations, and every variety of obstacle. A long ice runnel on the left flank of the Buttress climbed by Tiso and Marshall was named Smith's Gully, after their fellow climber had met with defeat—an ironic tribute by Marshall.

The North-west Highlands

The problem of reaching those remote outposts in mid-winter has deterred all but those who do not have to turn an honest penny. In any case, the scope is not, as one might suppose, unlimited. Only a few crags such as the Coire Mhic Fhearchair of Beinn Eighe accumulate snow and ice as do Ben Nevis and the Cairngorms. The Cuillins are particularly disappointing; and the climber's dream of a winter traverse of the Main Ridge has not been realised.

Ben Nevis

The Ben is the home of Scottish "Alpinisme". Here the rude forefathers of the S.M.C. . . .

> Did assault the shoots
> and won their way by unheard of routes
> *S.M.C. song*

Here, too, in January 1959 was conceived, after an unduly protracted labour, the first five-day climb in the history of British mountaineering.

In 1939 Ben Nevis was still to the forefront in Scottish winter developments. Green Gully, a product of that era, is still regarded as a most formidable ice climb. Its neighbour, Comb Gully, reputedly the hardest pre-war ice course, occupying ten hours on the first ascent, has recently succumbed in under an hour. Stop Press reports say that Dougal Haston has reduced the time to twenty minutes!

For a long time after 1939 there was a lot of traffic on the established routes but little or no original exploration. Meanwhile, on Lochnagar and Glencoe, winter activity far outstripped that on the Ben. The C.I.C. log-book records several cursory inspections of Zero and Point Five Gullies, but few serious attempts to force an issue. An atmosphere of impregnability had surrounded these two gullies for some time and the amount of undeserved publicity they enjoyed served only to divert attention from numerous easier unclimbed alternatives.

The turning-point came on a memorable week-end in February 1957, when near-perfect conditions gave us the opportunity we had been waiting for. A large party foregathered at the C.I.C. hut. Hamish MacInnes, temporarily unattached, suggested that Graeme Nicol and I should join him on his seventh attempt. As he pointed out, the gully was virtually his property; since most of his property was in the gully we could but agree.

The weather had improved overnight and Zero Gully was plastered with excellent snow-ice. I led the first 350 feet occasionally inserting an overhead ice-piton as a safeguard against a momentary loss of balance. It was exhilarating climbing on reliable snow although the extreme angle and long run-outs did not encourage any liberties. Hamish now assumed the lead and fought his way up the last big pitch—the great ice-fall barring the way to the upper snow trough. The last 600 feet were quite straightforward, and a race developed: Nicol arrived last, carrying the sackful of Hamish's ironmongery. Zero Gully had yielded in only five hours—a tribute to the exceptional conditions we encountered.

Two days before the Zero Gully episode, Len Lovat, Nicol, and I chanced upon an even more valuable discovery. Bill Murray had persuaded us to have a look at the far side of the North-East Buttress which faces the Carn Mor Dearg *arête*. The result was the Cresta climb, the first of a series of long, mixed routes on this, the forgotten face of Ben Nevis. The later routes, all led by Ian Clough and his fellow climbers of R.A.F., Kinloss, are probably finer than Cresta, which has now become a thoroughfare. Slalom and Frostbite hold the joint distinction of being the longest natural ice routes in Britain, and offer 2,000 feet of complicated route-finding. None of these climbs is desperate by modern standards and their former anonymity is all the more difficult to explain. The summer aspect of the cliff is depressing, and the recorded routes follow "the line of most vegetation". Yet it is often just such a crag that offers the best winter lines. In winter mountaineering one learns to set new values on long-established routes.

The winter revival on the Ben has continued with unrelenting vigour up to the time of writing. There are two distinct fields for exploration. One has led to the exploitation of the Last Great Problems (i.e. the training climbs of the next generation). The other has accounted for a host of no less worthy routes, which the average climber can savour without risking annihilation. Raeburn's Buttress, Number Two Gully Buttress, the North Face of Castle Ridge, the Italian and Staircase climbs all come into this category.

However, it is difficult to resist the lure of notoriety. The Saga of Point Five Gully was a case in point. Once Zero had been climbed it was inevitable that Point Five should come under siege, and when Joe Brown fell off the second pitch, its reputation was firmly established. The Creag Dhu were next on the scene. In appalling conditions, Cunningham and Noon got as far as the third pitch; here a miniature Niagara erupted through a hole in the ice and prudence won the day. MacInnes's first solo attempt was typically unorthodox. He descended the top 600 feet of the gully, "yo-yo fashion" on a lifeline of nylon ropes borrowed from his unsuspecting rivals. His subsequent re-ascent proved the upper section to be climbable—already a well-known fact. At Easter, 1958, when a ribbon of clear water ice delineated the route, he returned to the attack with Ian "Dangle" Clough. They planned their ascent on the principle of "a pitch a day": consequently, when we spotted them on the second pitch, they were already on their second day's climbing. Here Fate took a hand, and prolonged blizzards made the recovery of the fixed ropes a feat in itself!

In January 1959, these tactics finally prevailed, and Clough, Alexander, Shaw, and Pipes emerged triumphant at the end of a seven-day operation. Every night they recuperated in the C.I.C. hut—a disqualification in the opinion of a puritan minority (who alleged, furthermore, that a rest day had allowed the party to replenish their stocks from a Fort William blacksmith's). Whether Point Five can be climbed in a day, using conventional technique, remains to be seen.

A week later the Orion Face of Ben Nevis, "the Scottish Nordwand" was climbed on the first attempt by Robin Smith and R. K. Holt. This pair had already made a very hard ascent of the Comb Buttress by the Tower Face Route, and they tackled the Orion Face by the line of the Long Climb (Summer grading, V. S. Rubbers), finding the rocks plated with ice throughout. This twelve-hour climb was perhaps the finest performance of the season. It could only be rivalled by Jimmy Marshall's remarkable lead of Minus Two Gully, probably the most severe winter route on record.

On a lighter theme Marshall and I completed a first winter girdle of the Main Face crossing all the established routes at midheight. This was not such a *tour de force* as one might suppose; there is a natural traversing line most of the way and the difficulties are not extreme. We started from Observatory Gully and finished five hours later on the Carn Mor Dearg *arête*.

What of the future? The summer months in Scotland are now the off-season—a period when hungry Tigers sharpen their claws for the winter onslaught. Hence this essentially *personal* diary of recent events may well be outdated by the time it goes to print. The scope for original winter exploration in Scotland is still enormous.

Of one thing I am certain. This vigorous offshoot from the parent stem is a healthy one: it will flourish and bear fruit. Its principles are founded on the best traditions of British mountaineering, and it teaches virtues which are the essence of successful

Alpine and Himalayan climbing—speed, resourcefulness and, above all, accurate route finding. Nevertheless I would recoil from describing Scottish winter climbing merely in terms of training for (so-called) Greater Mountaineering. That would be heresy: the Scottish brand of winter mountaineering is unique!

Postscript

The above notes were submitted too late for publication in the May issue. Since they were written another season has passed and a few more "citadels" have fallen.

The season of 1959–60 was remarkable if only for a spectacular campaign on Nevis by J. R. Marshall and R. C. Smith. In the course of a week they succeeded (I quote Marshall) "in cleaning up all the outstanding problems in the Ben". It had been anticipated that Point Five Gully would yield more easily in favourable conditions, but few could have forecast that a mere seven hours would be sufficient for success. No artificial aids apart from the two ice-axes were used. Marshall writes with typical audacity—"We included Point Five as a gesture—it's a fine climb but a wee-bit old fashioned now."

As if the Orion Face Direct were not sufficient in itself, there is now the "Direttissima". This 1,600-foot route, probably the most formidable route of its kind in Scotland (familiar phrase), starts at the foot of Zero Gully. It goes via ice grooves to the bottom left corner of the basin. As distinct from its precursor, the new route continues directly up the face overlooking the basin by way of a buttress on the right of the Second Slab Rib. Eight hours were required for the first winter ascent.

Marshall and Smith also accounted for the following routes— all of them led for the first time in winter—the Great Chimney on the East Flank of Tower Ridge, Minus Three Gully on the North-East Buttress (incidentally this numerical classification is becoming so complicated that any further additions will be cal- culated to the nearest decimal point), the Comb by Piggot's Route, and a new route on Observatory Buttress.

The half-dozen or so parties who have led Gardiloo Buttress in summer will be somewhat nonplussed to hear of a winter ascent. In the current Nevis Guide, the summer climb ranks second to Sassenach for difficulty—perhaps a generous assessment but not a recommendation for crampons. Smith and Marshall attacked the Buttress by its central ice-fall, taking six hours for 400 feet of climbing.

The final event of the year was an impudent raid on Zero Gully by Robin Smith's party, which commenced at the criminally late hour of 2 p.m. and ended, very properly, at 3 a.m., after the party had run out of daylight quite early on.

It was a lean year for most other climbers. Clough is reported to have led Compression Crack on Raeburn's Buttress sometime in January. Our own modest contribution was the North Post of Creag Meaghaidh. J. H. Deacon (Climber's Club), George McLeod, and I were joined on that occasion by Pierre Danalet, a guide of Les Diablerets. The spectacle of a Swiss guide on a Scottish ice climb was both interesting and instructive. Let it be said that he acquitted himself with honour.

MacInnes was rampant in the Cuillins. Unhappily his plans for "shooting" a winter traverse of the Ridge came to naught owing to lack of snow. It is reported unofficially that plans were made to transport snow from Coire Lagain to the Ridge in rucksacks, for distribution at suitable points so that a false photographic record of the prevailing conditions might be obtained.

OVER THE SEA TO SKYE

From The Etchachan Club Journal, 1962

I HAD MADE foolproof arrangements to meet Hamish MacInnes in Skye; so had Chris Bonington. Now the source of Hamish's livelihood is shrouded in mystery and his movements are often unpredictable. So we were not surprised to hear that he had been suddenly recalled by the B.B.C. for what he termed "a most important assignment". Hamish was bound for the Faroe Islands. We gathered that he hoped to bring back to an expectant world a film record of the islanders and their customs. He urged us to team up in his absence on the grounds that we were not unreasonable types and should find each other's company congenial. The two letters could almost have been carbon copies.

To anyone familiar with the Llanberis Pass and its galaxy of X. Certificate climbs, C. J. S. Bonington needs no introduction. Abroad his exploits are equally well known. An impetuous debut on the Eigerwand with Hamish had been, so to speak, the first rung of a ladder that led to the summit of Annapurna II and membership of the British Alpine Club!

Knowing that he had just returned from his latest Himalayan campaign and was by all accounts outrageously fit, I awaited the rendezvous with more than a little trepidation. His letter was rather puzzling. It read as follows: "Do you like curry? I find it is the only way of disguising compo. If so, and with your permission, I shall purchase several pounds of best Patna rice and assorted spices. I feel this is an important point, so I thought I should consult you first. Dick hated it on A.II. Yours etc. Chris". I folded it thoughtfully in my wallet. Here surely was one in whom the garb of the Sybarite served only to conceal the rugged temperament of the seasoned veteran.

We met at Euston Station. He was easily recognizable—a tall incongruous figure in Alpine breeches and anorak, telescoped under the weight of two enormous rucksacks. His Service Unit, he confessed, had only allowed him a second class travel warrant, but there are no social barriers among mountaineers, and we bivouacked in the luxury of a first-class compartment, keeping intruders at bay with the strains of my accordion. The ticket inspector was our only visitor; he came to remonstrate but only to retire in confusion. Bonington's winning riposte, "But I can't stretch myself properly in a second-class compartment" was delivered with the composure of one who brooks no interference from petty officialdom.

Our schedule took in Torridon, the Applecross hills and Skye in that order, and I had visions of chalking up a new route for every day of the holiday. Such a programme made no allowance for rain, midges and unfriendly motorists, because we were desperate men, spurred on by a dream of the great "Faces Nords"—a dream shattered on the eve of fulfilment by our mutual insolvency. As if still under the spell, Bonington had brought with him two dozen pitons of all shapes and sizes, an assortment of wooden wedges, a necklace of karabiners, a set of *étriers*, and a special device for threading slings behind chockstones (said to be indispensable in North Wales). Had this mighty arsenal been brought to bear on some misty Highland crag, the effect would have been truly devastating. Our friends of the "white haired potentate", as Hamish calls them, would have disowned us forever. Fortunately, whereas my feeble protests carried little weight Bonington's rucksack carried a lot more, and he was forced—albeit grudgingly—to compromise.

Our first base was the Ling Hut in Glen Torridon. Although only recently leased to the S.M.C. by Coulin Estates, the hut has an atmosphere that is difficult to define—wistful perhaps of the early pioneers who trod these hills, and to whom once upon a time the secrets of the great corries were revealed. On the wall is Tom Weir's fine photograph of Ling and Glover, taken only a few months before the end of their long partnership.

From the hut it is but a short step to the Coire Mhic Fhearchair of Beinn Eighe; still bristling with unclimbed rock, despite the successive waves of embryo Sassenach exploration which have engulfed the nearby Carn Mor Crags and An Teallach.

On my last encounter with the majestic Triple Buttresses, I had come forearmed by Tom Weir with all the information about recent exploration.

Weir and Len Lovat were the first post-war climbers to meet with much success in the way of new routes. They were also the first to investigate the eastern facets of the three great buttresses where they found little trace of the conventional terrace pattern, so prevalent elsewhere in Torridon. Moreover the rock was not sandstone, but a rough quartzite set at an exceedingly fierce angle, yet so jointed as to present a bewildering array of cracks and *dièdres*: none of them looked easy, yet many offered that faint chance of success that is so often the hallmark of a classic route.

They prospected first of all on the Central Buttress face, and set up a couple of fine routes between the traditional buttress line and the edge of East Central Gully. But the two surviving strongholds—the eastern walls of the East and West Buttresses—were much more securely fortified. The latter, a precocious baby Eigerwand, looked heavy with menace, and in fact overhung slightly throughout its last 600 feet. On the East Buttress the upper 600-foot tier of vertical cliff continued leftwards for several hundred yards before petering out on the brink of Far East Gully. Here was a miniature Cloggy, in comparison with which the Rannoch Wall paled into insignificance.

The two Glasgow climbers, however, were intent on discovering a route that took in the complete left wall of the East Buttress so they started from the floor of the lower corrie. After eight hours of very severe climbing, they were forced to retreat only 150 feet below the skyline. In 1959 my luck was better and by concentrating on the upper tier I was rewarded with an excellent climb of little more than severe standard; on the three culminating pitches the correct solution proving in each case to be the least obvious one. This route, Gnome Wall, was probably to the left of the Lovat–Weir "tentative" but it would be an interesting experiment to link the two routes together.

So much for history. Our number one objective was the unclimbed East Wall of the West Buttress. Such a mundane name

seemed inappropriate to a face of this stature, so we christened it
The Wall of the Winds. A brief skirmish served, however, to
convince us that better weather was necessary for success. During
the climb it started to rain. Initially we were protected by the
beetling overhangs several hundred feet above but then the big
drips started and all the holds became moist and oily. From the
Meadow half-way up the cliff we wriggled up a deep contorted
chimney, left it by a thin traverse and continued up a steep
shattered crack—150 feet of very exposed climbing.

This left us on our last link with "terra firma"—a large but
precarious ledge, overhung above and undercut below; part of a
thin horizontal fault line slicing right across the middle of the
upper quartzite crust. We wondered idly if it extended all the
way along the face—if so what a magnificent natural line it would
be for a Girdle Traverse! Of more immediate importance it
offered us a safe escape on to the edge of West Buttress from where
we could climb to the top of the cliff without undue difficulty.

By now the rain was finding its way through my weatherproof
anorak, although Bonington with less flamboyant equipment was
still dry. I reminded him that it was only twenty-four hours since
we had boarded the Highlandman at Euston. A bivouac in étrier
and "cat's cradle"—exclusive privilege of the Faces Nords
clientele—would probably have suited him admirably but I was
motivated by baser ideas. We checked out accordingly, crossing
two pitches of severe standard, and abandoning a shiny new piton
as a peace offering to the Big Grey Man of the Mountains.

Two days passed before we returned. On the first of these we
visited a remote peak to the south of Glen Torridon—An Ruadh
Stac—which failed, though only by a few feet, to measure up to
Munro qualifying standards. For this if no other reason it had
come to be regarded by most climbers as a mere nonentity.
Even the Editor of the *Northern Highlands Guide* had little to say
in its favour:—"the precipitous north-east face of the mountain
looks very forbidding and the rock is untrustworthy—however,
there are doubtless climbs to be made".

This statement was, however, quite enough to stimulate our
imagination and the long toil through the peat bogs served only

to whet our appetite for the feast of new routes that was to follow. What Messrs Ling and Glover had achieved in Coire Mhic Fhearchair fifty years ago, we might now emulate on the North East Face of An Ruadh Stac!

Alas, perfection is seldom attainable: it usually exists only in the imagination. Two disjointed 300-foot tiers of cliff comprised all the live rock in the vicinity. In the circumstances we got away with a rather pleasant climb of very difficult standard by combining a route on each tier. The quality of the rock of the lower tier was impeccable (Bonington said "gneiss" or perhaps "nice") proving once again that sweeping assertions by "remote control" guide-book editors should be taken with more than a pinch of salt.

We made record time on the return leg to Annat after Bonington had scented female prey ahead and accelerated accordingly. Once more for him came bitter disillusionment: the elusive trio though nimble footed belonged to a category best described as matronly!

A day later we set out again for Coire Mhic Fhearchair. By the lochside we met a large group of earnest-looking men. Climbers, perhaps? Certainly not, we were assured. Their labours were only in the cause of science and their motives, unlike ours, were purely altruistic. We had indeed surprised them in the act of completing a Bathographic Survey of Lochan Coire Mhic Fhearchair. Hence the two men in the rubber dinghy, whose soundings were communicated at minute intervals to the group of eager computors on the shore; each momentous announcement preceded by the shrill blast of a whistle. Their staccato commentary was to accompany us throughout our climb and cause several false alarms. It only goes to show that nowadays it is impossible, even in a remote Highland corrie, to escape the march of progress. Mountaineer-scientists, tiny embryonic Slessers,* lurk behind every chockstone.

We had made a cache on top of the cliffs after our previous day's climb. In order to retrieve it we climbed the Central

* Dr. Malcolm Slesser, a prominent member of the Scottish Mountaineering Club.

Buttress. This was a fine airy climb though open to much variation. Before we finished, it had started to drizzle and The Wall
of the Winds had retired discreetly behind a watery shroud. As an
alternative, I suggested the Girdle Traverse that we had spotted on
Monday. My companion was unenthusiastic. "A mere scramble,"
he protested, "nothing more than a formality": but he came along
notwithstanding.

Half an hour later we had not only roped up but were searching
conscientiously for belays. The fault line was unmistakable: it cut
right across the Eastern Ramparts from the foot of Far East Gully
to the vertical skyline of the East Buttress. By no stretch of the
imagination could it be termed an easy scramble. Pitch succeeded
pitch, each exposed corner yielding only by virtue of the fault
line. Elsewhere there was nothing but a smooth unrelenting
verticality. We passed my tiny cairn marking the half-way point
on Gnome Wall. This climb was the only line of weakness that
I could determine on the upper palisade, but not so Bonington,
who viewed the crag with an eye of faith that had long since
become myopic from prolonged study of overworked Welsh
outcrops. He claimed to have spotted at least a dozen routes of
fine calibre.

The one pitch I remember vividly was that which led on to the
front of the East Buttress. Here, "a profound abyss drew forth
startled comments and there was talk of retreat". Instead, as
did the ancients, we "smoked a pipe over it and eventually crossed
the hiatus without incident".

Six hundred feet of continuously difficult climbing was already
more than we had bargained for, and so we saw no reason to
grumble when the ledge became more broken and accommodating. Except for one difficult gap we were able to move together
across the East and Central Buttress, although even here there
was only a small margin of freedom and we had to take great
care. Ultimately we reached the bed of West Central Gully
where only 150 feet separated us from the point we had reached
earlier in the week. This promised to be the most impressive
segment of the Girdle—a thin scar drawn boldly across the breadth
of a great unclimbed wall. Yet it yielded only three more pitches

of severe standard making eight in all, perhaps more, we had long since lost count. So ended a memorable day's climbing, which we rounded off in style by tacking on a new variation at the top of the West Buttress.

Our Torridon programme was now completed. We were tempted to stay on, for there is more unclimbed rock in Coire Mhic Fhearchair than anywhere in the Cuillins (or, for that matter, north-west Scotland), but we had a pressing engagement with the Cioch of Sgùrr a' Chaorachain, over Applecross way, and it was one we could not afford to miss.

For future reference, it might be noted that the Shieldaig bus meets the mail train at Strathcarron Station. We did not know this and got off at Stromeferry—the notorious bottle-neck of West Coast traffic. Here, according to the tourist brochure, "time stands still": so do long queues of irate motorists lining the roads on either side of the ferry. In the height of the tourist season there is more hot air vented at this remote spot than at many a Rangers–Celtic football match. The ferrymen belong to a different category. They stand aloof from the mob, performing their tasks with the unruffled calm and natural dignity of the Celt. Nothing short of an H-bomb could shake their composure. The tale is told by a hiker who saw his rucksack and all his kit engulfed by the clear waters of a Highland loch. The skipper turned to the ferryman responsible for the accident, and chided him gently for his mistake.

"Ach, James," he said, "you will really have to be more careful in future."

Hence the moral: "it is no use crying over someone else's spilt milk".

We had anticipated an early lift, but the only fellow traveller who showed any interest in our plight was a mongrel collie who accepted my last scrap of bread and then nipped me in the leg. In the end we had to trudge the full twelve miles and it was 6 p.m. before we reached the lower rocks of the Cioch. Almost simultaneoulsy the clouds opened and every crack became a waterspout.

We scrambled breathlessly up to the Half-way Ledge and along it as far as the Nose, where the big overhangs form a natural canopy. Bonington selected the dryest and hence most overhanging crack in the vicinity.

"Just keep an eye on the rope, I won't be a minute," he remarked laconically, lacing up his favourite P.A.'s.

True to his word he returned almost immediately, landing on the ledge in a heap.

"Mild XS," he muttered. "You have a go."

"I am going to try beyond the corner on your left," I replied. "At least that's the natural line."

"But that's a scruffy climb!" he protested. "Personally I'd rather admit I was defeated than resort to cheating."

This fairly roused my wrath. I have a proprietary interest in the Cioch dating back to our ascent of the North Wall in 1952 and our discovery of the five great buttresses in the Corrie beyond, and now this was the first time that I had heard the rock described as "scruffy". I counted it an unpardonable insult.

Paradoxically it was the Lion of Llanberis who led the first and only dirty pitch on the climb. Here were scanty clumps of grass and heather from which he recoiled with an expression akin to revulsion, as if picking his way through a freshly manured field.

"A fine orthodox line," I murmured as I passed him, "and even better things lie in store for us."

A rope's-length in the general direction of the Nose led to an open chimney of 60 feet, well furnished with holds. Then we were forced further rightwards to emerge upon a lofty balcony right out on the angle of the Nose.

Bonington's lead once more, and it looked like a desperate piece of work. I squeezed into a dry corner and lit a cigarette, resigning myself to a long wait. I was too pessimistic: 100 feet of rope snaked out in as many seconds and a triumphant yell resounded round the corrie.

"Come on man—it's incredible!"

It was indeed. Great rough excrescences sprouted everywhere on the Nose like an exuberant eruption of "acne vulgaris". What had appeared from any angle to be an XS pitch up an incredibly exposed slab turned out to be a glorious Difficult!

The rain poured down unheeded. I yodelled with gay abandon: Bonington cheered (his musical repertoire is strictly conservative).

Above us 350 feet of wonderful rock soared in brilliant crescendo to the topmost crown of the Cioch. The Cioch Nose—an eight years' dream—had yielded almost without a fight. Yet what a magnificent climb. It was "The Diff. to end all Diffs!" Bonington affirmed it could fit comfortably into one of his favourite Welsh crags, yet lose nothing to its new environment.

Nothing could lower our morale now; not even a night in a Youth Hostel, for which we paid more than an average B. and B. There was no time to prepare a meal before lights out (11 p.m.), so we chatted amicably with the warden before turning in on mattresses which had been stripped of blankets and pillows for hygienic reasons as we could not produce the regulation pattern sleeping sacks (Mark I). Next morning we completed our tasks to the warden's satisfaction and left in a hurry, clutching our newly won membership cards.

So at last we arrived in Glen Brittle. Bonington was still awaiting the return of his wallet which had lain by the roadside in Torridon for some days until a small boy found it and handed it to the postmaster. I reproached Chris for his carelessness and reminded him of the debt he owed to native Scottish integrity.

"Where's your jacket?" he interrupted.

I remembered. It was on the bus that we had just left—so was my wallet. . . .

We called at Cuillin Cottage and told Mrs. Campbell that we had both lost our wallets—by an extraordinary coincidence— and hence might not be able to pay for our accommodation until later.

"I don't know if it reassures you," I added gravely, "but I should perhaps mention that I am a member of the Scottish Mountaineering Club."

"Maybe so," said she, "but you have an honest face and that is a lot more important."

The week we spent at Cuillin Cottage was excellent in all respects. There is a tradition here of good homely food and comfort that dates back to the early days of Cuillin exploration and climbers of all creeds and denominations are welcomed with the same excellent hospitality.

When the sun shines on Skye, it catches everyone by surprise, so it was almost noon next day before Bonington and I got under way, still dazed by our luck with the weather. We had six hours for the round trip to the Coireachan Ruadh face of Mhic Coinnich, so we had to sprint. A new route on Sgùrr Thearlaich, of little merit, but conveniently near at hand, took us up to the ridge and from there we scrambled at breakneck speed down the Coruisk side and round to the foot of the most talked about crag in Skye.

Bill Brooker and Mike Dixon, the original explorers, had set up between them three outstanding routes—Fluted Buttress, Crack of Dawn and Dawn Grooves—the latter a more recent offshoot from Crack of Dawn. Brooker had avoided the steepest part of the Grooves and reckoned that if his route could be straightened it would give superlative climbing, "perhaps the best in Skye". This had been our original intention, but Bonington, who had already led Crack of Dawn and inspected Dawn Grooves, decided to go one better. He suggested attempting a completely new line to the left of Dawn Grooves. This was the steepest part of the Coireachan Ruadh face, an 800-foot sweep of vertical grey gabbro, its smooth uniformity only interrupted by the occasional cluster of black overhangs. It impressed me considerably, but I said nothing and tried to look bold.

By rights there should have been only one feasible line—an almost vertical water-worn chute. I climbed a token 80 feet and threw down all the loose rock I could find, hoping to demonstrate the futility of proceeding. However, while I roped down, Bonington disappeared round a corner on the right and I found him firmly established below a rather attractive dièdre, looking as pleased as the goose who laid the golden eggs.

"This is the route for us," he announced proudly, "and here is an old tin can to prove it."

As we were supposed to be climbing a new route, I did not see the force of his logic. However, as the holds on the wall of the dièdre were large and hospitable, it seemed pointless to waste time arguing. At 70 feet I came upon an old rusty piton, and pulling up on it sighted a tell-tale nylon sling at the back of the next ledge.

"No joy here," I reported. "They abseiled off. Maybe there's a slight chance to the right."

Treading delicately across the rim of the vortex, I reached the foot of another much fiercer *dièdre*. The only stance here was a sloping foothold, large enough for a roosting seagull. I hammered in two belay pitons, lashed myself into an upright position and beckoned encouragingly.

This was Bonington's day of glory. Few climbers of my acquaintance would have tackled this pitch, without the moral security of several piton-runners. For all practical purposes, it looked to be a completely holdless *dièdre*, all of 70 feet in height, and as near vertical as made no difference. He used one peg and then only because we knew that my belay would not support a fall of more than a few feet. For the rest of the way, Bonington and the rough Skye gabbro were inseparable as a courting couple. I realised for the first time the value of P.A.'s on a really thin pitch. Most of the current Welsh masters wear them: a few never take them off, even in bed.

"Hard severe" was his first impression, later corrected to "Hard Very Severe, perhaps Mild XS in boots". It should be added that this was intended as a face-saver for me. I found considerable difficulty. Happily the next pitch was a mere scramble—about Mild Severe perhaps. It landed me on a large ledge, from which I could peer down into Dawn Grooves on the right and contemplate gloomily the hopelessness of trying to avoid one's destiny.

We were firmly entrenched below the wicked cluster of over-hangs and again it was Bonington's turn for the trip into "No-Man's-Land"—the narrow borderline between the sublime and the impossible. Up to the roof he swarmed, oozing confidence, then came a pause. For a few seconds he flapped around below the eaves like a young eagle about to take flight for the first time. The symbolic significance was not lost upon me.

"Will it go?" I asked anxiously—"or will you?"

As if in answer to my question he suddenly lunged prodigiously, found something and twitched all over with gratitude. Then he was up around the corner and out of sight.

"It will go," he answered breathlessly, "but it is not easy."

Very Severe, on at least three counts, was my verdict. Above the first overhang was an incipient crack at the top of which I passed Bonington tied to a piton. The second overhang was breathing hard down my neck but out to the left was the sheer corner decorated with a fragile spike that beckoned invitingly. I grabbed it hastily, and it held. Almost at arm's length another spike appeared, massive and reassuring. I slapped on a nylon sling and breathed again. One last strenuous pull and I had reached the end of the major difficulties.

The sting was drawn and the venom spent. Henceforward the route threaded its way lazily upwards for 300 feet or more by deep chimneys and cracks, still steep and exposed, but bristling with huge heart-warming holds. Surely there was no other route in the Cuillins that could equal this one for technical difficulty or regal splendour!

We built a little cairn at the top and I smoked my last cigarette. Putting a name to a new climb is always a pleasant way of wasting time. "Crack of Dawn" was a noble precedent, intended to commemorate one of Brooker's infrequent early morning starts. Something similar seemed to be indicated. Dawn Addams and It Dawned were in turn rejected as being altogether too flippant and liable to provoke the godfathers of the crag. I suggested Alligator Crawl, because it was smooth and in the groove, but not all mountain lovers are jazz enthusiasts. Eventually we settled for King Cobra for reasons that will be obvious to most climbers on a closer acquaintanceship.

The rains came and we rested on our laurels, entertaining the company at Cuillin Cottage with tales of miraculous escape and hard-earned victory. We had once upon a time intended to camp on the beach but Bonington had struck up an acquaintanceship with the young lass who cooked the porridge and was reluctant to change his quarters merely for reasons of economy.

We had one other sunny day in Skye when we turned in a mixed bag of routes—three scrappy variants on the Bhàsteir

Tooth and a more satisfactory climb on Sgùrr a'Mhadaidh which we named Whispering Wall. It follows the edge of Deep Gash Gully opposite Thunder Rib and although a fine natural line of merely very difficult standard it had apparently never been visited. Thunder Rib on the other side of the Gully had been attempted several times and was still unclimbed. We had insufficient time on our hands to attempt the overhanging second pitch, but we saw nothing to suggest that it might not be climbed given "the right men high at the right time"* (i.e. a group of inebriated Scotsmen on Hogmanay night). It is certainly a fine looking buttress though not on a par with the Coireachan Ruadh climbs.

The last day of the holiday found us on the road for the Storr Rocks. We had been assured by several climbers that the rock here was no better than porridge, but with a distrust born of long association with rival scalp hunters we had been forced to investigate the place for ourselves. We could now confirm the accuracy of their reports. The rock is like porridge—in consistency though not quality, for porridge is a part of our national heritage and a feast fit for a king. This was not.

Nevertheless it is a weird, fascinating spot almost Dolomitic in contour. The rock is perhaps at its best on the Old Man of Storr and even there is dangerously loose. Don Whillans, who led the only recorded ascent of the Old Man two years ago, would be surprised to hear that local tradition credits the feat to a thirteen-year-old American lass who is reputed to have nipped up and down in her plimsolls. The date is not specified but it may be assumed that no pitons were used. It is also rumoured that the Devil lives on the summit.

One hundred yards to the north of the Old Man is another pinnacle overshadowed by its neighbour yet from some angles even more bizarre. Daylight can be seen through three ragged windows in the crumbling masonry, suggesting a fanciful resemblance to a ruined cathedral. The topmost spire looked as if it might yield to a strong push.

"How about that!" I cried enthusiastically.

* Robin Smith has since proved me correct.

"Very picturesque," Bonington commented briefly.

"I mean, as a route." He sat up.

"Now why should anyone want to climb a heap of disintegrating rubbish like that? You tell me."

Here was my cue.

"Because it is there," I answered (recalling an apt phrase from a climbing book).

For this was no insignificant mole-hill. It was a virgin summit modest by Alpine or even Cuillin proportions but nevertheless a potential Aiguille Bonington or Sgùrr Tom. We took the rope as an afterthought and lived to be grateful. After a scramble of 100 feet we came out on to the *arête* opposite the Old Man and had to readjust our scale of dimensions. There was still 75 feet to climb and it was not easy. We split it into three pitches in order to limit the momentum of any loose rock dislodged by the leader. A crash helmet would have been useful for the second.

At last, after a titantic struggle, Chris balanced delicately on the topmost block and performed the time honoured summit rites. It then occurred to him that the descent might present its own special problems. He would not consider climbing down by the same route and there was nowhere to fix a *rappel* rope. It was all very depressing. His only hope lay in adjusting the rope across the very tip of the pinnacle so that I could lower him down to safety, but the manœuvre was fraught with danger for two very obvious reasons. In the first place the rope might slip from its moorings: again, and more important from my point of view, the whole top of the pinnacle might break off under the extra strain. In the event nothing untoward occurred—otherwise I would not have lived to tell the tale—but it left me with an acute attack of the "heeby-jeebies".

It is tempting to consider how ironic it might have been for Bonington to have achieved the pinnacle of his desire only to be marooned there for all time. One pictures a statuesque yet almost absurd figure sitting cross-legged on its lofty pedestal, contemplating the passing crowds with a jaundiced eye and being fed periodically from a long pole. In climbing circles it would have perpetuated for all time the fame of the Aiguille

Bonington and for the tourist trade would have been an un-expected fillip—perhaps an even greater attraction than the Loch Ness Monster! Who knows? Alas for the historian, " 'tis of such stuff that dreams are made". Miracles never happen in real life—only in fairy-tales.

CAIRNGORM COMMENTARY

From The Scottish Mountaineering Club Journal, 1962

"Any fool can climb good rock," said Dr J. H. B. Bell, "but it takes craft and cunning to get up vegetatious schist and granite. . . ."

"We were bound for Lochnagar, the greatest citadel of vegetatious granite."

W. H. MURRAY (*Mountaineering in Scotland*)

IT WAS THE opinion of most climbers of the 'thirties that no worth-while routes had been recorded on Cairngorm granite. This was not misrepresentation but fact. With the exception of a few classic climbs (such as the Mitre Ridge of Beinn a' Bhùird or the Eagle Ridge of Lochnagar) exploration in the Cairngorms before 1946 had not gone beyond the Gully Epoch.

Most gullies are unpleasant. A Cairngorm gully is doubly so. It is the sort of place you would incarcerate your worst enemy; a dank gloomy prison where moisture seeps from every fissure and "all the air a solemn stillness holds"—save for a constant drip, drip from many a greasy moss-enshrouded chockstone and the occasional dull thud as another ledge sloughs away in a welter of slime and rubble.

The early mountaineers, who revelled in the false security of gullies and chimneys and spurned the hazardous freedom of the open face, must have found the Cairngorms a veritable Mecca. Here were any number of holdless muddy walls against which to erect a pyramid of stout fellows in tweed jackets, greasy constricted chimneys where they might squirm and wriggle to their hearts' content, and improbable through-routes streaming with icy water and black as Old Nick himself which "would just admit a cragsman of average girth."

It is a pity that so little exploration was carried out by the mud-bespattered pioneers, for their accounts in epic Victorian style would have made splendid reading. In fairness it could be pointed out that the few climbs they did pass on to posterity earned a notoriety out of all proportion to their number.

There was Raeburn's Gully in Lochnagar which on the first ascent in 1888 harboured a great block "surmountable only by the aid of an ice-pick hung from the upper edge". On the second ascent thirty years later, the main obstacle had become "an imposing two-tier pitch some 70 feet in height". Unhappily the famous Double Cave pitch was not destined for longevity, and following a rock fall in 1940 "not a vestige of it remained". The Editor of the *Cairngorm Club Journal* sang its requiem: "I regard this as a catastrophe of the first magnitude . . . fitting to be classed with the fall of Constantinople, The Union of 1707, Hammond losing the toss at Sydney, and things of that kind". A few years later I was one of a large party that had a grandstand view of the collapse of yet another entire pitch near the top of the gully. We had a special interest in this pitch because we had descended it only ten minutes earlier in order to attack the unclimbed chimney on the right wall of the gully. At least two of our number had come along merely to watch or pass ribald remarks, but by the time the echoes had died away and the clouds of dust had settled we had suddenly become a united party of six. Thus was made the first ascent of The Clam.

There was also the Douglas–Gibson Gully of Lochnagar. Like Raeburn's, it "changes its character from year to year"—to borrow a phrase from the pioneers. Raeburn himself made several unsuccessful attempts between 1897 and 1901; ultimately, he was lowered from the top and was "sufficiently discouraged by what he saw not to try again".

Up to the early 1940s the Cairngorms retained the aura of inhospitality ascribed to them by these early climbers. In 1941, however, a worthy champion emerged in the familiar colour of Dr J. H. B. Bell, who may be regarded as the patron saint of granite climbers and the first prophet of the true Gospel. None of us had ever met Dr Bell: to us he was merely a voice, thundering out a clarion call from his distant S.M.C. editorial chair. Yet he seemed to feel much as we did about the Cairngorm granite, describing the Eagle Ridge of Lochnagar, his favourite route, in fine authoritative vein as "for difficulty, narrowness and steepness altogether superior to any of the well-known Nevis ridges". His two companion routes on Shadow Buttress "B" and the Tough–Brown Ridge served to illustrate that there was no lack of sound climbing rock in the Cairngorms for those who had the initiative to find it.

It had been amply proved that the Cairngorm gullies had little to recommend them, but Bell was the first to demonstrate that the more exposed ridges, faces and buttresses of rough, weathered granite had as much to offer the rock specialist as many more highly-rated Scottish crags. His researches were to inspire young Aberdonian climbers after the war, for here a school sprang up owing little to any pre-war group. Many of its early struggles took place in that notorious Douglas–Gibson Gully, whose first ascent had in fact been made in 1933 by one Charles Ludwig (the first man to attach a skeleton to the spire of Marischal College and to cross the "Blondin" wires above Rubislaw Quarry).

Ludwig in fact set little store upon his Douglas Gully adventure, and described the route as "perhaps unjustifiable". Such a qualification had of course the unintended effect of securing for the climb the attention of successive generations of young aspirant V.S. men who may be relied upon to accept any open invitation to deride their elders. So for a time in the bad old days "before the dawn of reason", many young tigers were blooded in "Gibson's", often literally, so that the gully gained quite a reputation for itself. The more loose rock they pulled away, the more they uncovered, so that the standard varied from V.D. to V.S. in successive weeks.

It was not until 1949–50 that the winter ascent which had eluded Douglas and Gibson in 1893 was again seriously considered. Abortive attempts followed—probably the most spectacular being that on which George McLeod plummeted from the cornice almost to the lochside, a vertical height of some 800 feet. He had been turned back at the last pitch and, while roping down in the approved fashion, suddenly found that he was no longer able to maintain a grip with numbed fingers and slid down the length of the rope, rocketing off the end like a small shooting star. Deep powder snow saved him from annihilation; he escaped with bruises, and climbed up again to safeguard his companion's descent.

On 30 December 1950 "Goggs" Leslie and I emerged, shaken but triumphant, from a hole in Douglas Gully cornice, thereby ushering in a new era of winter expeditions on routes which had hitherto been regarded as solely within the provinces of the rock specialist. It was also our first première and earned grudging recognition from our more talented contemporaries together with admission into the select conclave that gathered in the Fife Arms, Braemar, on a Saturday night. We did not broadcast the principal factor in our surprise coup—that having climbed well beyond the point where we could have safely withdrawn and finding no belays for an abseil we had little option but to continue climbing. In the long run we both profited from this good fortune, and learned several important lessons. I cannot recall ever again suffering such agonies of apprehension on a climb.

Leslie and I had thus dramatically elevated ourselves to a peerage which I had first encountered two years before in rather humiliating circumstances. I was one of a motley collection of Gordon's College schoolboys who had chosen to spend Hogmanay in the Cairngorms, using as our base camp Bob Scott's bothy at Luibeg. We discovered that more than forty climbers were housed in various outbuildings and that we had been relegated to the stick shed as befitting to our lowly station, Minor snowdrifts formed inside the building and an indoor thermometer recorded 40 degrees of frost. Next door in the bothy, which was reserved for the hierarchy and where the heat from a blazing log fire drove one back to the farthermost corners, were two very celebrated mountaineers—Bill Brooker and Mac Smith. We soon guessed their identity by the excited buzz of conversation that signalled their return from a climb, the sudden hush as they entered the bothy, and the easy grace with which they accepted the seats of honour nearest the fire. Mac Smith was then (and still is) the chieftain of the Luibeg Clan—an all-round mountaineer who had taken part in almost every important summer or winter ascent in recent years. He knew the Cairngorms better than any of his contemporaries, and they would have been the first to admit it. The bothy armchair, which has only recently been vacated and converted into firewood, was Mac's prerogative—a rustic throne. Bill Brooker, "the young Lochinvar", cut a more dashing figure, the complete counterpart to Mac's slightly reserved manner. To all outward appearances he was merely another pimply-faced schoolboy like ourselves, full of wild talk. But then who could forget that this was the same young heretic who had but recently burst into the climbing arena with a series of routes which had defied the best efforts of preceding generations? With such a wealth of mountaineering experience behind him, you could overlook the lad's extravaganzas.

These were the real mountaineers—not mere "hill bashers" like ourselves who had that day tramped many an endless mile in search of a minor 3,009-foot Munro top away out in the middle of the Great Moss. We had built a little cairn on what appeared the most elevated undulation and been well satisfied with our day's achievement. These men spoke of icy vigils and gigantic ice-falls; routes that finished long after dark; remote bivouacs in faraway corries, riotous nights in bothies, late-night dances in Braemar and brimming tankards in the Fife Arms. Adventure, unconventionality, exuberance—these were the very elements missing from our scholarly conception of mountaineering which had led us with mathematical precision up and down the weary lists of Munro's Tables.

I do not know what impressions we left behind. A few of our number were kilted and this earned us the title of the "Horrible Heelanders", a name which stuck. I remember listening with envy to the two demi-gods as they planned the first winter ascent of Crystal Ridge, success already a foregone conclusion. Late next night when they did not return at the appointed hour, we spoke hopefully of a search party, but this merely earned for us the derision of the company. Their confidence was soon rewarded by the arrival of the victors, eyebrows caked with frozen drift, faces glowing with the heat of battle. . . .

A year later, in my first year at university, I became part-owner of a climbing rope. After some preliminary experiments, we started cautiously feeling our way up the well-trodden Mods. and Diffs. of Lochnagar and the Sputan Dearg.

At that time it was impossible to climb for long in the Cairngorms without becoming aware of the diversities of opinions and ideals that characterised the bothy set and stamped each of its members as a genuine eccentric, uninhibited by the conventions of society. Even the names by which they were known invited a wealth of conjecture—Sandy-Sandy, Ashy, Chesty, Dizzie, Sticker, Esposito, the Hash Kings. . . .

The Hash Kings might have been a secret society. Their hashes, which were compounded of every conceivable ingredient known to man, were justly famous. I never learned the names of the founder members, but on one of my early bothy week-ends I met a character who introduced himself with simple dignity as "Apprentice to the Hash Kings". Sad to relate, the Hash Kings have faded into obscurity, and the name itself has become abbreviated to Hasher, which is synonymous with bothymonger or nignog, and this is a very low order of animal life indeed.

Of a later vintage were the Boor Boys, a group of unruly youngsters from Aberdeen Grammar School who terrorised the bothies; among their numbers were Kenneth Grassick and Graeme Nicol, later to become respected sons of the S.M.C.

Then there were the individualists, although every man in that company wore the hallmark of an individualist. One remembers Stan Stewart who strummed his guitar on the back seat of the Three Fifteen. (The *Three Fifteen from Bon-Accord Square* was a special bus tactfully set aside for climbers by Messrs. Strachans Ltd., following incidents in which old ladies had been isolated at the back of the bus by a mountain of rucksacks, only effecting an escape, several miles beyond their destination, by a desperate hand traverse.) There was Charlie Smith, brows furrowed in concentration, whistling some obscure aria; Mac Smith and Kenny Winram arguing about the early New Orleans trumpeters; Jamie Robertson engrossed in Marx; Freddy and Sticker, the inseparables, plotting new routes in Coire na Ciche; Alex Tewnion, with binoculars and camera, in quest of some unsuspecting dotterel; Chesty Bruce resplendent in tartan shirt and wide toothy grin, with his band of camp-followers; Bill Stewart, who thought nothing of cycling out to Lochend Bothy for a day's climbing on Lochnagar, a round trip of 100 miles; and Ada Adams bound for Derry Lodge, to supervise the week-end "work party" from the Cairngorm Club.

There were three clubs in Aberdeen: the Cairngorm, the Etchachan and the University Lairig Club though, by and large, more reputable climbing was done on impromptu bothy week-ends than during organised meets. Only a few regular week-enders were active club supporters and perhaps most of these owed allegiance to the Etchachan Club, a splinter from the Cairngorm Club. The latter club, though nowadays flourishing and not lacking in initiative, seemed to us then rather moribund. Most of the members were keen hill walkers, but there was a notable lack of rock climbers. Even the club circular had an archaic quality, describing club meets as "motor coach excursions" and ending with the solemn injunction "Members are requested not to ring the Meets Secretary at his residence". We later found that the wording of the circular could be adapted with only minor alterations to a West Indian calypso tune, and the song enjoyed a fair measure of popularity among the nonconformists.

The Etchachan Club was in many ways the antithesis of the Cairngorm Club. The latter wined and dined in the Fife Arms, the Etchachan Club merely stopped for a half-hour break at any convenient pub; their meets were less expensive, but there was a certain air of austerity, not to mention frustration, in leaving a half-pint standing on the bar counter to sprint for a bus which moved off punctually on the half-hour.

The University Club, like most clubs of its kind, enjoyed an ephemeral existence. Certainly its most flourishing period was during the reign of Ken Grassick. It was his policy that a mountaineering club should not solely depend on the support of accredited mountaineers. A club could be run on popular lines if it supplied suitable entertainment for its members, not only in the mountains, but also in the valleys. His recruiting campaign was initiated by an advertisement in *Gaudie*, the students' newspaper, stressing the club's need for new blood. "*Qualified climbing instructors, including some of World Repute*" (this phrase was masterly) "*will be glad to show newcomers the ropes . . . climbers of (both) sexes welcomed . . . no mountaineering experience necessary! The bus will stop at the Inver Inn for refreshments, singing etc.*" The response was more than gratifying. Instructors were soon able to select their "clients" from a large number of applicants and bus meets were attended by upwards of seventy members. Not all came to climb, though nearly all enjoyed a little fresh air prior to the evening's entertainment. Thus it came about that a day meet to Lochnagar cost merely 5*s*. a head, and the ends justified the means.

We saw very few climbers from farther afield: it was left to local climbers to reap a weekly harvest of new routes. Most visitors to the Cairngorms came only to collect Munros, sleep a night at the Shelter Stone or pass through the Lairig. The few who sported nylon ropes, pitons and P.A.'s almost invariably courted asphyxiation in some foul enclosed chimney, or lost themselves in a vegetatious jungle on what should have been an honest straightforward line, misled by ambiguous descriptions in the existing guide book.

There were, of course, the Great Unwashed—itinerant, bearded Englishmen usually unemployed or unemployable, all of them friendly fellows, particularly when the scent of food was strong. They could be distinguished by their Mancunian accents, a preference for Glen Brittle Youth Hostel, and an enthusiasm amounting to adulation for a certain Joe Brown, then an unknown name in these remote parts. " 'E's incredible! . . . like a yuman spider! . . . 'e doan't cut 'and-'olds and feet-'olds in t'ice . . . 'e cuts a thin groooooove and lie-backs oop it!" (whistles of incredulity).

These hairy vagabonds were legion in the Cairngorms. One remembers Droopydrawers (an apt name this) who could imitate all the instruments in a jazz band and invariably did just that within seconds of introducing himself to a company of total strangers. His equal in megalomania was the man Bob Scott recalls as the "Birmingham Highlander". This gentleman wore his kilt in the manner of his professedly Scottish ancestors, i.e. *in modo naturae*. He took pains to advertise this, and it was therefore all the more fitting that it should have led to his undoing. One day when walking near the lip of a steep snowfield, he lost his footing and set off upon a long involuntary sitting glissade. Most of us are aware of the heat that can be generated through thick corduroy trousers. This gentleman had no such protection. He has not been seen around much lately.

Among other immigrants were the "Be Prepared" types, not all of them Scoutmasters. I once accompanied such a man. After relieving him of his pack for a short distance I was curious to discover its contents. The following items came to light—one hemp rope (for use in mist), guide book, maps, compass, pro-tractor, torch and spare batteries, one *Do-it-Yourself* first aid kit, one sleeping bag (against possible benightment), forty eight hours' rations (against further benightment), and a small tent (for indefinite benightment). He told me that the Cairngorms were dangerous mountains, and that it was unwise to take liberties with the elements.

This motley influx certainly added colour to the climbing scene, yet one could only deplore that so many were profoundly ignor-ant of the vast rock climbing potential. The existing *S.M.C. Guide* was partly to blame for this, the descriptions of routes being so inexact that in one instance a single route was described three times under different headings. Another route, hallowed by tradition—the Married Men's Buttress of Sgoran Dubh—has never in fact been identified since its inauguration in 1906 "when snow masked the lower rocks".

It was not until 1954 that plans were formulated for a new Rock-Climber's Guide to the Cairngorms under the joint editor-ship of Mac Smith, Mike Taylor, and myself, the three of us having received official S.M.C. sanction for our labours. Later on several other Etchachan Club members took an active part, but the main burden was shouldered throughout by Smith who had to compile a readable guide book from the various sources of information. He devoted six years of his life and a few grey hairs to this worthy cause. Thus, should the new *Guide* appear to be too partisan or too well laced with Vallot-type superlatives— (*une des plus belles, des plus difficiles, des plus importantes escalades etc.*)—then this is only to be expected from such a fervent disciple as Mac, who cannot have missed more than a few week-ends in the hills for sixteen years. No local climber past or present could pretend to claim such kinship with the Cairngorms.

Nor is Mac's enthusiasm so grossly unwarranted. It cannot be disputed that a lot of Cairngorm granite would benefit from a liberal application of weed killer; on the other hand, the north-east climber finds more exhilaration in opening up an exciting natural line on a 600-foot unclimbed buttress than in subjugating 150 feet of unscratched vertical outcrop. The latter calls for nerve and high technical skill but makes little or no demands upon the climber's route-finding ability and gives no expression to his imaginative talents. To my mind the magic of a great route does not lie in its technical difficulty or even the excellence of its rock but in something less readily definable—*atmosphere* is the term generally applied. A route should fulfil an honest purpose: it should follow a natural line of weakness up a natural obstacle and reach a logical conclusion. There are many so-called routes whose conception would not tax the mental faculties of an ape. They start from cairns set midway between existing cairns and follow straight lines up the cliff to other cairns at the top. Such routes portray complete lack of purpose, imagination or logic on the part of their creators. In the Cairngorms the climber's mental horizon is fortunately wider.

There is some loose rock in the Cairngorms. So much the better. Personally, I detest rock which is intrinsically rotten and whose security can never be accurately assessed, but loose rock is a natural hazard which may be safely negotiated by a leader not lacking in guile and judgement. I must confess to finding the impeccable gabbro on Sròn na Ciche pretty dull fare. The rock is too good. It is so riddled with holds as to be climbable almost anywhere and it demands no more of a leader than an average athletic physique and some technical ability.

In case this may seem to be a tirade against accepted values in rock climbing, I admit that the Cairngorms do not offer the same scope for severe face climbs as do the playgrounds of the West, Glencoe and Ben Nevis. The Cairngorms are now firmly established as a reputable rock climbing centre and it took several years of campaigning among the infidels to achieve this; hence it may now be freely conceded that Cairngorm Granite does not measure up to Chamonix Granite or even to Glencoe Porphyry for difficult sustained face climbs. If this appears to be a deliberate *volte-face* then it should be remembered that to destroy a myth you have to create another myth. The sober truth seldom satisfies, for most mountaineers are sceptics by adoption, if not by nature. The net result has been satisfactory and the Cairngorms are now accredited with no more than their fair share of glory.

The winter potentialities should be assessed in altogether different currency. In snow and ice climbing, the Cairngorms and Lochnagar yield to none. Their only rivals are Ben Nevis and Creag Meaghaidh, where snow conditions are infinitely more variable, and inconsistent. Glencoe can be discounted right away; the first prerequisite for winter climbing is a modicum of snow, and the recent mild winters have produced nothing worthy of that name below 3,000 feet in Glencoe, thus dealing a death blow to its traditional reputation for ice climbing.

The north-east climbers of the early 'fifties were all individualists but never rock fanatics. There are no crags in the Cairngorms within easy reach of a motorable road and a typical climbing week-end savoured more of an expedition than of acrobatics. If the weather turned unfavourable, then a long hill walk took the place of the planned climb. All the bothies were well patronised— Luibeg, Lochend, Gelder Shiel, Bynack, the Geldie Bothies, Altanour, Corrour and of course the Shelter Stone. At one and all you would be assured of friendly company round the fire in the evening. Everybody knew everybody and formal introductions were unnecessary.

It was a sad day for Lochnagar when, in August 1953, Bill Stewart fell to his death on Parallel Gully "B". Although his initial slip was a mere six feet, the rope sliced through on a sharp flake of rock and he fell all the way to the corrie floor. It was a cruel twist of fate to overtake such a brilliant young climber, and for many of the "faithful" it soured the love of the hills that they had shared with him. The numbers dwindled on the Saturday bus and the crags shed much of their glamour; the majority of the old brigade took to hill walking and ski-ing, where they could forget unhappy memories and still enjoy the camaraderie of the hills.

It was not long, however, before two new groups emerged from the crucible. The first were the Boor Boys, now masquerading under the more genteel title of the Corrour Club and including the aforementioned Nicol and Grassick. The flame of adventure burned as brightly as before. Nicol had read so many books about the Munich climbers of the *avant-guerre* that he had himself become pseudo-Teuton and spoke of all-night bivouacs on minute ledges "contemplating his destiny" like a Buhl. History records that after hurtling 120 feet to the Lochnagar screes before a large, impressed audience his first words to his rescuers were as follows:

"Turn me over and let me see the place where I fell. It wasn't V.S.," he cried bitterly, "only Hard Severe." He lived to redeem his lost honour and despite the trifling inconvenience of several cracked ribs was none the worse for his accident, being left without so much as an honourable scar.

His comrade, Grassick, had already fallen off once in the process of testing the security of a large block to which he had conscientiously belayed himself. Unhappily the block was loose: when it fell, Grassick fell too. He wasn't a dangerous climber in the accepted sense of the term—merely "accident prone", as they say in industry. This was borne out a fortnight after his first ascent of Polyphemus Gully, scene of previous marathon bids by Brooker. Grassick had just joined the short axe school but failed to realise that the new weapon had only limited application in the art of glissading. The Left Hand Branch of the Black Spout held only a fraction of its seasonal snow build-up, and lower down the gully quite a few sharp rocks protruded from the hard icy surface. Into one of these Grassick cannoned at high velocity, shedding his axe on the impact and finally coming to a halt on the pile of big boulders at the gully entrance. Several relays of stalwart climbers carried him down the mountain and the incident is still commemorated by two brief entries on the wall of the Gelder steading: *K. Grassick—climbed Polyphemus Gully— 6 hours*, and the postscript in different handwriting *K. Grassick— carried down—5 hours.*

An even more colourful occasion followed, on which Gordon Lillie dislocated a shoulder while seconding Kenneth on another Lochnagar climb. They made their way down to the nearest roadhead and were rescued by none other than Princess Margaret. Lillie sat miserably beside the chauffeur; while Grassick in the back seat made intelligent conversation with Royalty. Next morning the press reported the rescue on the front page and Grassick, never slow to seize his share of the limelight, was quoted as saying—"She was radiant. . . . I never knew anyone could look so beautiful. . . . Her pictures just don't do her justice"—a graceful tribute from a commoner of Grassick's lowly station. We looked in vain for his name in the New Year's Honours List.

The Kincorth Club under the joint leadership of Freddy Malcolm and Alex "Sticker" Thom were formidable rivals. The majority of their new routes were located in the Coire na Ciche of Beinn a' Bhùird, which came to be regarded as club property. The club headquarters was sited at the Howff, the exact location of which is still a secret for the excellent reason that the head gamekeeper turns a blind eye to its occupants. The construction is partly subterranean and is the eighth wonder of the Cairngorms, with a stove, floor boards, genuine glass window and seating space for six. The building materials were brought from Aberdeen to the assembly line by the herculean labours of countless torchlit safaris which trod stealthily past the Laird's very door, shouldering mighty beams of timber, sections of stove piping and sheets of corrugated iron. The Howff records the inaugural ceremony—"This howff was constructed In the Year of Our Lord 1954, by the Kincorth Club, for the Kincorth Club. All climbers please leave names, and location of intended climbs: female climbers please leave names, addresses, and telephone numbers."

"Freddy and Sticker's Howff" was not unique. It stood in a small village of howffs, three in number and together capable of accommodating an entire climbing meet. There was "Charlie's Howff" which had lock and key, a tiny door of Alice-in-Wonderland proportions, and a skylight—until some misguided individual fell through the latter, deceived by the almost foolproof camouflage. "Raymond Ellis's Howff", the third of the group, was entirely above-ground, with no attempt made at concealment. Five miles farther, and 3,000 feet up on Beinn a' Bhùird, you may still stumble upon "Mac's Howff", a cave of the Shelter Stone variety, made habitable only by the extraction of a giant rock tooth which yielded to the combined efforts of "a drill and a mason's four-pound hammer". "Mac's" was the first of the howffs, dating back to 1949, and it had been inspired by Jock Nimlin's article in the then current issue of the *S.M.C. Journal*. It did not enjoy any lasting popularity because of the marathon hike that it demanded after closing-time in Braemar—thirteen miles via Invercauld Bridge or nine miles if you chose to ford the Dee, waist deep in icy water.

More new routes were recorded in this period than ever before, though proportionally fewer climbers participated. Nor indeed was the exploratory trend due to any significant advance in skill or technique, because excellent climbs of Very Difficult standard or less were still coming to light. On the other hand, an early sign that the boom period was nearing or past its zenith was the relative increase in the number of first winter ascents, scope for which was still enormous. Developments had proceeded at such a pace that occasionally the first winter ascent of a route followed almost immediately the first summer ascent, and in a few cases actually preceded it, as with "The Scorpion" on Càrn Etchachan. As potential *Guide Book* editor, Smith's resources were severely taxed in keeping abreast, and those of us engaged upon checking route descriptions found it more profitable to anticipate new routes than fulfil our obligations with less glamorous second ascents. We had already agreed that any new route worthy of inclusion in a climbing guide covering such a wide area should at least exceed 200 feet in height and should follow a logical line up a recognisable feature. Without these limitations, guide book descriptions would have become hopelessly bogged down by technical data.

Eventually and inevitably, the first invaders began to arrive, precursors of a new régime, which was to challenge the Aberdeen climbers for the leading role in the development of Scottish ice craft, and whose élite were to make even more exacting winter climbs, routes such as the Orion Face Direttissima and Minus 2 Gully on Ben Nevis.

In these final years of isolation, two further outstanding climbers appeared: Ronnie Sellers, who did many routes of the highest standard, along with Jerry Smith, a likeable Englishman naturalised in Aberdeen. Two accidents in the same summer cost us these two friends.

For ten to fifteen years, the Cairngorm fraternity had existed as a closed community uninfluenced by the traditions of other clubs or denominations. During these years they had perfected a new brand of ice climbing by adapting Alpine snow techniques to the requirements of their native crags in winter. Virtually their only contact with the wider world of mountaineering was at holiday periods when a few enthusiasts reached the Alps, while others hitched a lift to Skye, the Lake District or Wales. Week-end exploration was curtailed by the shortage of car owners. Much more could have been achieved, but it would have lost the group its individuality.

Nearly all recent exploration has been from the Braemar side of the Cairngorms. Despite the wholesale exploitation of Aviemore and district as a summer/winter sports area and the seething hordes of humanity on the Speyside hills, very little has been recorded from that airt. Aviemore is too far from the main climbing crags to be of any value as a rock-climbing centre. The north-corries of Cairngorm and Cairn Lochan offer only scrappy climbs and the buttresses of Sgoran Dubh, though impressive as a whole, disappoint individually. Among the popularly acclaimed climbing crags only the Shelter Stone *cirque* is more readily approachable from Aviemore than from Derry Lodge, and this only since the new Ski Road was constructed.

Because they have no vested interests in the northern sector of the Cairngorm massif, north-east climbers generally have been indifferent towards the new chair-lift on Cairngorm, which might seem to pose a remote threat to their privacy. The chair-lift might unleash hordes of souvenir-hunters and salvation-seekers over the central Cairngorms: of these perhaps quite a few would come to an untimely end. Against this is the complete lack of inspiration and the gregariousness that characterise the modern tourist.

Ten years ago Coire Cas was as dreich a place as you might find anywhere in the Cairngorms. As a corrie it was wholly devoid of character. At the time of writing it contains one large continental-type chalet (with the hint of more to follow), a chair-lift which works occasionally, and on an average week-end in February, upwards of a thousand skiers of all shapes and proportions. I must confess that I now find Coire Cas more stimulating. Even for the mediocre skier there is a milk bar selling hot coffees and no lack of gullible young novitiates upon whom to practise one's skimanship, Knowledge of a few basic terms (*mambo, wedln*) and a nodding acquaintance with some of the Austrian and Swiss instructors is an undoubted asset. Skis may be carried or occasionally even worn; although in the latter case the least embarrassing course is to continue steadily ascending till out of sight (*langlauf*). Coire Cas is undoubtedly a colourful scene nowadays, and it owes this to superimposed humanity and not to the landscape.

Nevertheless the danger in the Coire Cas scheme is that it may be the forerunner of others which would threaten the finer and more remote fastnesses of the Cairngorms.

The peculiar fascination that the Cairngorms hold for so many climbers cannot be ascribed to any one special feature. Different facets of the mountain scene have their own appeal for different people. For myself I have always held that it is impossible to dissociate mountains from those who climb upon them. The Cairngorms are a compact group of mountains. The Cairngorm climbing fraternity has always been a closely-knit community, linked by similar ideals and aspirations. Good climbing and good company often go together: each is essential to the enjoyment of the other. In the Cairngorms they are inseparable.

THE FIRST WINTER TRAVERSE OF THE CUILLIN RIDGE

From The Scottish Mountaineering Club Journal, 1965

IT WAS A frosty moonlit night in February this year, and snow lay deep on the hills around the head of Loch Broom. I had just finished my evening's work when the phone rang. Anticipating a late-night visit, I lifted the receiver with weary resignation.

"Hello there! Is that you, Tom!" said a familiar voice. "I was thinking of pushing over to Skye tonight for a look at the Ridge. Naturally, I thought you might like to come along."

The enthusiasm crackling along the line soon left no doubt as to the voice. Who else but Hamish MacInnes would phone at this hour with such a preposterous suggestion?

"It's great to hear from you again, Hamish," I replied cautiously. "Could I perhaps phone you back in an hour? I would need to make a few trifling arrangements, you know."

"Of course, of course," he conceded magnanimously. "Perhaps an hour would be sufficient, and if I haven't heard from you by then, I'll just set off." Sixty-five minutes later I rang him up. "Hello again, Tom, I thought it might be you," he bellowed cheerfully, "you're just in time. We're about to leave."

"We!—Who is we?" I asked suspiciously.

"Davie Crabb and myself, who else? Didn't I tell you? Oh, of course, you wouldn't know. Well, when you didn't phone back I asked him to come instead. It's unfortunate that you've got everything fixed up." His voice took on a sententious tone. "Three is a bad number for the Ridge—far too slow and they eat too much. Why don't you find a fourth? Anyway I can't stop to talk now. See you tonight at Sligachan? The last ferry from Kyle leaves in three hours, so you might just make it, if you hurry."

I swore violently as the line went dead. My mind went back to the occasion several years ago when I had received a postcard which briefly announced, "Meet me at Molde on 25th June at 3 p.m." Molde is a tiny place somewhere up a Norwegian fjord. I already knew of Hamish's violent fits of enthusiasm, so I had thought of phoning him at his home in Glencoe on the appointed day and announcing my arrival in Molde. I had abandoned the idea. He would have commiserated briefly and then asked about the snow conditions. . . .

I remembered, too, the scraps of information scattered haphazardly through Hamish's letters, that had a simplicity often shattering in its impact—viz.: "If you receive no reply to your next letter you will know that I have gone up the Amazon in search of a new species of long-tailed monkey. It promises to be a really interesting project."

It was eight years since our last climb. That was a red-letter day in February 1957 when with Graeme Nicol of Aberdeen we made the first winter ascent of Zero Gully on Ben Nevis, at that time the most difficult winter route on the mountain (*S.M.C.J.* (1958)). It is curious that we had never joined forces again.

My annoyance at MacInnes' premature departure for Skye was eased next day by the news that he had stuck in a snowdrift near Cluanie and retreated to Glencoe to carry out essential repairs on his car.

Meanwhile I had been phoning up various likely partners. Eric Langmuir, the Warden at Glenmore Lodge, was immediately enthusiastic. Eric was an old friend and a very experienced Alpinist. It so happened that another mutual climbing acquaintance, Graham Tiso, was visiting the Lodge when I phoned so that he too became entangled in the plans.

The same evening a small, wiry individual wearing a climbers' safety-helmet arrived at our door looking for a "doss". It was none other than Brian Robertson. He had hitch-hiked from Fort William in a fish lorry and wore the keenly expectant look of a man who has wandered many days in the desert and suddenly stumbled upon an oasis. His arrival could scarcely been better timed.

The following evening found us at Sligachan. We had chosen to attempt the Ridge Traverse from the north because this would enable us to abseil several sections where the reverse direction would involve very severe ice-climbing. Langmuir and Tiso had left immediately on receiving our S.O.S. Tiso's van was piled high with every possible and impossible item of climbing equipment.

We phoned MacInnes in Glencoe and told him snow conditions appeared excellent and we would be starting at dawn. If he hurried he could just catch the late night ferry. It says a lot for his superb sang-froid that he was able to accept this information with no show of emotion and to inform us in a detached tone of voice that he would be unable to leave for several days due to previous commitments. On the other hand, he could well have been clairvoyant.

I had already made one attempt on the winter traverse of the Main Ridge, and I knew of at least a dozen others, including six made by Hamish himself with different companions.

It was three years almost to the day since my own visit. On that occasion Richard Brooke and I arrived in Skye together with the worst blizzard of the winter. Between Sligachan and Glen Brittle our car stuck in a snowdrift. There was a dance on that night and we were joined by several carloads of frustrated merrymakers. This was fortunate because we soon found ourselves at a hastily arranged Ceilidh in the kitchen of the nearest croft.

Next day we staggered to Glen Brittle through two feet of newly fallen snow. Getting from there to the summit of Garsbheinn, the southernmost point of the ridge, was even more harrowing. In summer this is an easy three-hour walk. It provided us with six hours of undiluted misery floundering in snow seldom less than thigh-deep. On the ridge itself we were due for further disillusionment. Throughout its entire length the Cuillin Main Ridge had been stripped of every particle of snow by the westerly gales. It was, in fact, the only area of bare ground in Skye. There was no point in tackling it under what amounted to summer conditions.

We could have completed the climb in less than twelve hours from end to end, but we would seldom have had to cut steps and there was no advantage in wearing crampons. We found the

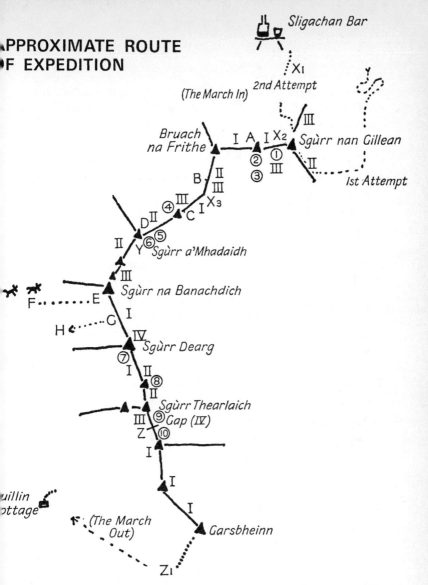

APPROXIMATE ROUTE OF EXPEDITION

Roman numerals indicate approximate degree of difficulty, graded as I to V in the *Cairngorms* guide-books, in *true optimum winter conditions*. A, approximate scene of the *Affaire Tiso*; B, bivouac Langmuir–Tiso; C, bivouac Patey–Robertson; D, bivouac Moriarty–Tiso; E, bivouac MacInnes–Crabb–Patey–Robertson; F, route of supply team and dogs; G, where sacks were jettisoned; H, where sacks were recovered; X₁, ₂, ₃, here Robertson was sick; Y, Crabb loses half a crampon; Z, the MacInnes rope trick; Z₁, the 2,000-foot glissade. Circled numbers indicate abseil points: on S. to N. traverse each would indicate III to IV difficulty. EQUIPMENT NOTES: (i) At least one member used a MacInnes Ice-Axe. (ii) Many articles of Tiso equipment were thoroughly tested. (iii) Dogs appeared by kind permission of H. MacInnes. (iv) Robertson reports "loss or theft" of one piton.

harder pitches little more difficult than in summer. Our retiral disappointed the locals, for whom the Winter Traverse had become something of an out-of-season attraction when so many rival groups of climbers were vying with each other for the honour of being the first.

I was rather disillusioned by this visit. It began to look as if the Cuillins, because of their proximity to the warmer Atlantic, seldom if ever come into condition for winter climbing. The essential ingredients for success appear to be a heavy snowfall without an accompanying wind and followed successively by a thaw and an equally rapid freeze. A further essential is that the weather must remain favourable for at least two days. All these conditions seldom concur during the course of a Skye winter. It is hardly surprising that I had had to wait three full years, after my first attempt, before returning to the fray.

On this occasion, as events were soon to prove, it was the climbers and not the Cuillins who were out of condition. In direct contrast to my previous visit there was no snow at all below the 2,000-foot contour, but above this level the fantastic jagged skyline of the main ridge was crusted as white as a Christmas cake. The conditions were perfect—iron-hard *névé*, ideally suited to front-point cramponing. We intended to carry two ice axes per man. An ice-pick in either hand as additional points of contact would serve to narrow down any element of risk involved, since we planned to climb unroped for most if not all of the way along the ridge. Without twelve-point crampons we would have needed to cut thousands of steps and might easily have spent the better part of a week on the climb.

Because of an unduly late start we did not reach our first objective, the top of Sgùrr nan Gillean, until midday. All four of us carried heavy rucksacks full of bivouac equipment.

We traded valour for discretion by ignoring the challenge of the direct route via the Pinnacle Ridge—a jagged crescendo of glistening ice-towers Himalayan in its unaccustomed winter garb. Instead we climbed the Tourist Route which spirals up the back of the mountain. This was a much longer approach and I am not convinced that we saved ourselves any time.

Near the top we were suddenly enveloped in dense cloud that had been building up over the Sound of Sleat all morning. Big flakes of snow began to fall—sporadically, but with ominous insistence. We began the tricky descent of the West Ridge believing that the weather was going to deteriorate further and any subsequent effort would be merely a formal concession to the occasion, calculated to save face on our return to Sligachan. Consequently there was little urgency and we indulged our fancy by finishing off the delicacies which were to have soothed our bivouac.

Soon we came to where the ridge narrowed in a jagged sword-blade of gabbro. Here we were forced to rope up. Half-way along the icy tightrope the snow-encrusted Gendarme held us up for half an hour. Eventually we discovered that a doubled rope reached the snowfield below on the north side. It was then simple to by-pass the Gendarme by an abseil and an easy horizontal traverse, regaining the Ridge at the next col.

Here, Robertson and I reverted to climbing solo. Langmuir and Tiso had roped up at the start and were already far behind. Although we sympathised with their conscientious approach we considered that the traverse would take three or four days if we were ruled by traditional precepts. We had only enough food for two days and in any case only a rabid optimist could expect Skye weather to remain fine any longer than that. The first instruction in the climbing manual is to "climb as if the rope wasn't there". We had no need for pretence. Anyone who has made a regular practice of climbing solo over a period of years must of necessity be a competent climber. If such was not the case, he would be dead. Nature has effective methods of eliminating the unreliable individualist. I am not making a case for solo climbing —merely pointing out that most solo climbers are not the unprincipled fanatics that some authorities claim but are essentially dependable and well-adjusted companions.

Time was once again important. As if to mock us, the cloud barrier had dispersed and the afternoon sun lit up a dazzling panorama of snow-capped peaks from Ben Nevis to Torridonia. There was no longer any possible justification for giving up.

A long abseil from the top of the next peak landed us on the

Bhàsteir Tooth—a clean-cut prow of black rock starkly outlined against the universal snow blanket.

Descending the Coruisk side of the Tooth we eventually reached a point where a 300-foot rope, doubled through a piton of doubtful integrity, just reached the foot of the cliff. The abseil was largely free and because of a slight bulge half-way down we could not verify that the rope in fact reached the bottom. I offered Robertson the privilege of the lead. Some time after he had disappeared from sight, the rope suddenly went slack. As there was no simultaneous scream I gathered he had reached the bottom under control.

The Ridge was now easy for a long way. The other two had just arrived at the top of the Tooth but we decided not to wait for them as we intended to stop at least an hour before dark, to prepare a communal bivouac. This would let them catch up.

Only now had we begun to move at a respectable pace, as muscles became attuned to the rhythm of front-point cramponing. A quick stab with the crampon, a punch with the ice-axe spike— right foot—right hand—left foot—left hand—so on it went, hands and feet working like pistons, pricking out a thread-like tattoo-line across the glistening *névé*. We could count from memory the rock holds we had used since Sgurr nan Gillean. These were the climbing conditions which one dreams about, but in practice seldom encounters. In sixteen years' winter climbing in Scotland I have never found better. The creaking of crampon points was sweet music to the ear.

Two hours later we came upon a perfect site for the bivouac— a curving snow wreath directly below the west peak of Bidein, Druim nan Ramh. Tonight there was the merest breath of wind, but no sooner had the sun sunk behind the Hebrides than it became so cold that we were forced to excavate a 3-foot deep trench, wide and long enough to accommodate the four of us.

We were so preoccupied that it was dark before we realised the second string was considerably overdue.

"A bit odd," I ventured after a long silence. "When did you see them last?"

"Not since the Tooth," Robertson confessed. "You don't

suppose there was any particular reason for all that shouting about an hour ago?"

"I could only just hear it," I said, "so it could hardly have been anything too drastic."

"On the other hand that sound must have carried quite a distance," commented Robertson gloomily. "At least two miles, I'd say at a guess."

I had been thinking the same thing, but had not wanted to say so.

"Anyhow," I remarked with a feeble attempt at optimism, "they must have bivouacked by now because it's so dark they wouldn't be able to see their own feet, far less climb. In any case I haven't heard any shouting for a long time."

"There may be a very good reason for that," he observed dryly. "It's a bit of a bind, after digging such a flaming big hole. . . . Still, you never know—it might make a fabulous grave for Tiso. . . . Perhaps he's gone and hanged himself," he suggested brightly.

Robertson must have the Second Sight.

The next time I opened my eyes it was broad daylight and the sun must have been up for over an hour. Once again the weather was beyond reproach. I levered myself out of my ice-encrusted cocoon and peered blearily over the rim of the snow-hole. Our bivouac site commanded a view of the whole ridge back to the Tooth. It was as empty as the back row of a cinema during the National Anthem.

With a resigned gesture I switched off the torch, a pathetic little beacon that had shone bravely but to no avail throughout the night. "I'm afraid that's it," I remarked tonelessly. "I suppose we ought to go back and look."

Robertson was visibly depressed. "Remember that bit in Gervasutti's book where the German fell off the overhang for the third time? What did Gervasutti say? 'Though my heart was near to breaking I let him down.' You can understand how he felt," he said bitterly.

We split up, Brian retracing our tracks along the crest of the Ridge while I descended into the western corrie to search the base of the cliffs. It pays to be realistic on these occasions.

About an hour later the corrie resounded to a volley of oaths, "What are you doing down there?"

"I—am—looking—for—your—dead—bodies," I replied spitefully, giving every syllable its last ounce of venom.

"Sorry—can't make out a word you're saying. Why—is—Brian—up—here? Did—you—fall—off?"

I gave up and sat down on the snow in an attitude of despair. Getting no further reply to their shouts they all eventually descended the corrie.

It was an exotic story. Told against the background of a cloudless sky and the Cuillin Ridge in unique winter conditions, it sounded like a bad joke.

The trouble began because Tiso was too conscientious. Having abseiled down from the Tooth and thus tested the piton to most people's satisfaction (he was the heaviest member of the party) he took an extra precaution. He knotted a loop on the double rope, stepped into it and swung with his full weight on the rope. This would have been all right if it had not been for three significant factors. The rope had reached him at a slight angle; the slope fell away at a slight angle; and he was wearing crampons. When his gyrations ceased he found himself 5 feet off the ground with one crampon entangled in the loop. In an effort to free it he turned upside down. . . .

He was now hanging by one foot with his head caressing the snow. It was a unique and quite irreversible position. Physiologists have stated that a man hanging freely in space from a rope around his waist expires from suffocation in somewhat less than twenty minutes. (I can't imagine how they arrived at this hypothesis.) Probably no one has calculated the life-span of a man hanging from one foot, but it is reasonable to assume that his condition will steadily deteriorate. Hence it was not surprising that Tiso's initial distress signals had carried a distance of two miles.

Up above, Langmuir was in an unenviable position. It was obvious that some stirring drama was being enacted at the foot of the cliff, but the bulge concealed it from view and also distorted Tiso's colourful commentary. There was only one way to find out. This was to descend the fixed rope which was stretched taut as a guitar string. He had no spare rope to rig an abseil and it would have been suicidal to try to climb down without protection. He used the only safety device available—a thin nylon sling which he attached to the main rope by a Prusik knot. Every time he adjusted the knot to a lower position, his other hand clutching the rope had to take his full body weight. Where the rope ran over a projection, the situation became even more hazardous. His downward vista centred round the upturned sole of a Tiso Special Climbing Boot, behind which he could see the congested features of the leading Scottish distributor.

Half an hour later, his herculean task accomplished, he unhooked the unfortunate Tiso with a flick of the ice-axe and both collapsed on the snow in utter exhaustion.

Not surprisingly, they had been unable to get much further along the Ridge before darkness forced them to bivouac.

We had been prepared to be critical. Instead we had to admit that they had done extraordinarily well to extricate themselves from a nightmarish situation. It could have happened to any of us and in retrospect had its lighter moments, but at the time the outcome could have been serious.

So ended our first Cuillin adventure. I might not have been so despondent had I known that we would be returning to Sligachan before the week was out.

I phoned MacInnes, as I had promised, with the news of our defeat.

"So you didn't get up," he remarked before I had even spoken.

"How on earth did you know that?"

"Well I heard that conditions were almost spring-like, so I knew you wouldn't bother pushing on with it. Quite right. It would have been daylight robbery to claim a first winter ascent."

"What do you know about it?" I replied huffily. "You weren't even there."

"Ah, you forget that a friend of mine, Peter Thomas, lives at Glen Brittle," said Hamish in his "matter-of-fact" voice.

I returned the gauntlet. "If that's what you think, go over and see yourself."

"All right," he said thoughtfully. "I think I will. I'll find Davie Crabb and we'll be on the road in an hour. See you at Sligachan. . . ."

From the road outside the hotel, MacInnes was prepared to admit he was wrong. That was about all he was prepared to concede. "Tom—this idea of yours of getting Peter Thomas to carry the bivvy gear up to Sgùrr na Banachdich is all very well, but Davie and I have been thinking and we reckon it's cheating. You know, of course, what everyone will say?" he added darkly.

"You think it's cheating? Well, look at it this way—I've already carried a heavy rucksack as far as Bidein and that's almost as far as Banachdich. I'm damned if I'm going to do it twice in a week merely to keep the records straight. I want to enjoy the climb— so does Brian. If we happen to find a couple of rucksacks on top of Sgùrr na Banachdich just before dusk we shall accept their existence as an Act of God and put them to good use. Peter Thomas is agreeable?"

"Oh yes, he is quite willing to help out but wonders if you are happy about the ethics of the thing."

"Overjoyed," I said, "and so will you be when we take your packs off you after you've collapsed with exhaustion. . . ."

Once more we stood at the top of the abseil from the Bhàsteir Tooth. The weather was perfect, the snow beyond reproach— only the time of day differed from the last visit. It was merely 11 a.m. Our rapid progress was due to two factors. We had our own recently made tracks to guide us. There was also a hint of rivalry between the two pairs of climbers—the merest suggestion, but sufficient to cause a gradual and insidious acceleration in the combined speed of the party. All the way from Sligachan we had been forced to put up with MacInnes's Lifemanship gambits. He appears to be entirely unaware of his talents in this particular field, so that his comments are usually unanswerable.

"That was a tricky bit, eh, Davie? The boys made it look quite easy! It only shows how carrying a pack can upset your equilibrium. Makes an easy pitch into a very severe."

Or again . . .

"Please don't let us hold you up, lads!" He was hammering along like a steam engine at the time. "It's going to be a terrible cold night for you if you don't reach Banachdich tonight. I know quite well you're both keen to get ahead." We were in fact finding considerable difficulty in keeping up but we had a measure of excuse for our poor showing. MacInnes and Crabb had gone religiously to bed at 9 p.m. the previous evening. Robertson and I had stayed up until 2 a.m. at a Ceilidh, exchanging stories with mine host, John MacLellan, former Scottish Champion Athlete of the Heavy events. Several other convivial Sgiathanachs had joined the group around the fire. An accordion, a mouth-organ, a tape-recorder and a bottle of whisky were ideal ingredients for an impromptu Ceilidh. The whisky circulated briskly. I am not hang-over-prone—Robertson unhappily is. He had been unable to resist the fiery *creutair* and the temptation of getting something for nothing. We had got up at five, roused by an alarm clock. We could have slept till midday and it was a long, long time before I could convince myself that we had slept at all. On the way up the mountain Robertson had been stopping every half-mile to be sick, and I imagined he might give Sgùrr nan Gillean a miss since he had climbed it only a few days before. I soloed up the gully leading to the final col on the Pinnacle Ridge and then made my way with some difficulty up the most direct route to the top, being forced to cut steps for the last 400 feet. Despite this I arrived a little in front of MacInnes and Crabb who had climbed the West Ridge, finding the Gendarme tricky.

The four of us were climbing unroped and Robertson and I were ahead of the others by about ten minutes when we reached the crucial abseil, the scene of Tiso's solitary penance. History almost repeated itself. I was half-way down the aerial section when a freak knot appeared on the rope below me. Next minute it had jammed squarely against the karabiner at my waist and I was left spinning round and round on the rope like a frustrated marionette. Desperate situations call for desperate measures: I eventually solved the problem by hammering the knot through the karabiner.

It was only when we were about to retrieve the abseil that I realised that the knot was on the "wrong" half of the doubled rope. Sure enough, it jammed again in the eye of the abseil piton. There was no easy solution this time. We would just have to wait for MacInnes and Crabb to free it.

Then I noticed they were preparing to abseil down an altogether different part of the wall somewhere in the neighbourhood of Naismith's Route.

"Climb down a bit this way. That's the wrong route," I called up persuasively.

"It looks O.K. to us," said Hamish, "and will save minutes in any case."

"You realise that if the rope's only 150 feet long, it won't reach the bottom?"

"Of course it will. I happened to measure this pitch last summer. It is exactly 135 feet from top to bottom."

MacInnes has such an impressive array of facts and figures at his fingertips that one occasionally doubts their authenticity. However, his voice carries such conviction that one hesitates to argue.

"Actually it would help us if you could come down the same way; our rope is jammed, and you could chuck it down to us." I felt like the small boy who asks for his ball back from the next-door garden.

The practised Lifeman never exploits such an obvious confession of failure. Instead he pretends to ignore it altogether, although his face shows that he has had to make a conscious effort to do so.

"Pity about that," remarked Hamish, in an abstract way as he handed us a neatly coiled rope. "We must have lost at least ten minutes on that little mishap. Can't be helped, of course. These things do happen."

We mumbled our apologies and offered to take our turn of carrying the packs.

"I'm feeling fine," said MacInnes, who indeed looked it. "How about you, Davie?"

"Never felt better," replied that stalwart with his usual loyalty.

"Thanks all the same, Tom," the gallant hero continued, "but you have to get to Banachdich for 4 o'clock and we'll manage to struggle along."

I was beginning to question which pair of us was labouring under the bigger handicap. Without rucksacks we should have been half as fast again as they were, but with Hamish in his usual superb physical condition this was an impossibility.

I must admit too that we were dismayed to discover how effortlessly Davie Crabb was keeping pace with MacInnes. For a man who had only recently entered the limelight he was making light of snow and ice problems that would have caused most veteran Alpinists to demand the protection of a rope. I had always understood that although reigning tigers might surpass their elders on short routes of extreme technical severity they lacked experience to move fast and competently over average difficulty. I was now finding out, like many others, that this is another myth as ridiculous as the tale that our modern climber only betters the achievements of his forefathers by excessive use of pitons and slings. In climbing, as in any other competive sport (which climbing most certainly is), a man's ability and achievements must only be measured against the yard-stick of his contemporaries.

We passed the site of our previous bivouac shortly after midday, a much-improved performance. At the top of the snow gully between the Central and West Peaks of Bidein we grappled with our first pitch of actual rock climbing. Even so the vital holds were hidden under blue ice and had to be bared with the axe. Although merely a "muscle-loosener" in summer this was now a pitch of severe standard. Having duly appropriated the Central Peak we abseiled back to the col, passing the other pair on the way up.

From here to Sgùrr a'Mhadaidh was no more than a walk. That is to say, you could have fallen and escaped with your life. This could not be said of any other part of the Cuillin Ridge in the conditions we found it. There was a sufficient depth of iron-hard snow on most of the ledges to incorporate them into the uniformly steep slopes which fell away from the Ridge—itself a tortuous knife-edge of snow. We could never hope to find more perfect climbing conditions.

Two successive abseils from the twin towers of Sgùrr a'-Mhadaidh launched us upon the long middle section of the Ridge Traverse which leads successively over the summits of Sgùrr a'Ghreadaidh and Sgùrr na Banachdich. Here are no outstanding rock problems, but in winter a steady succession of minor difficulties which would greatly reduce the pace of a roped party. Fast progress on this part of the Ridge is absolutely essential if one is to complete the traverse in two days. Indeed if a climber has not the confidence and experience to cope with this section unroped he would be ill-advised to attempt the Ridge Traverse.

There are climbers who advocate moving together, carrying coils, on this kind of terrain. My own view is that in these circumstances the rope is rather a hindrance and a hazard than a means of protection: if no belays are taken then any protection is largely illusory. Quite apart from this, very few climbers climb with the same margin of safety if they are clutching a coil of rope in one hand.

Although now enveloped in mist the party continued to advance in loose order. Robertson was still vomiting periodically, about twenty minutes behind me. I could gauge his progress from the occasional sounds of ice-axe or crampon. At least half an hour behind him were MacInnes and Crabb. Why they were no longer challenging was not obvious. Later it transpired that a most disastrous thing had happened. Davie Crabb had broken a crampon. For a time, MacInnes even considered abandoning the attempt. In effect, Crabb was climbing with one foot and a heel, the toe of his unprotected vibram-soled boot stubbing uselessly against the glassy surface. He roped up behind MacInnes.

I knew nothing of this and by the time I reached Sgùrr na Banachdich sounds of pursuit had long since faded. Visibility was down to ten yards and I was aware of a gnawing doubt whether we would ever be re-united with that all-important rucksack containing the bivouac gear and food rations for the next twenty-four hours. Supposing Peter Thomas had left it at the wrong place? We had only an hour of daylight to seek our salvation.

Suddenly and quite unexpectedly I came upon the tracks of a dog. A few yards further were more dog tracks and a trail of clearly defined footprints leading towards the summit of Banach-dich. I heaved a profound sigh of relief.

The supply party—consisting of Catherine MacInnes, Peter Thomas, and Hamish's two Alsatian dogs—had passed this way an hour earlier. A few more steps and I came upon the rucksacks, neatly stacked against the summit cairn. It was a poignant moment.

Here, too, was a cryptic message scratched on the snow which read, "A I MET". I decided that MET must be Peter Thomas's initials. Perhaps he preferred to be called Peter just in order to be complicated (some people do). In that case A I would be a symbol of self-congratulation, like patting oneself on the back. Why shouldn't he congratulate himself on his hard work— perhaps nobody else would? It seemed a logical explanation. Only afterwards did we discover the significance of this message left by Catherine MacInnes for her unpredictable spouse. De-coded it meant "Weather forecast—continuing fine". Character-istically, he was no wiser than we were.

As I had not seen anyone for several hours I was quite relieved when Robertson appeared about twenty minutes later. By this time I had discovered a well-protected ledge for a bivouac and half an hour later when the other pair dropped in we had already excavated a level platform capable of holding four in some dis-comfort.

"It looks a bit cramped," MacInnes remarked critically. "I rather fancy digging a snow hole. How about you, Davie? It would be good practice if nothing else."

I waited with interest to see if Hamish intended to carry out such a prodigious threat. In the end he settled for another smaller ledge a few feet to the side.

A vague element of insularity still coloured the remarks that wafted across the icy no-man's-land between the rival bivouacs.

"This is excellent soup, Davie. What's it called?"

"What's after the baked beans, Brian?"

"I don't know whether I *could* eat any more if I tried!"

"This is a palace!!"

"I could live here quite happily for a week!!!"

"I reckon the packs were worth the effort. Makes you sort of feel that you have earned it all."

"That was a great idea getting the packs sent up. Organisation! —Pity we had to stop!—I could have gone on for hours!" etc.

In fact, the organisation was far from perfect. We had assembled the contents of Peter Thomas's rucksack in a hurry on our return from the Ceilidh. Our choice showed little discrimination and a lack of consideration for our porter's feelings. Catherine MacInnes told us later that he had eventually opened the rucksack out of curiosity and asked with disgust, "Is this a bivouac or a birthday party?" There was some truth in his complaint. The contents included three packets of margarine, a large tin of salt and a half-gallon can of water.

We had selected a fine vantage point for our bivouac. Anchored by ropes and pitons, and secure in the warmth of *duvets* and sleeping bags, we could pass away the evening by identifying the numerous lighthouses off the west coast of Skye. Nearer at hand the lights of Glen Brittle beckoned like a friendly beacon. How easy and pleasant it would be to glissade down the long slopes of Banachdich! In an hour we could be sitting by a warm fire. In the morning if we rose early we could be back on the top by dawn and nobody would know we had deserted our posts. . . .

At some unearthly hour I was awakened by a light fall of snow and the dawn ushered in a cheerless morning. Grey tentacles of mist clung to every cranny on the Ridge and fresh hoar-frost covered the rocks. It had been one of the coldest nights of the winter. Although I had fallen asleep in comparative luxury, I awoke in misery. Condensation inside the polythene bivvy-bag had soaked inexorably through sleeping bag, *duvet* and trousers. As soon as I got up, my clothes became as stiff as cardboard. Then the primus refused to work in the cold and we had to borrow Hamish's butane stove. It was almost 9 o'clock before we finally got under way. We climbed with the agility of four knights in full armour.

Fortunately it was an easy start to the day. At the col between Banachdich and Sgùrr Dearg we jettisoned all the spare rations and bivouac gear. MacInnes, ever cautious, placed his rucksack under a prominent boulder: I slung my own with utter contempt in the direction of Glen Brittle and watched with gay abandon as it finally disappeared from view, 1,500 feet below, in one final gigantic arc. Robertson followed suit, although with mixed emotions. It was the first time he had wilfully abandoned his precious ironmongery and there was a nostalgic look in his eyes. (Both rucksacks were recovered intact the following morning, less than an hour's walk away from Glen Brittle.)

We now had to keep our first appointment of the day. The Inaccessible Pinnacle of Sgùrr Dearg was an unpleasant customer to meet so early in the morning. Easily the most impressive summit pinnacle in Britain, it is considerably more intimidating in mid-winter. We began by examining the north end of the Pinnacle—the so-called "Short Side". It was plated from top to bottom with black ice. The ascent can be quite awkward on a wet day in summer, yet Hamish was confident that he could force a way up even in these conditions.

It promised to be a long teethy struggle, and I do not enjoy watching life-and-death drama for the same reason that I would not pay to watch circus acrobats: I become too personally involved. Consequently, I left the other two spectating and walked round towards the other end of the Pinnacle. Suddenly, I had an impulse to investigate the "Long Side". Although reputedly a much easier climb than its counterpart, it is at least twice the length and might now present similar technical difficulties, for the angles of both routes are roughly comparable. After 50 feet of climbing, undertaken purely for reconnaissance, I became unpleasantly aware that I was now committed to the climb. After 100 feet, I would have given a great deal for rope protection and a belay. There was little time to cut extra holds. The very edge of the *arête* had been denuded of snow by the sun, but even so there was less than half the summer quota of holds. When I came to the short vertical step where one usually pauses before stepping up on to a rather thin bracket, I decided that it was time to enlist Robertson's assistance. Unfortunately he was out of sight and apparently beyond recall because nobody appeared to

investigate my shouts. There was no sense in hanging on indefinitely for a last-minute reprieve, so I chose to continue while I still
had some strength. As so often, no sooner had I made this resolu-
tion, when everything suddenly clicked. Crampon points bit
tenaciously into thin wafers of water-ice, woollen gloves clamped
down firmly on rounded verglassed holds and before I even had
time to consider the penalties of failure, I was already over the
difficulty and scrambling up the last few feet to the top. Total time
for the ascent—ten minutes—Standard—a good Severe—and I
had to suppress an urge to dramatise my sudden appearance on the
top of the Pinnacle. It was gratifyingly effective nevertheless, as
MacInnes was at grips with the "bad step" and in a position to
appreciate a top-rope. (Although, knowing Hamish, he would
obviously have fought his way up in time.)

I pulled up an extra length of rope from the base of the Pinnacle
and belayed MacInnes from one rope, leaving the second for use
as a handrail.

"This fixed rope isn't much good, Tom. It will swing clean off
the rock. Can't you flick it across to your left?"

"All right, I'll do that," I said, "but I'll have to let go your rope.
O.K.?"

"No! Not on your life. I'm relying on this rope for support."
Most odd, I thought. I am obviously belaying him with the wrong
rope. By ordinary standards, Hamish ought to be in mid-air.

After jugglery, we had a second rope secured top and bottom,
and the rest of the party made free use of it to clamber up and
down the Pinnacle. (We were not to know that merely forty-eight
hours later the second victorious pair to complete the Traverse of
the Cuillin Ridge would be persuaded by our tracks into tackling
the Short Side of the Pinnacle. One was the indefatigable Tiso:
the other the formidable J. Moriarty, the Not-So-Gentle-Giant,
"Big Elly" himself. This was a sterling performance as our quartet
would be the first to confirm.)

The first of the two redoubtable strong-points of the Cuillin
Ridge had been out-manœuvred and overcome. Now only the
Thearlaich-Dubh Gap remained. The early morning mists were
dispersing rapidly, the sun shone on a dazzling landscape and for

the first time we dared to contemplate success. If the weather was not going to stop us nothing else would.

We glissaded down the long snow chutes of An Stac and climbed the twisting aerial stairway to Sgùrr MhicCoinnich. From the summit eyrie, one after another we spun down the 150-foot abseil which hung clear of the cliff like a spider's thread. So on to Sgùrr Thearlaich by a left-flanking traverse on 100 yards of creaking snow that threatened to avalanche but held firm. At the top of the Great Stone Shoot we turned aside to pay homage to Sgùrr Alasdair and a magnificent viewpoint.

We were all impatient to come to grips with the last difficulty on the Ridge—the Thearlaich-Dubh Gap. It needed only a few seconds' inspection to confirm that its ascent under present conditions would be exceptionally "thin"—corresponding to a summer grading of "Very Severe" and rating high in that category. An evil veneer of ice obscured every wrinkle on the wall. Without crampons any ascent would have been out of the question, but where were there big enough incuts to support the front points of a crampon? I did not fancy peeling off backwards. Someone did this some years ago and paid for it with his life. A glance at the jagged boulders which lined the floor of the Gap recalled this incident.

Moriarty and Tiso must have come to the same conclusion two days later. Although they had already dealt with the difficult "Short Side" of the Inaccessible Pinnacle they failed to climb out of the Gap and had to abseil all the way down to the corrie floor, only regaining the Ridge after a slight detour.

We were most reluctant to take this diversion from a Ridge Traverse. Robertson therefore prepared to hurl himself at the last hurdle in a fervour of martyrdom.

At that moment MacInnes, who had yet to descend into the Gap, made a novel suggestion. "If you just hold it a minute, lads," he shouted, "I might manage to get a rope over to the other side."

Surely, I thought, someone would have discovered this solution long ago, if it in fact existed?

However, there are few who can rival Hamish's flair for

improvisation. "The fact is, I've been here investigating in the summer," he confessed (familiar phrase, I thought), "and there's a pointed rock on the other side that will take a direct pull from below, supposing I get the rope to lie behind it."

With the very first cast his rope wrapped itself neatly round a projection at the top of the wall. Most men would have sweated blood and tears to achieve this. Only one thing troubled me. It was obviously not the same projection that Hamish had aimed at.

"How do you know this rope is safe, Hamish?"

"I don't," he replied in his abstract way.

"Well, how are we to find out whether it's safe, if you can't tell us from up there?"

MacInnes was the model of patience. "Try climbing up the rope," he remarked encouragingly. "I'll be most surprised if it comes away."

"You won't be the only one," I thought.

Now followed the Moment of Truth, beloved of mountaineering chroniclers—the Throw of the Dice that was the difference between success and utter disaster. Even if the whole of my past life did not flash across my subconscious mind as is supposed to happen on these occasions, I still remember the enormous relief when I pulled myself over the top to find the rope securely jammed. We had broken the Last Barrier. Success was assured.

One abseil remained. Then we coiled up the rope for the last time and each of us wandered silently and independently along the final mile of scree-speckled Ridge to Garsbheinn, the final outpost of the Ridge. Beyond lay the blue Atlantic, warm and inviting in the afternoon sun. Down there by the shore a different world awaited us—a world of colour and contrast. In one searing whooping glissade of 2,000 feet we returned to it. It was indeed good to be back. Our two-day journey in the winter Cuillin and the twelve-hour "tarantella on ice" when crampon tips and ice-axe spike were our only contacts with tangible reality, now all seemed a strange and wonderful fantasy.

A little older in wisdom, a little younger in spirit, we marched back over the moors to Glenbrittle. Down there in Cuillin

Cottage, Mrs Campbell would be waiting for us with supper. It was a long-standing invitation that we fully intended to keep. . . .

There are many ultimates in mountaineering and every generation finds its own Last Problem. The five others who shared the first winter Traverse of the Cuillin Ridge probably feel the same way as I do. There are many harder and more exacting routes, and many more still to be explored, yet I feel confident that the Winter Traverse of the Main Ridge will always retain its place as the greatest single adventure in British mountaineering.

It would be presumptuous to be conceited about the success of our own exploit. We can only be grateful that we were lucky to find this superb climb in superb winter conditions. If any individual honours are awarded then they should go to Davie Crabb and Brian Robertson who completed the Ridge on half a crampon and half a stomach respectively, thereby revealing—in Hamish's own phraseology—"a determination that is truly Scots".

CLIMBING THE OLD MAN OF HOY

From the Scots Magazine, December 1966

> See Hoy's old man, whose summit bare
> Pierces the dark blue fields of air.
> Based in the sea his fearful form
> Glooms like the spirit of the storm . . .
>
> MALCOLM, 19th-century Orcadian poet

"THE OLD MAN of Hoy?" said our fellow passenger. "You'll see it when we round the headland."

We jostled for position, responding to every lurch of the *St Ola* as that time-honoured vessel pursued her rugged course through the seven conflicting currents that separate Scrabster from Stromness.

The speaker was uncompromisingly Orcadian. He had been telling us a story about a "Continental", a gentleman from London. Now he was recounting the wonders that awaited us on the Mainland, as he called the largest of the Orkney Islands.

"From the Mainland you'll have to hire a private boat to cross to Hoy. There is a service boat, but it leaves Stromness just before the *St Ola* arrives."

I was not surprised, since I had already learned that the Hoy passenger service sailed twice weekly and that unfavourable winds or tides could prevent a landing or force the intending visitor to land on the wrong island.

"And what would you be expecting to find in Hoy?" inquired the informant.

"You probably won't believe this," I replied. "We hope to climb the Old Man."

He looked at me oddly, although he was too polite to register amusement. He advised us to contact an old man living in an isolated cottage at nearby Rackwick Bay. This man made a practice of descending the cliffs opposite the Old Man to recover driftwood from the shore.

"He'll be glad to show you the way down. You'll be able to get a photograph of the Old Man from the bottom, and that is as far as you can go. The Old Man cannot be climbed. Even the British Army couldn't do it. And they used rockets to try to get a rope across the top!"

"My two friends over there," I said proudly, "have both climbed the north face of the Eiger."

He glanced discreetly at Chris Bonington and Rusty Baillie. "You mean the two gentlemen who are being sick?"

I could appreciate his lack of faith. Bonington, his features mottled green, was a shadow of the bearded giant who had figured in many mountain dramas. Sharing his paroxysms was the swashbuckling adventurer from Rhodesia, Rusty Baillie, now instructing at the Adventure Centre in Dunoon. The man who had got a lift from Mombasa to Aden on a passing Arab dhow had capitulated in the Pentland Firth.

With Rusty were three more seaworthy companions, his wife Pat, their baby, and a dog. We were bound for Ultima Thule with ropes, pitons, cameras, a cradle, and a dog bowl scattered in happy confusion across the deck. Unorthodox, we did not appear a team of professionals.

By contrast our goal, the Old Man of Hoy, off the starboard bow, gave every foretoken of belligerence. As if aware of the impending threat to his privacy, he had drawn about his lofty cowl a dark pall of cloud. From the great breakers that dashed against his feet a white plume extended across half a mile of turbulent sea. Objectively the Old Man consists of 450 feet of Orcadian sandstone resting on a granite plinth. The pillar never tapers from the base to the square-cut summit, nor does the maximum diameter ever exceed 100 feet, yet this extraordinary freak of nature must have weathered some of the island's most violent gales.

The monolithic pillar did not always have such unique symmetry. An old print depicts the Old Man with a short second leg on the landward side. When this broke away it formed a 50-feet high escarpment of tumbled blocks, connecting the pillar with the mainland of Hoy. It is easily accessible now, even when high seas are running, although improbable local legends tell of days when a daring skipper might sail his small fishing boat through the narrow channel isolating the Old Man from the shore.

Legendary, too, is the chronicle of the first ascent. An elderly but athletic islander was reputed to have scaled the pinnacle as the result of a wager.

On regaining *terra firma*, he discovered he had left his favourite pipe on the summit and had to repeat the climb. It was a refreshing story, and if the theme was an old one, the tail-piece was undoubtedly new. It was less refreshing to our egos to discover that some of the locals still believed it.

The Old Man, a mountain peak in its own right, had long appeared utterly unscalable. Nowhere else around these shores is there a sea stack of such majestic proportions or one whose ascent by the easiest route involves free climbing of extreme technical difficulty, allied to skilled application of the most modern mechanical aids.

Height for height it is considerably more spectacular than the final 450 feet of any Alpine peak of my knowledge. Since I first started climbing in 1948, I've met many climbers interested in the mysterious Old Man. Some considered it impossible to climb, on photographic evidence alone; others like myself concluded that the rock must be rotten.

But the word "impossible" has no permanent place in a climber's vocabulary, and the Old Man had been an unfulfilled date in the diary for several years before we arrived. For once all my arrangements were beyond criticism. Stepping off the *St Ola* we were escorted to an excellent dinner in Stromness. Later a motorboat ferried us across the narrows to a pier on Hoy's north shore, where a van waited to transport us across to our headquarters on Rackwick Bay. Dr Johnstone of Stromness had put his summer cottage at our disposal and we were so used to good fortune that it came as no surprise to find we were in the nearest house to the Old Man, a mere forty minutes away.

It would be well to admit that Bonington's visit was not wholly recreative. He had signed a contract with a well-known Sunday newspaper to photograph and climb the Old Man of Hoy by a specified dateline. This lent a sense of urgency to the affair and accounted for much of the deadweight we carried to the start of the climb.

By noon the following day we had assembled a vast armoury on the isthmus below the pinnacle—ropes, pitons, bongs, karabiners, slings and nuts, the stock in trade of the modern climber, the "Meccano man". In the good old days stalwarts would have attempted the Old Man fortified only with moral courage, as W. H. Murray describes it. We took a more materialistic view, preferring degradation to decimation, a not unreasonable attitude.

Having loaded his various cameras, Bonington announced that the climb should now commence.

"Unluckily for me the climbing game is my bread and butter, mate," he explained forcibly and at some length. "You two carry on and enjoy yourselves. I have to stay behind with the cameras. I hope to join you on the last pitch, of course, so I'll need fixed ropes for following you up on *jumars*" (clamps).

This seemed like a rather unequal division of labour, but when the piper pays, one must alllow him to call the tune.

It was difficult to choose between the four separate facets of the pillar for sheer ferocity. Each offered a chance of success, but every proposed route led to a gap impossible to bridge without complicated engineering. The Old Man's profile was nowhere less than vertical and the most promising cracks were sealed off above and below by short brutish overhangs. Eventually Bonington glanced at his watch.

"You have now been here for almost two hours," he remarked in his best Sandhurst accent, "and you have yet to make a start. To be quite frank, I think you should attempt the side opposite the cameras to make my task a little easier."

We accepted this proposal with some misgivings and I led off from the saddle. The rough Orcadian sandstone looked good and decidedly felt good until without warning a perfectly formed hold suddenly disintegrated into small fragments. Most alarming was the absence of any pre-existing fracture line that might have accounted for this. We had to conclude that the rock itself was so soft and brittle that it could break away almost anywhere.

Loose rock is an accepted hazard on most Scottish climbs, and with experience can be handled safely. Intrinsically rotten rock is always dangerous because no amount of experience can entirely eliminate the risks involved. We could only minimise them by inserting a peg every ten feet to reduce the potential length of a leader's fall, a pessimistic but necessary precaution.

The first 80 feet, up a rickety pedestal inclined against the main face, were not particularly difficult, and I spent some time picking away rotten rock. It was often hard to decide what should be left and what discarded. It would have been quite easy to have stripped the face entirely of holds.

At the top of the pedestal was a large ledge, the essence of comfort had I not shared it with a young fulmar petrel. When molested these birds have a characteristic and unpleasant trait—they eject a foul-smelling oil from their throats into the face and eyes of any intruder, leaving a pungent odour on skin and clothing which no amount of scrubbing or deodorant can remove.

Their aim is remarkably accurate up to 6 feet, although the wily bird usually holds its fire until it cannot miss. An authoritative source informed me that this is merely a basic fear reflex. Experience has taught me otherwise. There is an element of cunning that could only emanate from the higher brain centres.

To combat this, we used a long wire to persuade the birds to discharge their ammunition before we entered the target area. But they resolutely refused to retaliate until it was profitable for them to do so. Some of the hardier specimens had to be bodily evicted from the nest, a risky procedure when hanging by one hand. We were careful not to harm the young birds, although they often tried our patience.

By the time Rusty arrived I was liberally spattered with oil and partly digested offal.

"You must hand it to the little basket," he said, sniffing the air appreciatively. "He really hates you." The feathered friend responded to his remarks with a hoarse belch.

"Your best bet would be to push on up the face and lead out left," I suggested, glad I wasn't leading. Above us the South Face swelled out with foreboding, overhanging throughout most of the next 200 feet. This ledge marked the undisputed frontier between the realm of free climbing and the unknown hinterland dominated by the "wee iron men". These pitons and bongs dangled neatly from Rusty's waist-belt, jangling rhythmically as he climbed.

He had gained a few tentative feet when he gave a hollow curse and hurried back to the ledge.

"There's another of those petrels up there," he said, wiping his brow. "I didn't stay to argue, and I'm certainly not going back." He disappeared round the right-hand corner.

The East Face was slightly more overhanging, but facing land and keeping the off-stage director in good spirits. "Do you know, Tom," he shouted, "that really looks quite dramatic from down here. Will you tell Rusty to hold it for a second? I'm not quite ready for him yet."

It was quite dramatic. Rusty descended a few feet, and, relying on rope tension from above, clawed his way across the abyss until he squeezed himself breathlessly into a small niche below a huge overhanging crack. Two hundred feet of air lay between his boot soles and the jagged boulder field at the base of the Old Man. Every hand-hold gave way as he touched it, dropping like an overripe coconut into space.

After a few tense moments we heard the welcome ring of a soundly placed piton. A short time later he had secured a traversing rope which could serve as an emergency lifeline. We remained linked by two full-weight nylon ropes, one clipped into Rusty's pegs as a security rope, the other hanging free as further protection. After a few feet the crack widened, and he exchanged the ordinary knife-blade pitons for wide angle pitons, called bongs. We had only a limited supply, since they cost a pound each, so Rusty often had to drop back on his *étriers* (stirrups) to remove all but the bongs essential to the second man's ascent.

Soon he passed out of sight above a roof, and I could only guess at his inch-by-inch progress from the nervous twitching of the nylon plumbline which soon hung 10 feet away from the rock face. If the worst happened I would be able to arrest his fall on one of the many pitons to which his rope had been clipped, but if he no longer had the strength to climb up his own rope and make contact with the face I would have to lower him 200 feet to the ground. This would have been difficult, since our rope was only 150 feet long.

How near we came to disaster remains a secret known only to Rusty. He told me afterwards that he reached a point where the angle ceased to be vertical, and, encouraged by a few rounded incuts, he dispensed with 100 per cent protective measures, against his better judgement. Without the restricting fetters he could force the pace for a few feet before inserting a peg upon which to recuperate. Soon he was firmly wedged in a short hanging chimney below the main roof. A few more inches would have brought good holds within reach.

At this crucial moment his sweaty fingers started to slip on the powdery sandstone, and simultaneously one foothold crumpled and fell away. For an instant he hung suspended in space from his shoulders, jammed squarely across the chimney. A desperate contortion enabled him to drive home a life-preserving piton in the remaining wall. He slumped back in his *étriers*, drained of nervous energy.

"That was the nearest I've been to a peel for some time," he announced ruefully as he rejoined me on the launching platform.

I nodded sympathetically, not mentioning I had been more pre-occupied in lighting up a cigarette than minding his rope. It had never struck me that on a long artificial pitch Rusty might meet any difficulty that could not be easily solved with a hammer.

It was an obvious cue for us to retire and reconsider the verdict. The implications of this narrow escape were not lost on us. Either traditional precepts of rock-climbing would have to go overboard or we would. Nothing was certain on this crumbling colossus but the due fate awaiting a carefree climber.

When we returned next morning we intended to use pitons to safeguard every move if necessary. Rusty first consolidated the previous day's gains, and then wedged his way backwards out of the inverted chimney until he could tap a trembling piton into a hairline crack above the overhang. Clipping a stirrup into this, he swung clear of the roof, only to find that the continuation of the crack still tilted slightly outwards for a further 30 feet. The battle, it seemed, was far from won.

Chris thought otherwise, for an unexpected burst of cheering roused me from my three-hour reverie. Unfortunately I took the applause to mean that Rusty had completed the pitch, and, taking advantage of the respite, began to unpack my overdue lunch. Frantic signals from the shore recalled me to duty, and I had no chance to satisfy my appetite until mid-afternoon, when Rusty finally overcame the pitch, the hardest on the climb.

Bonington's belated arrival from the ground floor roused my cynical displeasure. I suggested graciously that he tie on to the end of my rope in order to supervise the de-pegging operations.

"Sorry, old chap. I have to be quite frank about this, I'm afraid —the de-pegging is your problem. I will be prussiking up the fixed rope alongside so that I can take thrilling action shots as you climb."

Swearing under my breath, I submitted to the insistent demands of Rusty's top rope. Under its reassuring guidance I slid down the fixed rope on a karabiner fixed to my waist-belt and gained the foot of the crack. My climbing style is ill-suited to a mammoth de-pegging campaign. I know of no more subtle way of inadvertently strangling to death. The higher one climbs the more complicated becomes the tangle of *étriers*, ropes, slings, nuts and pitons which are recovered. Eventually exasperation gives way to despair, and the unfortunate second becomes enmeshed in a spider's web of his own making.

Bonington's cameras clicked busily. He was thoroughly enjoying his trip hovering over me like an inquisitive vulture.

This pitch held Rusty up six hours, discounting his efforts of the previous day, and I took two additional hours to restore the crack to its pristine savagery, aided morally and materially by the top rope. By the time we were all reunited in a cramped triangular niche at the top of the crack the lengthening shadows cast by the Old Man indicated that we must spend a third day on the climb.

This 450-foot sea stack was taking more time than the North Face of the Eiger! Even more ridiculous was the suggestion mooted by Chris and Rusty that we bivouac in this undignified, not to say cramped, situation. We had come a mere 200 vertical feet from the starting point. The Orcadian well-wishers who had come along to satisfy their curiosity had long since lost interest in the snail's pace and gone home.

"I'm off down," I said decisively. "I'll remember to give you a call in the morning." No man enjoys a bivouac when he knows that home comforts are just around the corner, and Chris and Rusty were no exception. After a rapid descent we rigged the doubled rope to await our return in the morning.

"Today we must succeed," Bonington announced, "or we will be too late for the Sunday edition." He had become increasingly edgy since the possibility of failure first dawned on his commercial soul.

It was my turn to lead, on territory well suited to my peculiar talents. The average angle had relented but the next 50 feet re-sembled hard-baked mud at best. It was useless trying to insert many pitons in the friable cracks. The few pitons I left behind were carefully re-inserted by Rusty when he followed me up, since he distrusts any scaffolding he has not erected with his own hands.

In three separate pitches we gained 200 feet in little over an hour. The diminished angle of the rock, now nearly vertical, greatly increased our climbing speed, and the colonies of fulmars that hugged even the smallest ledge made this no place to linger.

I was surprised to find myself at the foot of the final 80-foot crack, Bonington's allotment, and was tempted to press on. Although from a distance it appeared hostile, the Old Man's headpiece was compact sandstone offering generous holds which could be freely exploited without fear of sudden retribution.

While I brought up Chris and Rusty I had an opportunity to appreciate our magnificent situation. The surge of the waves against the base of the Old Man was no more than distant murmur on the wind. Only the mournful howls of Rusty's faithful hound reminded me of the world we had left behind. Once you climb the first 100 feet, you are no longer consciously aware of any added insecurity. As you climb higher there is a unique sense of physical detachment and height ceases to have any morbid significance. We were higher than St Paul's Cathedral, and by the time we reached the top we would be level with the new Post Office tower, London's highest building.

Any lingering doubts about the climb's success were quickly dispelled by Bonington, who tackled the final crack with the energy and skill of a dedicated climber. As he swung gleefully up from the crack the rope dropped cleanly from his waist to the coils at our feet.

A single forlorn cheer heralded our arrival at the top.

"Where are all the crowds? Where is everybody?" I demanded impetuously. Climbers are brought up to scorn the public gaze, but, like Walter Mitty, every man has his pretended moments of glory.

Yesterday the clifftop had been alive with spectators. (Nine, all told. I counted them.) Today not a soul had turned out to witness our triumph. Like the Beatles arriving at an empty London Airport, we were already forgotten heroes.

"We could always build a cairn," prompted Chris.

"Or light a bonfire," Rusty suggested, with his sense of the spectacular.

We carried out both suggestions. The top of the Old Man is a spacious plot of sun-scorched heather. In our enthusiasm the fire got out of hand, and only collective action saved us the inconvenience of a fast abseil down melting nylon.

"It wasn't really too bad, after all," Rusty concluded. "Next time we'll try it without pitons."

"In that case, you can count me out," I said. "There won't be a next time."

And for once I really meant it.

THE OLD MAN OF STOER

From The Scottish Mountaineering Club Journal, 1967

There have been three Old Men in the news recently. The first Old Man is of Hoy, in the Orkneys; he is 450 feet, Very Severe, and fell to Baillie, Patey and Bonington last year; and is described under *New Climbs* this issue and in the popular press. The second Old Man is of Storr, in Skye; according to Patey he is "160 feet high, repulsively loose and Extremely Severe", though the report (*S.M.C.J.*, xxvi (1956), 54) makes him 220 feet, Very Severe; anyway, he has remained aloof since Whillans' visit. The third Old Man is of Stoer, off the Stoer peninsula north of Lochinver; he is described on p. 116 of the *S.M.C. Northern Highlands Guide* as "evidently quite unclimbable". He is not. He is over 200 feet high, impeccably sound, Hard Severe, and his first ascent is described below.—*Ed.*, *S.M.C.J.*

"CAN WE BORROW your ladders again, George?"

My friend, the hotel proprietor, agreed without batting an eyelid. Years in the catering trade had taught him the customer is always right however irrational the request.

"I hope they bring you better luck this time, lads," he remarked affably. "Useful piece of equipment, a ladder. I've often wondered why they never used them on Mount Everest."

"It would have been too much of a novelty," I suggested, glossing over the horizontal ladder in the Ice-fall, de Saussure on Mt Blanc and, of course, *étriers*. Ladders stick up, *étriers* hang down; the principle's the same.

However, we lashed the ladders to the car without prolonging the discussion. George was not alone in misinterpreting the role of the ladder in the plan of attack. Our sporadic visits had become a source of speculation to the crofters of the Stoer peninsula. It is not every day that peat-cutting is agreeably interrupted by the passage of four wild-eyed men carrying ladders over the moors towards Stoer Point. They formed their own conclusions.

"Climbers, that's what they are. With climbing tackle. And them thinking to climb the Old Man of Stoer with a wee bit of a ladder that won't reach a quarter of the way up the side of it. They will be asking for a 200-foot ladder next. And they will not be finding it here; no, nor in Lochinver either."

The peat-diggers were not in the least surprised when the first two attempts failed and we returned like Sir John Cope, bearing the news of our own defeat; sagging under the yoke of two ladders, twin symbols of our incompetence. Tales of intractable tides and gale force winds carried no conviction; they had not even crossed the hill to watch. Once a West Highlander forms an opinion, he stays beside it.

Today there was only a solitary digger at the peats. "Back again," I shouted enthusiastically. "Third time lucky." He nodded wisely and continued his digging.

Brian Robertson muttered into his embryo beard. "There's one thing I've been noticing about you," he grumbled. "Everything we do, it turns out to be an epic. Even the simplest things. Take yesterday, for instance. . . ."

We had gone for an hour's run in the car, and had not returned until long after dark. This was because we had encountered a gate which was usually unlatched but which on this occasion was firmly padlocked. To save time and energy I had tried to nudge it open; and shattered the car's headlights. . . .

"That was sheer misfortune," I claimed, "Today we've left nothing to chance."

"You can say that again," interposed Paul Nunn, half throttled by the rungs of his ladder. "How often do you do this sort of thing? I've been on some daft games in my time, but this is the daftest. We carried less gear in the Dolomites."

Paul Nunn and Brian "Killer" Henderson from Buxton and Tyneside respectively, were two leading English tigers whom Robertson had ensnared on the Etive slabs and persuaded to come with us. "Wait till you meet Killer," he had promised me. "The man's a born craftsman. He makes all his pitons out of scrap metal."

Killer lived up to his reputation. "How about this, then?" he said, producing from voluminous pockets yet another sample of his genius. "I reckon this little job'll come in handy today. You've probably never seen one before, have you?"

I had to confess I had not. I could not even guess its function.

"Nice little job," he repeated, returning it to his pocket. "A nice clean finish, too."

"How much?" I asked.

"Some things are beyond price," said Killer.

The Stoer peninsula is a huge golf course; short cropped grass, not a tree for miles. From the little hill above the Old Man you can see all the north-west peaks spread out like inverted flowerpots.

Amid this pastoral setting the Old Man of Stoer rears up with startling suddenness.

"My God!" said Killer (or words to that effect).

His reactions were understandable. Well-thumbed Northumbrian breastworks pale before a 200-foot virgin pinnacle.

"It's like a kind of a symbol," he mused. "What a size. . . ." He enlarged on the idea at some length, with apt recourse to Greek mythology.

"How do we cross the water below it?" interrupted Nunn, who had been regarding the problem from a less aesthetic standpoint.

"That's the purpose of the ladders," I explained. "Lash them together and you've got a 30-foot span."

Manhandling the ladders down the mainland cliff was quite difficult. To save time we scrambled down a 200-foot fixed rope with the ladders balanced awkwardly round our necks. The penalty of a slip was instant decapitation.

It was going to be a race with the tide. Despite consulting the West Coast Pilot and other official sources, it seemed I had made yet another miscalculation. In less than an hour the reef on the far side of the channel would be submerged, leaving us without a landing place for the ladder.

I was secretly worried about the ladders. I had a shrewd suspicion that as soon as the first man reached the rope lashing which secured the junction, the two ends would fold up like a clasp knife, bearing the unfortunate pioneer straight down to the sea-bed.

Then I had a better idea. "Do you see that rock in the middle? If I can reach that with a single ladder, I can pull the other after me and use it to cross the next gap."

Once committed, I wasted few minutes. By the time I had clambered on to the reef both launching pads were awash. The 15-foot wall on the edge of the reef presented a tricky problem for bare feet until I remembered I happened to have a 15-foot ladder with me. Elementary, indeed.

Earlier on, there had been talk of swimming across. Warm sun and placid sea beckoned, but the three landlocked climbers resisted the temptation. A fine specimen of the Atlantic, or grey, seal had moved in for a closer inspection. This mammal is harmless, but of playful disposition; his attentions can be quite embarrassing.

We seemed to have reached an impasse. Robertson was in an unco-operative mood. He was not prepared to get wet. He was not even prepared to get his rope wet. Killer was reluctant to surrender one of his artistic specialities to anchor the Tyrolean rope, for he had guessed (correctly) that it would be left behind. I was obviously in a hopeless position to bargain; so my rope and pitons were used.

It was therefore consoling to watch Robertson getting wet. He took every conceivable precaution, but forgot to allow for the weight of ironmongery and the elasticity of nylon rope. By the time he had slid down to the half-way mark his rucksack was submerged and the water lapped about his ears, "Pull, man!" he gasped. I responded energetically and landed him in a flurry of spray.

"The tide seems to be coming in much faster," said Nunn doubtfully. "I think we'll stick around here for a while. You can chuck us a traversing rope once you're up the first pitch."

"What happens if we don't get up the first pitch?"

"That possibility had crossed my mind," he admitted. "At a guess, I suspect you'd have difficulty keeping afloat. But you can't grumble: few men are given such a powerful incentive to succeed."

This situation was tailor-made for Robertson's ideology. He

recalled a passage from a favourite author—*To go on was impossible, to retreat unthinkable.* . . . . "This is why we must go on!" he cried with Teutonic frenzy.

The first pitch resembled one of those gritstone problems where many fall and few prevail. The waves were breaking at Robertson's feet and the seal began to bob up and down in excited anticipation of two new playmates. In these situations I usually climb well.

The landward face of the Old Man is plumb vertical for the first 100 feet. I use this overworked term deliberately. Any sharp intake of breath would displace the climber from his holds, and there is no promise of a respite for a very long way.

I had only gained 12 feet when I found myself edging leftwards by two horizontal cracks ideally spread for the hands and feet, but separated by slightly bulging sandstone. A soft-shoe-shuffle took me to the corner of the face and out of sight of the audience; I stepped into warm sunlight and a hanging gallery of jug-handles. Barely a minute later I reappeared, on the first ledge 60 feet up. Robertson, with his usual bravura, tried to bludgeon a way straight up the wall, only succumbing after a struggle to the persistent lateral tension of the top-rope. This enforced detour tore him from his principles, as he now reminded me.

"Let a seagull defaecate from the topmost pinnacle, and that is the route I must follow," he announced, echoing the sentiments of his hero Comici, first Apostle of the Direttissima Doctrine.

Fortunes had been reversed, and now Nunn and Henderson were faced with the unpleasant prospect of ascending a 120-foot Tyrolean rope to join the assault. Even with our height advantage we found it difficult to throw the rope across to them; so we tied on a hammer as a range finder. The first cast with the hammer shaved Nunn's head but he grabbed it on the recoil with a spectacular leap nearly ending in the fiord. The two experts Robertson and Killer then took charge of their respective ends in order to tension the Tyrolean rope by means of *jumars*. This soon became a most complex operation, as each man was so committed to his own theories he had no time to check on the activities at the other end.

But eventually all was ready for the aerial crossing of the shore party. Robertson and I turned our attention to the next pitch. So compelling was the technical interest of the whole climb that the only implication I drew from the catastrophic possibility of the Tyrolean rope snapping was the personal inconvenience of being stranded indefinitely on the Old Man of Stoer. Two phantom lighthouse keepers waiting for the relief that never came. . . .

This second pitch was undoubtedly the crux—perhaps Severe, although it looked much harder. Large safe handholds led up to the overhang and Robertson could have been up it in a fraction of the time if he had not chosen to insert a security piton at the most awkward point.

I found him sharing a cave with a young bird. "A fulmar petrel," I announced. "Now, there's something peculiar about fulmar petrels; I remembered reading about it in a bird book."

"Anyway, this one seems to be choking," remarked Robertson.

The bird's neck had swollen hugely; its eyes glared. It looked as if it had something urgent to communicate.

It had. Its beak shot forward, opened, and drenched us in foul-smelling slime. I recalled the fulmar's peculiarity.

Robertson's cave was overshadowed by a considerable overhang which he had already inspected before deciding to belay. I lack conviction on considerable overhangs, so I decided to try my luck once more on the landward face, improbable as this had looked from the shore. The main bulge lay below me now and the angle had reverted to the perpendicular. Vast jug-holds took me diagonally rightwards to a small eyrie. From this, a well-concealed chimney offered a one-way ticket to the summit. There was a good stance and plenty of cracks, but when I had selected the appropriate blade from the pack I realised I'd left my piton hammer down at the last belay.

Not caring to call attention to this rather elementary mistake, I pushed on, vaguely aware that I had accumulated a peel-potential of some 120 feet. That figure did not worry me unduly, as I have a healthy disrespect for the rope, which I regard as a link with tradition and a reasonable assurance against the leader falling alone; the stronger the rope, the better his chances of company.

The chimney was V-shaped, bottomless and harder than I had thought. It was also the communal cuspidor of a thriving community of fulmars on the ledge above. I went into it back and foot, hood pulled down, P.A.'s skidding on avian regurgitations, breathless to the top. My exit was the signal for every fulmar in sight to release the final salvoes. Then up a short layback crack and almost as the rope went taut I wriggled over the top on to the summit bed of sea pinks.

It took Robertson some time to realise he had reached the top. He reckoned he was entitled to the fourth pitch and was quite put out to find he'd run out of rock. For an hour we lay in the sun waiting for the others. We passed the time bombing the seals with divots. Seeing a small movement on the distant Tyrolean rope I slung a divot at it and was surprised when it yelled back.

"What's happening?" we demanded.

Distant unintelligible noises. Finally Killer arrived at the end of the traverse rope and disentangled himself on the shore. His voice was suddenly audible. "What the blazes held you up? We got fed up waiting and we're going back."

"We've been shouting for you for the past hour."

"Come off it! We heard you shouting at each other."

"Nonsense," I said. "Come on up. It's a great climb. Three times bigger and better than Napes Needle."

"Stuff Napes Needle!"

"How about a few pictures, then—for posterity?"

"Sorry, mate—film's used up."

"Englanders!" Brian muttered. "You can't depend on them for anything."

We baled out on a 150-foot abseil which hung straight down to the first belay platform. Robertson came down last, and it was some consolation to the watchers on the shore when the rope jammed and he had to climb back 140 feet on Hiebeler clamps to free it. Before leaving he handed me a rope end.

"Tie this to a piton," he said briefly.

"Which piton?"

"Any piton."

I did as I was told, then set about cleaning up the stance.

About to extract the last piton, I noticed that the rope attached to it gave a twitch each time I tapped the peg.

"Don't you think you ought to leave that piton where it is?" Nunn shouted across.

"Why?"

"I think it would be a kind gesture," he said. "It's holding one end of the double rope and your friend is climbing up the other."

"Oh." Reason dawned slowly.

"Don't worry about it," he consoled. "Everybody makes mistakes. Some make bigger mistakes than others."

"Very true," I admitted.

And so the return was uneventful.

Note. Nunn and Henderson reached the last belay stance. Several months later the author took part in a second ascent by this route with a party of fellow-veterans from the north-east—K. A. Grassick, W. D. Brooker, the Rev. S. Wilkinson and J. M. Taylor. Grassick and Taylor swam, the rest linked ladders. They estimated the standard at Very Severe. It was the first ascent led by a clerical gentleman. All agreed that the sandstone is the finest of its kind in Scotland—quite distinct from the neighbouring vegetatious cliffs.

CREAG MEAGHAIDH CRAB-CRAWL

From The Scottish Mountaineering Club Journal, 1970

I'll put a Girdle round the Earth in forty minutes........
PUCK, *A Midsummer Night's Dream*

NOTE THE WORDS of Alasdair "Bugs" McKeith, Editor of the Creag Meaghaidh section of the S.M.C. *Central Highlands Guide* (1968):

"The Girdle Traverse of the cliffs of Coire Ardair . . . is certainly the longest potential expedition of its kind in Great Britain (8,500 feet) . . . and still awaits its first complete ascent. The climbing is nowhere excessively difficult but the entire traverse would probably justify a high grading on account of its length and seriousness. Remarkable situations are abundant and the exposure, which is often Dolomitic, is almost certainly unrivalled in Scottish winter climbing."

These comments have given me great comfort in the last few months. I did not make them: McKeith did. One of the oldest gambits in the climbing game is to borrow superlatives from early pioneers, e.g. *In the words of that great authority Lionel Terray.* . . . Such statements are invariably taken at face value. They never fail to impress and are, naturally, irrefutable. Never pat yourself on the back. Get someone else to do it for you. It shows good taste, good breeding, proves that you are a likeable chap and also provides a good opening for a climbing article.

"I don't get much excited about girdles," said Don Whillans gloomily, "especially 8,000 foot ones."

"But it's perfectly simple!" I insisted. "You have two parties starting simultaneously from opposite ends, crossing over in the middle. The left-hand party led by a right-handed leader and the right-hand party by a left-handed leader."

"Look mate," he interrupted, "do you know what you want to do? You want to team up with a crab. It's got claws, walks sideways and it's got a thick 'ead. This isn't a climb, it's a bloody crab-crawl!"

There is an air of finality in that sort of remark which does not invite contradiction. I knew better than to argue and we compromised with the Great Gully of Garbh Bheinn.

A fortnight later a party of five returned to the empty arena of Coire Ardair. We stopped below the plastered crags to watch Peter Gillman shuffling hesitantly across the frozen loch. We laid bets that he would fall through but to everyone's surprise the ice held firm. Apathy set in.

"It's a pity about the late start," said John Cleare.

This was putting it mildly. It was after midday, and in mid-February that does not allow much daylight for what Dennis Gray once prophesied would be a two-bivouac expedition.

Jim MacArtney and Alan Fyffe failed to respond. They looked as optimistic as two slabs of their native Aberdeen granite.

For MacArtney there were compensations. He was partnered by his girl friend, Mary Anne, on her second major ice climb. Although not ideally qualified for "Britain's longest potential expedition", she was more than decorative, keen to succeed, and probably the fittest member of the party.

"There's at least one consolation," said Cleare, "we should get enough photographs to keep my Editor happy."

We were not consoled.

Peter Gillman, his Press Colleague, now announced that he had all the necessary material for his article, and that he ought to be getting along. Since this was the first time he had been within conversation range and we had not yet started to climb, we were impressed by his talent for improvisation.

It was not long before we got the message.

"Would you mind lacing up your crampons properly?" chided Cleare. "I can help if you like. I may be using some of these illustrations for instructional purposes, and we don't want to set a bad example, do we? Incidentally—I should warn you that I may want to swap positions on the rope now and again, just to get the best angles."

I was well aware of the implications of this remark, having climbed with John for several years. A rope of five with a leap-frogging snap-happy photographer is as mobile as a constipated caterpillar. That was why I evolved a plan.

"Look here, John," I said off-handedly. "I'll climb unroped. That will leave the rest of you free as a party of four or as two pairs, and I can go ahead and give perspective for your long shots."

I could see from the dark look on MacArtney's face that he realised this was goodbye, but being an understanding lad he kept his mouth shut.

"Splendid," said Cleare. "We'll give you a shout when we want you to stop."

Once round the first corner of the Traverse, I found I was not only out of sight but also out of sound. In fact this was the last I saw of them, although from time to time I left encouraging arrows on the snow to show I had not forgotten it was a team effort.

Once in a while it is very refreshing to climb alone. The practice is traditionally indefensible. I will therefore attempt to defend it.

There are two cardinal precepts in mountaineering: 1. The leader must not fall. 2. The leader must climb as if the rope was not there. The first commandment is self-evident. No useful purpose could be served by a leader falling except to provide his followers with belaying practice. For the second commandment, there is only one way to ensure that a leader climbs as if his rope was not there—take away the rope. Now, it is also a fact that two men climbing unroped are no more secure than one. *Ergo*—the best solution is to climb solo. Q.E.D.

By tradition the climber who habitually climbs alone is regarded as reckless. Nothing is further from the truth, because if he were other than safe, he would be dead. The main attraction of solo climbing is the freedom of movement one enjoys. The sensation is akin to coasting down the motorway after being held up at every set of traffic lights in Glasgow. You keep in top gear and your performance improves correspondingly.

The Winter Girdle of Creag Meaghaidh is the ideal circuit for this kind of abandoned gaiety. The technically difficult sections are not very long, yet the rest are not of hands-in-pocket category. It is the sort of place where you might feel obliged to rope up if you had company. Not because a rope could afford any real security but as a gesture to the exposure. In summer the line of the Winter Girdle is an intermittent narrow ledge seldom more than a few feet wide, diminishing to a minus quantity at several points, and it offers an 8,000-foot gangway across some of the most inhospitable walls in Scotland, with a lot of rock overhead and a lot of air underneath. The only breaks in this Iron Curtain are the few isolated winter routes already recorded, and none of them are easy. The line of weakness goes sideways all the time instead of up and down, which makes this girdle more logical than others of its class. In fact, the most extraordinary thing about an 8,000-foot ledge is that it should exist at all, but probably there is the usual geological explanation.

In winter it ceases to be a ledge and becomes a silvery band of high-angled snow-ice, a string of tinsel stretched across one and a half miles of crag. The snow banking on the ledges squeezes the climber out into the footlights, ensuring appreciation of the environment. This is equally impressive and oppressive, the free-fall potentials adding up to 500 feet in some places, a long way without a parachute.

The first two segments of the Girdle Traverse, The Scene and Apollyon Ledge, are little more than *hors d'œuvres* to the main course—the Post Horn Gallop on the Central Cliffs. Both introductory sections had been explored by McKeith and written up as separate routes, although his gradings and times seem excessive. The Scene, which crosses the broken buttress left of Eastern Corner and finishes in Raeburn's Gully, appeared to merit a winter grading of 2 instead of 3. The crossing, unroped, took only thirty minutes for 1,000 feet as against the $2\frac{1}{2}$ hours allotted. Although a solo climber moves at least twice as fast as a roped party the prevailing conditions were far from ideal—an unusual amount of black ice and heavy aprons of unstable wind-slab.

The Scene, however, is the most practical corridor to the next segment, Apollyon Ledge, and this is certainly worth inclusion. It crosses the gigantic bleak wall of the Pinnacle Buttress, 1,000 feet high with an average inclination of at least 80°. This is the only part of the Creag Meaghaidh cirque which promises rock climbing, the rocks here being too steep for vegetation; so far nothing has been done. Only two winter routes breach the main face of the crag. Both follow shallow water-courses and are exceptionally fine. The left-hand one, known as Smith's Gully (attempted by Robin Smith but climbed and christened by Marshall), had only had two ascents and is one of the really great ice routes of Scotland, exacting enough to satisfy anyone's tastes. As I crossed this legendary giant by an easy snow ledge midway between two appalling ice bulges, I felt I ought not to be there, having cheated in some indefinable way.

Gillman's ant-sized figure at the loch-side reminded me too vividly of the scale of things. I was glad when he stopped shouting. He evidently believed that he alone, from his special vantage point, held the key to the situation and he was trying in some unintelligible way to bridge the 1,000-foot gap that had opened up.

I waited a token ten minutes, but as there was still no sign of Cleare and his camera-party finishing The Scene, I gave them up as a lost cause and, scuttling across the rest of the snow ribbon, rounded the edge of Pinnacle Buttress, with the Main Face in full view ahead.

Up to now I had not seriously considered completing the Girdle Traverse in an afternoon, as I began with only six hours of daylight for a mile and a half of traversing. Totting up the guide-book estimates for the component sections gave 15 hours for the complete Girdle. My idea had merely been to go as far as I could without risking benightment and to get off the face—up or down —before nightfall. Now, with seven hours of guidebook time already condensed into 1½ hours and 4½ hours of daylight remaining for 8 hours' scheduled climbing, I was beginning to catch up with the clock, and an intriguing pipe-dream was beginning to look practicable.

Ten years ago Richard Brooke and I made a diagonal line across the Central Face, the Post Horn Gallop. This now formed essentially the critical third lap of the Girdle. From memory I knew I could scarcely hope to halve our original 5 hours, as we had then enjoyed superlative hard snow-ice. However, 5 hours itself would suffice, providing nothing unexpected cropped up afterwards.

Once or twice a climber has one of those days when angles recede, when the impossible becomes possible and he is caught up in his own impetus. I found myself relying implicitly on front points and the spikes of two short axes. Steps were rarely needed, and this meant an enormous saving in time.

Whatever the source of my elation, it was certainly not my reserves of armoury, which consisted of two ice-screws and one diminutive ring-spike—no selection for a crisis. My boots, equally uninspiring, were making one of their final farewell appearances. As with ageing Prima Donnas, money—or the lack of it—was the reason for these repeated performances. Earlier in the day I had been able to waggle my big toe through a large hole in the leather. This had then seemed an amusing party trick but I had now lost the point of the joke and, for all I knew, the point of the toe as well.

Post Horn Gallop shares a common start with the Last Post. From the bed of Easy Gully a 60-foot ice colonnade points the way. A few weeks earlier Carrington and Higgins were so delayed on the Last Post they had to spend a night on the plateau. I could still see a few dimples on an enormous ice bulge probably marking their ascent. Knowing the high calibre of that partnership, I decided to look elsewhere. The alternative was a long horizontal traverse above, across a smear of metallic ice. Every axe blow jarred and the monotonous cutting began to take its toll before I eventually reached easy snow bands above the ice. A few minutes later I ran into company on the South Post.

Earlier, I had seen signs of life in both South and Central Posts and calculated that I must be on "collision course" with both groups. Like unsuspecting stags upwind, they seemed completely unaware of my approach, so I had time to decide upon an opening pleasantry that might make my entrance from the wings seem less dramatic or flamboyant.

"Excuse me, can you tell me the time?" I said, with studied nonchalance. The leader glanced down.

"Three o'clock," he said briefly, and resumed step-cutting.

I was somewhat disconcerted by the lack of interest. Solo climbers don't grow on 1,000-foot ice faces. Not even a polite inquiry about my intentions. . . . I passed on with deflated ego.

The Centre Post encounter was more encouraging.

"Excuse me, can you tell me the time?"

"To hell with the time, mind my rope! . . . Wait a minute, who the blazes are you?"

"I'm just passing by," I replied chillingly, "but I'll have to nip up this next pitch before I can get out of your way."

He was visibly impressed. "I'll come down and give you a belay, if you want to take over."

It was a generous offer. He seemed unaware that he had already got up the worst part. I did not enlighten him and made full use of the three ice-peg runners he had already fixed. The last bit was still awkward enough, and I had to use one of my two precious screws to overcome a projecting boss of ice.

"Well done!" he cried. "Now, would you mind giving me a top rope?"

I could hardly object, despite the ominously lengthening shadows, but I was more unhappy when he arrived empty-handed.

"Where's the ice-screw?" I demanded. He nodded gloomily towards the gulf.

"They'll never get up without it," he said, "we'll post it on to you."

I forgot to leave my address, and was most surprised to find the screw in the mail a few weeks later. This sort of thing restores one's faith in humanity.

I hurried along towards the North Post trying to make up for lost time, but impetuosity nearly landed me in disaster.

Below the upper ice slopes, the North Post splays out in a lofty canopy, seamed by discontinuous diagonal cracks. I was half way down one of these before I realised I had selected the wrong crack. It is usually simple to reverse a descending move, but this time it was not. I tried once and failed. The second time, as I stepped back, the windslab ledge suddenly heeled off into space

1. Number 2 Gully Buttress, Ben Nevis

2. Winter traverse, Cuillin Ridge

old man of hoy   450′

SOUTH FACE   EAST FACE

final crack (hidden)

S E arete

upper chimney
hidden

HAVEN

traverse round S·E arete possible

line of climb variable

MOUTH

virgin
wall

GALLERY

overhanging crack

pendule

PILLAR

causeway

3. The Old Man of Hoy – 450′ high

4. Old Man of Hoy: Star Performers. *Left to right*, Joe Brown, Dougal Haston, Christian Bonington, Ian McNaught-Davis, Tom Patey, Peter Crew.

5. Tom Patey and Joe Brown, St. Kilda 1970

6. On the Rakaposhi expedition. Note hands bandaged and gloved to prevent infection after frostbite

7. Am Buachaille

8. The last 1,000 feet of Fiva route (March), Store Trolltind on right,
Trolltinder Wall on left. X marks highest point reached

and I was left in the posture of a Praying Mantis, crampon points digging into verglassed slabs. It was a moment of high drama—and horror—best contemplated in retrospect. Hanging on by one gloved fist jammed behind some frozen heather roots, I had to extract the small ring-spike from my pocket and batter it into the only visible crack. It went in hesitantly for an inch and seemed to bite. Then the crack went blind. Time was running out, as my supporting hand was rapidly losing sensation. I tied off the ring-spike at its base, and somehow threaded the rope, using my teeth and one free hand. I was now faced with a 20-foot diagonal rappel to reach a big ledge on the far edge of the canopy. If I missed it or swung off backwards. I would be spinning in space with little prospect of regaining the cliff face. I didn't spare a thought for the piton. It had to hold and it did.

I arrived in a rush, sinking hands, knees and toes simultaneously into a mound of powder snow. At the same instant the last ice-screw came adrift from my waist and dropped silently out of sight. I yanked the double rope, hopefully, to retrieve the ring-spike, but it held firm.

Once teeth-chattering subsided, I set off along an easy boule-vard that seemed wide enough to accommodate six old ladies walking abreast. The route unwound easily, across the snow bowl of Staghorn Gully and round into the crags of the Inner Corrie where the firm crisp snow faced the north wind. I was now on the Last Lap—so far an unknown quantity. I checked out the routes: The Sash, Diadem, Will-of-the-Wisp, Cinderella, The Prow. To look back on the line of steps weaving up and down like a switchback gave a perverse sense of artistry. On Will-of-the-Wisp I met another party and made my stock inquiry about the time; they would obviously have to hurry to avoid bivouacking.

Eventually only the Quasimodo Traverse separated me from the window and "journey's end", but on this unfamiliar ground I selected the wrong ledge system, emerging in Crescent Gully below, instead of above, the crux pitch, and also within easy glissading distance of the corrie floor. High above I could pick out the proper line, right out on the edge of nowhere. It was tempting to call off and head for the hostelries, but this would have meant avoiding "the sting in the tail", referred to in the guidebook: "*On no account should this pitch be avoided.*" With that sort of recommendation, it would be really nasty. Exercising considerable self-discipline I climbed back 300 feet.

The route petered out half-way across an incredibly steep wall; so steep that even in mid-February it held very little snow. There seemed to be no future on that vertical skyline, but the directions were explicit. There would have to be some enormous "jug-handles" somewhere. I moved gingerly out on to a projecting block which immediately threatened my balance. Groping wildly, I found I could sink my right arm behind the block and start brushing away the snow drapery from the next ledge. All the time I was being nudged off balance by the bulge overhead and survival depended on a succession of unseen Thank God holds.

Even when I learned that all the holds were there I was still relieved to find a good ledge beyond the corner. I stopped and pulled in the abandoned rucksack. The access route to the Quasimodo Traverse now comes up from below and offers the last escape from the recommended line, but one takes the honourable path by a long airy traverse almost exactly like the preceding pitch. This unexpected second "sting in the tail" has been graced with the extraordinary title of Positively 64th Street. I was uncertain what particular hippy significance was attached to the name apart from the author's obvious intentions that it should not be overlooked. Every step brought me a little nearer safety and the corrie floor rising up in welcome.

Quite suddenly it was all over. I had run out of rock and emerged on to broken outcrops and screes overlooking The Window. Learning to walk again was almost too much and I fell flat, slithering head-first down the snow. I scrambled up and yelled exultantly. Fortunately there was no-one within earshot and by the time I met the others I had recovered sufficient composure to submit to their back-slapping with measured calm. "It had been an interesting climb, rather over-rated but still worth a visit. In better snow conditions I could have chopped off another hour. A four-hour schedule might be adequate, etc."

These are enlightened times and this kind of line-shooting

kidded nobody, least of all MacArtney. There was an amused glint in his eye. "It's really made your day, hasn't it?" he said.

Postscript. When I wrote up this climb, I was not to know it would be the last occasion on which we would all climb together. Less than a year later Jim and Mary Anne died together on Ben Nevis, betrayed by a freak windslab avalanche near the top of the Italian Climb. If I had been writing a memorial for Jim MacArtney I could have selected many better or more appropriate climbs than this one. He had spent a frustrating afternoon under the lens of Cleare's camera and because of repeated delays they had to call it a day not far beyond Apollyon Ledge. In normal circumstances Jim would have been in his usual position, well out in front, but despite the frustrations he enjoyed that day as he enjoyed every other day, wet or fine, that he spent in the mountains, and it was because of his enthusiasm that it became for all of us a day worth remembering. That was the measure of the man.

PART II
Abroad

THE MUSTAGH TOWER

From The Scottish Mountaineering Club Journal, 1957

AT THE BEGINNING of April last year I was pretty much at a loose end. I had been all set to join Mike Banks and Hamish MacInnes on the Anglo-American Expedition which was said to be going to the far-famed Mustagh Tower in the Karakoram. Personal expenditure was to be minimal, and we might even reap a profit. But it was not to be. As sailing date came near and it became a question of finding £500, I could see no solution to the problem; so I withdrew.

A few days later I was bemoaning my bad luck when the phone bell rang. It was John Hartog, leader of a "rival" expedition to the Tower, inviting me to join them. He was brief but to the point: "Can you come to the Himalayas in a fortnight?" It was to be a small expedition of four, run on modest lines, with Ian McNaught-Davis and Joe Brown completing the party. What was more, the costs were within the scope of my pocket. So I cast personal integrity aside and joined the enemy forces. As I could not cancel my job immediately I followed on by plane three weeks behind the others, who had gone out by sea. I joined them at Rawalpindi where they were making final preparations before flying to Skardu in Pakistan Kashmir. There was no sign of Banks and Co., but we heard a rumour that they had decided to go for Rakaposhi instead.

Our own party was a curious combination, inasmuch as none of us had climbed together before. Only Joe had been on a previous trip to the Himalayas, though both Mac and John had expedition experience behind them on Ruwenzori and in Spitzbergen respectively. My own "climbing abroad" had been confined to the Alps, and in my post as expedition doctor I was even less well equipped, having only just qualified. However, I was assured that my services would not be required. The flight to Skardu was an exciting affair, during which we had a close-up view of Nanga Parbat as the plane passed within a mile of the top.

Skardu is the starting point for most Karakoram expeditions now that an air lift has replaced the long trek from Srinagar. We engaged 100 Balti porters here for the approach march. There is no need to describe the eleven days' march up the Shigar Valley to the Baltoro Glacier. It is also the way to K2, Gasherbrum and the other Karakoram giants, and has been written up in several mountaineering books. However, a word about the Mustagh Tower itself is perhaps indicated. It had no real history behind it; in fact there had never been an attempt on the mountain, though many expeditions have passed by on the way to K2 and ought to have responded to the magnificent challenge of the great obelisk. On almost every side the walls fall 5,000 feet sheer to the glaciers. Armchair climbers have been put off by the famous photo by Vittorio Sella, which shows the Tower from its most terrifying angle. Indeed, it is mainly because of this photo that the Mustagh Tower has passed into the category of so-called "impossible" peaks. However, no peak is impossible until it has been attempted. Now that the world's highest mountains have all been climbed, expeditions tend to be more attracted by difficulty than altitude. Hence it was an obvious choice and we considered ourselves lucky in being first in the field. There are two main ridges on the Tower, the North-West and the South-East. After a preliminary reconnaissance, we plumped for the North-West Ridge. There was little between them as regards difficulty, but the other seemed more exposed to avalanche in the lower reaches.

Right away we had porter trouble. Our four Hunzas, who claimed to have carried Hermann Buhl off Nanga Parbat, decided that the equipment we had supplied for them was hardly up to standard; so we had no option but to take leave of them at an early date and engage four of the local Baltis. No doubt they were out to prove themselves against their traditional rivals, the Hunzas. Anyway, they did an excellent job of work, and we never had cause for complaint on this score throughout the expedition.

It had been our intention to limber up on the Baltoro Spires above the glacier, but these now revealed themselves as a loftier edition of the Chamonix Aiguilles, all sheeted in ice. We had therefore, to break tradition by acclimatising on the Mustagh Tower itself. Access to the 20,000-foot col at the start of the NW. ridge is by the Chagaran Glacier, and this is guarded at the foot by a 2,000-foot ice-fall. Accordingly we set up base camp at 14,000 feet immediately below the ice-fall, and set about solving the first problem. No doubt about it, the party's *élan* could hardly have been surpassed at this stage. We had already dismissed the Mustagh Tower as "climbed" and were making plans for our next objective, Masherbrum!

For a start everything went well. We found a way up the left border of the ice-fall and established Camp I at 16,000 feet on the only patch of stable snow in the vicinity. Here, alarming new crevasses were appearing every day and we could only conjecture what would happen if one revealed itself underneath the tent. Instead of this our main difficulty was in maintaining the tent floor at ground level. A tremendous amount of melting and evaporation of snow goes on under the direct action of the sun's rays, so that after a few days the tent is left perched on a ridiculous pedestal, rather like a museum exhibit, and has to be re-pitched. Above the ice-fall the glacier shelved back at an easier angle for about 1½ miles, to abut against the 6,000-foot vertical face of the Tower. At this point Camp II was to be erected. John and I found a reasonable route for porters through the heavily crevassed upper glacier which we marked with little black flags.

From the top of the glacier a great 45-degree ice-slope of 2,500 feet slants up to the col at the foot of the NW. ridge. This was the first real trial of strength, and Joe advanced to the attack, armed to the teeth with ice pitons. He returned with John in the evening, somewhat discomfited; they had been forced to retreat owing to lack of time when still a good 800 feet below the col, and they reported that the innocent-looking upper snow slope was, in fact, hard ice with a thin layer of unstable snow on top. However, their staircase saved us many hours on the following day, and we arrived at the difficulties early on.

Further ascent was indeed laborious; each step required twenty blows with the ice-axe pick, and in any case soon melted away in the heat of the sun. Obviously we would require fixed ropes all

MUSTAGH TOWER (FROM THE WEST)

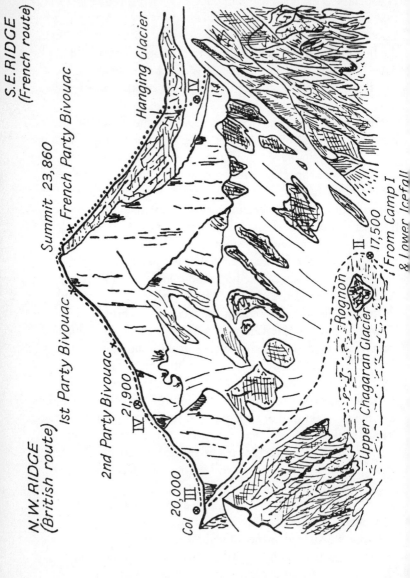

N.W. RIDGE
(British route)

S.E. RIDGE
(French route)

1st Party Bivouac

Summit 23,860

French Party Bivouac

Hanging Glacier

2nd Party Bivouac

21,900

IV

20,000

Col III

Rognon

II
17,500

From Camp I
& lower Icefall

Upper Chagaran Glacier

the way on this upper part if we were ever to get our porters as far as the col. Ice-pitons were a rather dubious anchorage, and so we decided to force a way up the snow-covered rocks on the right. This last 800 feet took five or six hours and included several very "dicey" pitches, but, once it was all roped and the necessary rock pitons in place, we felt sure our porters would manage to cope satisfactorily. What did upset us was the view from the col. We hadn't seen the North Face before, but thought that it could hardly be any worse than the other faces of the Tower. In fact there was little difference, except in so far as it was plastered with ice and snow which lay at an incredibly steep angle. Consequently we would have to take every pitch on the NW. ridge absolutely direct, and our route seemed comparable to the lower part of Observatory Ridge under bad winter conditions—quite a problem at 20,000 feet.

We returned and informed the others of this new problem. Already there was an undercurrent of feeling that we should scrap our projected route and take a look at the SE. approach. Bad weather was imminent, so we descended to base to sit out the storm and conserve our precious foodstuffs at Camp II. For a week it snowed without remission and the squalor inside the tent reached new depths of degradation. Everybody was rather apathetic. The only episode of interest was the Mystery of the Meat, the mortal remains of two goats who had accompanied the expedition. These were parked in a crevasse and disappeared piece by piece. Failing any logical explanation the porters were suspected, until one morning we discovered leopard tracks in the vicinity of the camp. Riaz told me I had nothing to worry about— a leopard does not attack unless hungry!

However, we were to be given a rude jolt. For a few days we had heard rumours of strange sahibs on the Baltoro Glacier, and our porters quoted them as saying they were going to climb the Mustagh Tower. This couldn't be true. Surely Banks was miles away on Rakaposhi. Then a letter arrived from Guido Magnone, leader of a French Karakoram Expedition. He had every intention of climbing the Tower and was, in fact, this minute, encamped below the SE. ridge. The wily man had been in the area now for ten days, and so ensured a good start on the first lap to the summit. There was great indignation at this, for we had understood their primary objective to be Hidden Peak. Instead, here they were on *our* mountain! A dispatch deploring competition was sent round to the French, and we awaited results.

It soon had the effect of producing the conqueror of Fitzroy in person. We got only a few minutes notice of his approach, and despite our frantic attempts to appear as professional as possible, the tent was still in a state of wild chaos when Magnone and Paul Keller appeared at the door. We had expected to find a grim *face nord* austerity in our rivals, but the opposite was the case. The arch villain, Magnone, was in fact a most charming personality, though his Parisian volubility was rather wasted on Joe and myself, who knew but little French. Nevertheless, it wasn't long before an *entente cordiale* was established, and both parties were wishing each other success, blaming all the confusion on the Pakistan Government. Magnone went so far as to hope the British would get to the top first, and he promised to send us round some cognac, if they had any left over. In the afternoon, both parties now on the best of terms, they left to rejoin their companions, Paragot and Contamine. Despite this we were left wondering just how far they had advanced up the SE. ridge, for when we sounded them on this they were noticeably reticent.

A 20,000-foot mountain mass separates the Chagaran and Younghusband Glaciers and it is linked to the Mustagh Tower behind by a high ridge. This effectively prevented the two rival parties from spying on each other. In any case the veteran British mountaineer is noted for his imperturbability, and we resolved not to ignore the edicts of our forefathers by joining in a race to the summit.

When the fine weather came at last, we carried imperturbability to its extreme by delaying our return to the Tower for a day or two in order to bag two peaks of 18,000 feet near our base camp. Then, almost reluctantly it seemed, we set off through several feet of new snow for Camp I. Joe and I continued to Camp II as the advance guard, reaching our destination just before nightfall. Disaster! We had collapsed our tents in textbook fashion before the blizzard, and they were now invisible under several feet of snow. Luckily Joe spotted an ice-axe sticking out, and we could fix the position to start digging. It was long after dark before we could crawl into the frozen tent and start thawing out our sleeping bags. The following day was wasted.

Next morning the snow was firmer and bearing weight. Joe and I were again the navvies, but we didn't envy John and Mac who had to safeguard the porters up the great ice slope, swaying under their 50-lb. packs. This time we really went at it with axe and hammer and laid out a fine staircase up to the col, furnished for most of the way with ropes. Despite the fact that this would have been rated quite a difficult ice climb at home, we could now rely on the porters continuing the lift unaided for the next few days.

All four of us were now lodged at the col at 20,000 feet, and we set out for the initial attack on the NW. ridge. We could only see the first 1,000 feet of this ridge, and beyond this, on what we hoped was easier ground, Camp IV was to be established. It was this section which had appeared almost impossible on our first visit, but we were surprised to find how much the angle leaned back when we really got to grips with the difficulties. No doubt about it, however, the slope was still exceptionally steep and we were having to cut handholds almost continuously. Soon the snow changed to hard ice, and we moved right towards the ice-covered rocks on the brink of the great West Face. The climbing here was exhilarating, quite exposed, but very sustained. Each pitch took about an hour to lead and the difficulties seldom fell below Severe in standard. Again it was fixed ropes all the way, but after a pitch had been led once, the major difficulties were over. We were three days on this 1,000 feet before we reached a site suitable for Camp IV. In the evening we would slide down to our Camp III on the col and next morning pull ourselves up the ropes to the previous day's highest point.

It was the last of these days that marked the start of the final bid which was to carry us to the top. Following a vague report from the porters that Riaz, our liaison officer, was at death's door, I had descended the ice slope to find him in remarkably good spirits and awaiting my arrival with hot coffee. Cursing my unfamiliarity with the Balti tongue, I returned to the col next day to find that Mac and Joe had left as the first assault party carrying with them the ingredients of Camp IV.

They didn't return in the evening, so we assumed things had gone according to plan and followed on next day as the supporting party. Above where the fixed ropes gave out our predecessors had been unable to spare any to leave behind, so we had some exciting "free" climbing on the remaining 400 feet to the top of the first easement in the ridge. Any stones dislodged here dropped absolutely unhindered, in an awesome silence, for 2,000 feet down the West Face. As I topped the last, slightly overhanging pitch my eye ran quickly up the remaining 2,000-foot ridge to the top. Suddenly I spotted two little figures outlined on the snow, almost at the summit. I shouted down the news to John that the Mustagh Tower was "in the bag". Then I noticed that they were still moving up! Obviously they had decided to cast discretion to the winds and emulate Hermann Buhl by sleeping out on the summit.

We reached Camp IV in another half-hour and prepared to spend a most uncomfortable night. The tent itself was perched apologetically on an insecure heap of rubble that Mac and Joe had collected, and John, who was too slow off the mark, found himself occupying the outer berth. The only primus had ceased to function, and we were denied not only warm food but also water, which was much more serious.

Despite the early hour—6 a.m—it was almost a pleasure to get up and away from the tent next morning. We couldn't cook a breakfast and had no excuse for delay. John packed in all his bivouac kit, but I rebelled against the drudgery of a heavy rucksack and took only the minimum of spare clothes. Anyway, the ridge looked quite straightforward compared to what lay behind us and I couldn't see what had held the other two up. For the first two hours we gained height smoothly on easy ground, reminiscent of Tower Ridge in winter. Mac and Joe had reappeared below the skyline and were proceeding downwards slowly and cautiously. We met them about 9 a.m. just below the steep upper section and heard their story.

We were only at the start of the real "climbing", they announced. The 800 feet immediately above our heads had occupied six hours of their time. For most of the way it had been a struggle through three feet of soft snow lying on a substratum of hard ice, and set at a very high angle. They had left a huge trough marking their line of ascent and, quite apart from the obvious avalanche danger, it had been extremely exhausting work. At 5.30 p.m. they had reached what appeared from below to be the top, only to see the true summit 200 yards away along a knife-edge ridge which dipped to a small intermediate col. The col was the limit of their advance. Only two short rock pitches separated them from the goal, but they were both very exhausted, and in any case it was 6.30 p.m. with only one hour to darkness. A small scoop in the ridge below the first summit served as a bivouac site, and they prepared for all the horrors of a night out at 23,000 feet. In the morning they were both very weak, though miraculously immune from frost-bite. They resolved to descend immediately so that they could vacate Camp IV that day and ensure a comfortable night's lodging for the second party. It was a very gallant action on their part to sacrifice their own chances of reaching the top, though by gaining the near summit, a mere 10 feet lower, they had, to all intents and purposes, made the first ascent of the Tower. For there had been no indications that the French had beaten us to the top.

Our own task was now much easier. The overnight frost had consolidated the snow, and we had a regular ladder of steps all the way. We put the main slope behind by 2 p.m. and carried on up a little rock rib towards the summit ridge. Magnificent climbing this and not at all what you would expect at 23,000 feet; almost vertical rock, yet sprouting jug handles everywhere and offering grand exposed pitches of merely Very Difficult standard. Despite the rareness of the air, we got as much pleasure from it as from a climb at sea-level. At 3 p.m. we stood on the West Summit, looking across to our other objective, and already aware of mounting exultation. Just as I emerged on the summit cornice I thought I heard a shout from John below me. Then I realised that it came instead from the direction of the SE.

ridge. Suddenly I spotted the French, tiny specks on the snow, encamped on the hanging glacier, 3,000 feet below us. They had actually been prospecting their route through binoculars when two figures appeared out of nowhere at the summit. We now had a valuable eye-witness proof of our ascent!

Continuing from the col, a small rock pitch of Severe standard gave us a little trouble, as we were in too much of a hurry to remove our crampons. Only two rope lengths to go, and a knife-edge *arête* of snow swept gracefully up to the summit cornice. With mock dignity befitting the occasion, each insisted that the other lead the way and we argued it out with great spirit. At last John was persuaded to advance the remaining ten feet; I followed him and we shook hands solemnly on the summit. The usual summit rites were restricted to photography, as we had forgotten to bring a flag along with us on the expedition. Bill Brooker had promised to present me with a Scottish Lion Rampant before I left Aberdeen, but unfortunately all the flags he had inspected in the shops were too expensive. In any case we couldn't afford to waste any time here as there were only three hours of daylight left for the descent, and a bivouac at 23,000 feet is a sobering thought.

We started down at 4.30 p.m. John, who probably carried the heavier pack, was going very slowly, whereas I was in a regular fever of impatience. My bivouac equipment was far too inadequate, and visions of Annapurna passed through my mind. At one point the bowline round my waist worked loose as I came down last, but I carried on regardless and rejoined John, holding the end of the rope in my hand. He was justifiably indignant.

Darkness came on quite suddenly, as it always does in the Himalayas, when we were still an hour away from the camp. There was nothing for it but to bivouac where we stood, and we established ourselves in a half-filled crevasse as a shelter against the night breeze. Within an hour or so the temperature dropped to subzero levels and the icy-cold draughts coming up from the depths of the crevasse did nothing to improve matters. I had removed my boots and stuck both feet in a rucksack, but John's laces were frozen and he decided to keep on his boots. However, he could feel his toes moving and took this as a sign that all was well. Dawn came at last at 4 a.m., but it was still two hours before we could start down. Both my boots had frozen stiff and would not go on my feet. I had to thaw them out under my shirt. John had to take over the lead down to the camp as I was experiencing violent paroxysms of shivering, so much so that I could hardly keep my hands on the holds. Such were the consequences of leaving some of my bivouac kit behind and having to keep rubbing my legs most of the night. It was only later, when John removed his boots, that he discovered the extent of his frost-bite. He had not noticed his feet going dead, yet, beyond doubt, they were in a very bad way. Tired as we were, we managed to massage the blood back into his feet, but not to the toes which remained a dirty-white colour.

Next morning bad weather appeared to be imminent so we had to continue downwards. John was very tired and unwell. All the fixed ropes were left in position: we had little inclination to remove them. Not far above the col I shouted to Mac and Joe to come up and meet us, in order to help John with his pack. They, too, were still very exhausted after their ordeal. So the four of us staggered back into Camp III. Joe and I, in response to a message from below, continued down to attend to a case of T.B. pneumonia among our porters at the Base Camp. Next day John and Mac experienced the final whims of the mountain. Descending the great ice slope, they were involved in a small rockfall, one of the boulders ripping the rucksack off Mac's back, but luckily without personal injury.

It took John not far short of a week to reach Base Camp. We had only three fit porters, and it would have been impossible to carry him. When he arrived his frost-bitten toes were already black, and as he would eventually require surgical treatment, we were anxious that he should start down the valley as soon as possible. It was agreed that he must be carried all the way, but our own porters for the return carry were not yet due for some days.

Then news arrived that the French had reached the top six days after us and were preparing to leave immediately. With their assistance we might be able to speed up John's departure. I decided to pay them a visit at their Base Camp, both to offer my congratulations and to consult their medico, Dr Florence, who was a recognised expert on frost-bite. That evening I fared sumptuously on a five-course meal, which left me thinking that there was a case for nationally sponsored expeditions after all. The French were in great form and full of superlatives about their climb. I was reminded of the classical descriptions of climbs in the Vallot Guide: "*Itineraire audacieux et superbe, l'un des plus beaux et des plus difficiles des Karakorams.*" They had been forced to bivouac on the ascent, tied to ice-pitons well below the summit, and had only avoided a second bivouac by 600 feet of abseiling in pitch darkness, with one torch between the four climbers. The grading was "*extrêmement difficile*", and 3,500 feet of fixed rope had been left *in situ*.

Next day both parties held a grand reunion dinner at the British Base Camp. It was decided that John and I would accompany the French down the valley, while Mac and Joe remained on the Baltoro for a few more days to take photographs of the Tower from its more sensational aspects. A stretcher being unmanageable, John was hoisted into a chair of sorts, perched high on a porter's back. Sixteen men carried him in turn, frequently having to cross steep cliffs and mud banks where the least slip would have been fatal. So we proceeded down the valley for eighty miles and then managed to hire a small fleet of *zoks*, or goatskin rafts, racing each other down the last thirty miles to Skardu. John then flew back to England and later underwent extensive surgery to both feet in a London hospital.

The Editor has asked me for a few general impressions of the Karakoram. The most striking thing is the number of famous unclimbed peaks all within a twenty-mile radius of the Mustagh Tower—Masherbrum, Hidden Peak, Broad Peak, Paiju, the Trango Towers, Crystal Peak, Mitre Peak and Bride Peak. All remain virgin. The main Trango Tower is the most extraordinary rock feature I have seen anywhere. Cut off on every side by walls as steep and long as the West Face of the Dru and attaining a height of over 20,000 feet, it poses a magnificent challenge in this new Golden Age of Himalayan climbing. Even the Mustagh Tower itself still holds its fascination—the traverse of the mountain would be a tremendous expedition.

There is an enormous amount of rock about, and nearly all the main peaks offer mixed routes of very high standard, comparable in severity to the great Alpine *faces nords*. There is not much snow plodding, often the most exhausting type of climbing at this altitude. The rock is granite, which is sound on the lower Baltoro spires, though above 20,000 feet on the Tower it tended to be very shattered. Snow lies at a steeper angle than I have encountered in the Alps or Scotland and seemed to be relatively more stable, for we saw few major avalanches. Powder snow and verglas on the rocks, however, offer a problem, and for this reason I found the climbing on the NW. ridge very similar to the Lochnagar buttresses in winter.

Acclimatisation gave us no worries, though 23,860 feet is, of course, small by Himalayan standards. The weather also was kind to us. We had one period lasting a month of almost continuously fine weather. We reached the top on the eighth day of that fine spell, though, as events proved, we could have afforded to spend much more time on the final bid.

Any comparison of the two routes is not really justified, though, from both accounts, there appears to have been little between them as regards difficulty. The angle of the NW. ridge is slightly steeper, but to compensate for this the French had more difficulties to face in the lower stages. The first party to complete the traverse will be in a better position to judge!

RAKAPOSHI—THE TAMING OF THE SHREW

From The Scottish Mountaineering Club Journal, 1959

NO ONE COULD describe Rakaposhi as a friendly mountain. It is a tempestuous Himalayan virgin, and flatters only to deceive. Although, as Mike Banks remarked pointedly, "It hasn't claimed a victim yet", it has at least made a creditable attempt. On the last three expeditions, there have been fourteen falls, and unwelcome suitors have had to run the gauntlet of avalanches, collapsing cornices and an electric storm. Obviously its courtship should be conducted with resolute firmness. . . .

Curiously enough the 1958 British Pakistani Forces Expedition selected Rakaposhi as a safer alternative to their original choice of Disteghil Sar. Banks, our leader, had a say in the matter, for he had led the 1956 Rakaposhi attempt when a combined British-American four-man expedition (B.A.K.E.) failed only 1,500 feet from the top (25,550 feet). He attributed their failure to bad weather, lack of manpower and the inability of the porters to carry beyond Camp II at 19,000 feet. Another factor, perhaps not insignificant, was the fact that all the participants, liaison officer and porters included, had fallen at least 100 feet at some time in the course of the expedition. The American, Bob Swift, collected the laurels here: he had been charged during an electric storm on the Monk's Head and taken two weeks to recover!

The first name to be associated with Rakaposhi was that of Martin Conway, doyen of Himalayan explorers, who in 1892 pronounced the mountain "quite climbable if the upper part of the SW. ridge can be reached". Yet it was not until 1938 that Vyvyan and Secord, employing rush tactics, climbed a 19,750-foot peak on the NW. ridge within a week of leaving Gilgit. Here a deep gap, impassable to porters, prevented farther progress. After the war Secord returned to the attack with Tilman and two Swiss climbers Gyr and Kappeler. They gained the NW. ridge beyond the impasse, but again it was not a route for laden porters. Climbers

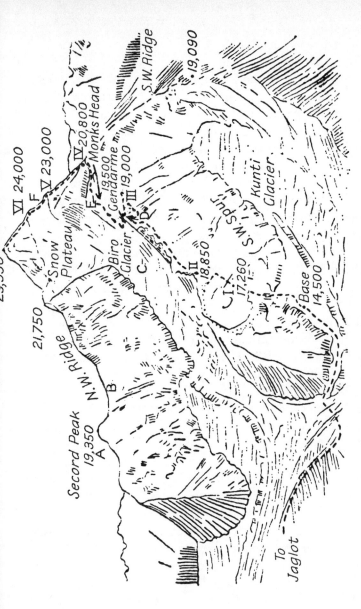

WEST FACE OF RAKAPOSHI (as if seen from SW. at a height of about 20,000 feet)

A, Secord and Vyvyan, 1938 (19,350 feet)   B, Gyr and Tilman, 1947 (*a.* 19,000 feet)   C, Tilman and a Sherpa, 1947 (*a.* 16,000 feet)   D, Tilman and others, 1947 (*a.* 19,500 feet) (The Gendarme)   E, Band, Fisher, Tissières, 1954 (*a.* 20,500 feet)   F, Banks, MacInnes, Irvine, Swift, 1956 (*a.* 23,400 feet)
...... Route on to the SW. Spur followed by 1947, 1954 and 1956 parties.   ----- Route followed by 1958 party (*Map after Shah Khan*)

were only beginning to recognise the perverse nature of this obstinate monster: from afar the NW. ridge appears to be an easy thoroughfare.

The same party were the first to put Conway's theory to the test. They attacked the SW. spur, the obvious stairway to those alluring upper slopes of the SW. ridge (see diagram). The spur presented problems of no mean order, perhaps outwith the scope of pre-war mountaineering in the Himalayas. From the first subsidiary peak of 19,000 feet the crest of the spur, heavily corniced to the north, ran back on an undulating course for $1\frac{1}{2}$ miles with little net gain in height before merging into the face below the feature known now as the Monk's Head. Half-way along this ridge Tilman came to a halt at the top of a razor-edged blade of snow, the Gendarme, and was moved to utter famous words cherished by subsequent expeditions, "hopeless, hopeless". He referred to the 1,000-foot ice slope of the Monk's Head which confronted him and barred the way on to the SW. ridge at 21,000 feet.

The dossier would not be complete without including the summary of the strong Austro-German Expedition of 1954, among their numbers Heckmair and Rebitsch: "the mountain appeared unclimbable by any of the routes we prospected". A debonair Cambridge undergraduate party followed hard on the heels of the Germans. Their adventures are described by George Band in his book, *Road to Rakaposhi*. They quickly realised that the SW. spur was the only feasible route and, although hampered by unwilling porters and Wrangham's temporary departure through a cornice, they succeeded in forcing a route up the face of the Monk's Head. Band described this as his "finest day's climbing in the Himalayas". The door to the inner sanctuary was open.

In the summer of 1956 came the four B.A.K.E. stalwarts—Banks, MacInnes, Swift, and Irvine. Hamish MacInnes, a Spartan Scot, was put in charge of food supplies, with dire results. His final letter from New Zealand advised them "to prepare to live like peasants!" Nevertheless they succeeded in roping the Monk's Head and establishing two camps above this on the SW. ridge. From their top camp at 23,000 feet they made their summit bid, but mediocre conditions forced them to give up after climbing only 500 feet.

A few lessons had been learned. Three camps were necessary above the Monk's Head. Banks was convinced that their top camp was too low to launch a successful summit attempt. For maximum safety six men must be firmly established above the Monk's Head, a summit pair and supporting parties at the other two camps. To achieve this the porters would be required to carry at least to the top of the Monk's Head and this would only be practicable after 4,000 feet of fixed rope had been installed. Thus Rakaposhi, although not enjoying the exalted status of a Dyhrenfurth "*Acht Tausender*", promised to offer problems of organization and transport quite equal to those encountered on the greater peaks.

Most of the team of nine had previous expedition experience. Mills and Deacock had been in the Army expedition to Alaska; John Sims had visited the Labord Himalaya with the R.A.F. team in 1955; Richard Brooke joined us direct from a winter in the Antarctic with Hillary's party. (With another expedition to the Arctic to his credit he perhaps holds a unique record.) Banks had considerable Arctic experience and of course had led the 1956 Rakaposhi bid, while I had already visited the Karakoram with the Mustagh Tower party. Dickie Grant, a Commando climbing instructor, joined us as a last-minute substitite for Lester Davies. The two Pakistani members were Raja Aslam and Shah Khan and upon the latter the success of our expedition hinged. He was the uncle of the Mir of Hunza and his presence was likely to inspire the Hunza porters with a sense of urgency! Brooke and Sims were survey officers, and the Survey of Pakistan had supplied us with Sahib Shah, a veteran of several expeditions. I envied the three of them their task, as the area had already been mapped several times. My own appointment as physiologist was an unpopular one—with my fellow climbers and myself.

On 12 May the expedition left Gilgit. Rakaposhi is perhaps the most accessible of the greater Himalayan peaks, with an approach march of a mere three days from Gilgit if jeeps are hired for the initial sixteen-mile drive up the Hunza Gorge. Unfortunately we were held up the best part of a week at 10,000 feet by heavy snow-fall which discouraged our poorly shod coolies. It had been an exceptionally severe winter and Banks reckoned that conditions higher up would be equivalent to those of late March in an average season.

Base Camp on a lateral moraine of the Kunti Glacier occupied the same site as that used by the three post-war British expeditions. Our main party settled in on 20 May, but Banks and I had mean-while pushed ahead to reconnoitre a possible short cut on to the SW. spur, which would avoid the long traverse over the first 19,000-foot peak and bring us to the crest not far below the Gendarme. Here we would establish Camp II at the site of the Cambridge Camp IV, a substantial gain.

We reached a height of 17,400 feet on the first day, and erected Camp I on a minor shoulder abutting against the main face. Much labour was expended on digging in to the 45-degree slope, where perhaps a snow-hole would have been more satisfactory in the long run.

The rest of our projected route looked quite feasible, but more heavy snowfall enforced retreat. We felt sufficiently confident, however, to give the "go ahead" to stage one on the expedition schedule. This consisted of ferrying forty man-loads up the 3,000 feet of steep snow below the camp: in the steep gully leading up to the shoulder we fixed the first thousand feet of rope to safe-guard our porters. Soon everyone (including a few half-hearted Jagloti auxiliaries who had been enticed by the promise of a pair of boots) was engaged on this thankless task, and the language was hot enough to melt the virgin snow.

Every evening it snowed. The previous day's tracks were invariably obliterated by morning, and the dreary routine of breaking trail, often thigh deep, had to begin again. The riotous evenings at Base with my accordion and a vigorous percussion section led by Grant did much to relieve the monotony. They were also responsible for the premature broaching of the crate of whisky with which we had intended to celebrate our success on the mountain.

A day came when Rakaposhi decided to show her mettle.

Richard Brooke, always an excellent companion on an ice climb, had accompanied me on a reconnaissance of the next stage of the route, the 1,200-foot face leading up from Camp I to the crest of the SW. spur. For once it was a glorious day and our spirits rose as we climbed. Great ice slopes fell away below us to lose themselves in the depths of the Kunti Glacier, 4,000 feet below. At 11.30 a.m. I was only 200 feet from the crest. The snow was excellent for kicking steps with a firm surface crust. Suddenly a shout broke the stillness. "I say, I'm certain I felt the slope move just now." I made a mental note for the physiological diary: "Brooke, hallucinations, not yet fully acclimatised."

His next shout, seconds later, was drowned in a dull roar as the whole slope avalanched. An area about the size of a football field broke away above and below us. At the instant we felt ourselves moving we drove our axes firmly into the stable underlying *neve* and hung on grimly. A tremendous weight of snow piled up against my body, but just as the pressure became unbearable I managed to deflect it past me with a mighty heave. The crisis was all over in ten seconds and perhaps a minute later we saw the debris spill out on the lower slope 2,000 feet below.

The silence was broken by Richard, picking his words deliberately with an admirable display of sang-froid as befits an Alpine Club member. "This place is distinctly dangerous. I propose that we turn back." This time I needed no persuasion and promptly abandoned my ice-axe as an anchor for the 800 feet of rope we carried. On the way down we collected my smaller second axe which had fortunately lodged in the slope by its pick. The two of us were stunned by the incident This was giant windslab on a scale beyond our experience. Indeed, despite similar episodes of a less serious nature later on, I still regard myself as quite unable to forecast the stability of Rakaposhi snow. The snow that day was the firmest we had met on the mountain!

More was to follow. A few days later another blizzard forced us all down to Base Camp. At the height of the storm Shah Khan, Raja and the porters sallied forth from Camp I intent upon a rapid descent to Base Camp. It was, in fact, considerably faster than they had anticipated. Without warning a huge powder snow avalanche swept out of the mist, picked them up effortlessly and deposited them 1,000 feet nearer Base Camp. They were unharmed but minus most of their kit and quite euphoric. Our initial enthusiasm had lost much of its sparkle, and the porters were beginning to develop strange illnesses.

A week later we returned to the scene of the first avalanche to find that the snow above the cleavage line was still in a highly precarious condition. Belayed by the others I went up the last 100 feet like an ibex. Once we had all assembled on the crest, Brooke and I descended on a tight rope and with a jump sent another huge mass of snow plunging down the face. This time most of the route above Camp I was cleaned of debris, and with the addition of another 1,000 feet of fixed rope the way was open for the next lift. Camp II went up a short distance along the ridge, within easy striking distance of the razor-backed Gendarme which reared up steeply for 400 feet.

For several days I was detained at Base Camp looking after Raja Aslam who had developed a recurrence of his malaria. During this time John Sims was performing heroics leading the Gendarme in waist-deep powder snow. Both sides had to be roped for the steep slope on the far side could be a death-trap to a tired party retreating in a blizzard. When I joined Brooke and Grant at Camp I we were able to leap-frog the top party and proceed to establish Camp III below the Monk's Head. On the mile of ridge beyond Camp II there is no net gain in height, and despite all our hard work we were only a little over 19,000 feet.

Still the bad weather persisted. One night a violent thunderstorm hit us at Camp III and vivid flashes of lightning illuminated the interior of the tent. The mornings were usually fine and found the three of us hard at work on the "Rakaposhi treadmill". We attacked the 1,000-foot, 45 degree slope of the Monk's Head, as did our predecessors, by the left edge next to the abyss of the Biro Glacier. Every 100 feet we left a great hole in the snow where a piton had been planted deep in the ice substratum. Near the top, where the angle steepened slightly, Warwick Deacock's long aluminium stakes proved invaluable for anchoring the ropes.

After three days' work the route was completed and the summit plan could go into operation. The first stage was a single combined lift by all members and porters to the top of the Monk's Head at 21,000 feet. Only Shah Khan remained at Camp III, suffering from altitude headache.

The Monk's Head belied its reputation for difficulty: it was no harder than the North Face of the Plan in the Chamonix Alps— and the porters justified their selection by making short work of the face, although aided throughout by fixed rope. They had climbed farther than their fellow Hunzas on the earlier expeditions, and much of the credit was due to Shah Khan. We could now afford to dispense with their services for the last section of the route up the SW. ridge. The next day we shifted camp from the top of Monk's Head across half a mile of desolate plateau to a more satisfactory site below the first of the three great steps of the upper ridge With complete lack of foresight we moved all the essential kit including the tents in the first carry, and on the second trip discovered that the driving snow had obliterated our tracks. Visibility was nil and we could only proceed by the feel of the old tracks under the fresh snow. With only one hour of daylight left we found the new site, thus avoiding the bivouac to which our stupidity had nearly condemned us.

On 23 June the seven of us attacked the first 2,000-foot step. Mills, Deacock, and Sims shouldered all the essential equipment for the last two camps: the other four of us carried only our personal kit and were to form the assault team. It was a difficult choice for anybody to make, for each member had acclimatised well and was going sufficiently strongly to make the top. Indeed, we still hoped that the weather would allow us all to make an attempt.

Above 21,000 feet the snow had consolidated under the influence of the bitter north-west wind which sweeps the ridge, and the going was immediately easier. Crampons were now a benefit, but we often had to kick steps in the hard snow, as a result of which most of the team were to lose at least one toenail from mild frostbite. At least the avalanche danger was past; we saw no windslab above the Monk's Head. In the early afternoon we staggered on to a level shoulder above the step, the first

available camp site on the upper ridge and the site of the B.A.K.E.
top camp in 1956. As elsewhere there remained not a trace of their
visit, a bitter disappointment as their top three camps had been
left fully stocked for the second attempt which never material-
ised.

The support party left us here and we settled down in the two-
man tents to spend a cold but reasonably comfortable night.
Even during the day time the temperature seldom rises above
freezing-point on this exposed ridge. Mike and I, benefiting from
our experiences in 1956 when we both climbed above 23,000
feet, had acclimatised a little faster than the others and were to
make the first bid for the top from the next camp (Camp VI).
Richard Brooke and Dick Grant would sleep another two nights
at Camp V before moving up to make their attempt.

By so doing they were able to relieve us of all but personal
kit on the next day's carry up the second step. A thin spine of
shattered rock broke the uniformity of the 1,000-foot face and
saved us hours of step cutting. The wind was strengthening
and we often had to shelter in the lee of the boulders to restore
circulation. Despite our 40-lb. loads we were all four moving
well, and in an hour had passed the highest point reached in 1956.
Near the top of the face the steepening rocks forced us leftwards
on to a 50-degree slope up which Richard battered out a ladder
of steps. At 1 p.m. we made an abrupt exit from the face on to
the broad upper plateau which straddles the mountain from the
NW. ridge to the SE. ridge. Through the drifting snow we could
see the rocky summit pyramid shining dimly in the afternoon
sun. It looked so near that Grant and I were tempted to carry on.
However, it was not long before he and Brooke were prevailed
upon by the wind, now almost gale force, to get back to their
tent while they could, leaving the two of us at Camp VI.

Mike and I lay awake far into the night, listening to the blizzard
raging outside. I estimated our chance of success as very slight as
the food supply would allow the two of us only one attempt.
We picked at our oatmeal biscuits half-heartedly, consoling our
protesting stomachs by calling down the wrath of Allah upon the
head of the absent food officer. Jimmy Mills was the next most

unpopular man to the physiologist at the high camps. The fact that he had made a scientific study of his subject and condensed the daily quota of calories into a pocket-sized carton earned him none of the credits he anticipated.

We woke at 6 a.m. on 25 June to the roar of the blizzard. Mike was almost suffocating under the weight of snow piled up against the tent wall. A peep outside to collect snow for making tea revealed an icy inferno which sent a cloud of spindrift billowing into the tent. We ate a leisurely three-hour breakfast; as Mike remarked, "there's no need to hurry". *Duvets*, windproofs, every article of clothing went on. At 9 a.m. I stuck my head out and, with what I hoped was a debonair laugh, said, "Here goes." We had only gone a few paces when we realised that the sky was quite clear, although this was only a minor consolation as we seldom glimpsed the sun in the driving spindrift. The gale force must have been 60 m.p.h. To face directly into the wind would have been to invite immediate frostbite.

We had 1,500 feet to climb and no technical difficulties to stop us, yet we had to fight for every step. The crampons were in the rucksack, but it was far too cold to remove our gloves long enough to strap them on, and so we settled into the mechanical routine of step kicking. For a long time we seemed to get no nearer to the summit rocks, intermittently visible through the snow streamers. Mike was complaining of numb feet and I had to stop several times to massage the life back into my hands.

As we learned later, Brooke and Grant were also fighting the gale in a gallant attempt to make the summit from the lower camp. They had to give up after 500 feet when they realised the impossible nature of their task. It proved to be their last chance of the success they deserved.

After four hours we were on the shattered rocks of the summit pyramid and moving more confidently. The difficulties were only moderate, but the last 200 feet of the SW. ridge narrowed to a knife-edge with an enormous void on the Hunza side. We used the very crest of the ridge as a hand rail, with the gale threatening every minute to tear us from our holds and toss us over the brink. Twenty feet from the top I found a convenient boulder on which to scratch the initials of the expedition. Mike passed me and at 2 p.m. crouched uncertainly on the summit, a crazy pedestal of loose blocks. I staggered heavily after him, intent on placing my shoulder on the very top, and succeeded in bruising my already numb fingers.

Ten minutes were sufficient to snatch a few random snapshots and to bestow our curses on the landscape; ten minutes of shivering misery as a climax to a year's preparations and six weeks of physical drudgery! I felt I could sympathise with the man who wrote, "The reason I enjoy climbing is because it is so entirely irrational."

We fled before the gale. The ascent had taken five hours, largely due to the appalling conditions: we regained the tent in ninety minutes. It had collapsed, half buried in the drift. In the process of digging it out I punctured my air mattress with a crampon spike, condemning us both to a miserable night on the remaining air bed. To make matters worse my bruised fingers were now badly frostbitten and Mike had numb feet. Luckily we had with us some anti-frostbite tablets.

During the night the sky became completely overcast, and in the morning the visibility was only a few yards. We left at the deadline of 12 noon and were lucky to strike the way off the plateau on our first cast. Near Camp V we were deceived by the mirage of an apparently huge *sérac* looming through the mist into considering ourselves lost. Banks blew himself hoarse on his whistle without evoking any response from the occupants of the tent. Then the sky cleared momentarily to reveal the camp site 100 yards away, and we realised the futility of our distress signals. The deserted tent lay flat on the snow. Inside was a note from Richard: "11 a.m. Tent roof tore today in the gale. Getting out quickly. Hope to hell you made it."

Two hours of daylight left. Spurred on by the thought of a night in a crevasse, we unroped and moved together, glissading wherever possible. This was no longer an orderly retreat but a rout: everything was sacrificed for speed. Suddenly shouts came through the mist. Our companions had heard our voices and were coming out to meet us. I was never more thankful to see anyone in my life, even if it was Jimmy Mills behind a cine-camera, fired with a Stobart-like enthusiasm. A few minutes later we were tucking into a huge plate of chocolate porridge, the *specialité de la maison*. Then followed the less pleasant intravenous injections for frostbite, an operation complicated by Banks dropping the candle. Finally the sleeping-bag and oblivion.

That was virtually the end of a successful campaign which had lasted only five weeks. A few days of inactivity at this altitude leave their mark, and no one was keen on mounting a second assault. In any case the bad weather showed no signs of improving. Forty-eight hours later everybody was back at Base Camp. Camp IV was salvaged by the simple expedient of tossing the tent down the Monk's Head, thereby causing the porters some alarm. They ran all the way to the foot of the face, mistaking the sack for a falling sahib!

There is little more to add, save that the Hunza apricots are the most luscious fruit known to man, and on our return to the valley we did them full justice.

WITH ARNE RANDERS HEEN ON THE ROMSDALSHORN

From The Scottish Mountaineering Club Journal, 1959

IN MARCH 1959 I accompanied an official Marines' ski-ing course to central Norway. My performance on the "boards" did not lead me to believe I was destined to stardom, so the prospect of a fortnight's training with Norwegian Army instructors was not encouraging. However, I knew the Romsdal Alps, a sort of Scandinavian Chamonix, to be within easy reach of our base at Dombås, and it seemed likely that I could arrange a week-end's leave.

On 10 March the Oslo express rolled into the tiny station of Dombås and disgorged a score of jubilant Marines; to the relief of the other passengers who had long since lost their enthusiasm for singing. We were met by two lean giants, who introduced themselves as our instructors (the cult of fitness is a disease indigenous to Norway). Jensen, the chief instructor, who spoke only a little English, delivered a brief speech of welcome: "I like men who like ski-ing. It will be hard work, but you will be happy. Perhaps you will come again."

Next day we were introduced to our skis. The courtship commenced with a ten-kilometre chase through a forest, in the course of which I lost the skin of both knees in a brief encounter with a tree. Fortunately the skis were unscratched so the incident passed without comment. Ski-ing in file at intervals of five yards is not without its hazards, and a single collision is transmitted like a chain reaction to the end of the line. One unlucky individual opened his eye on the ski stick of the man in front and was removed to hospital; as Jensen sadly commented: "It is always the keenest ones who are hurt first."

I was initiated in the mystic rituals of ski-waxing. It was grimly ironic to spend the early hours of the morning rubbing in wax in order to increase one's speed on the downhill. I had owned a pair of skis for several years, blissfully unaware of the existence of ski wax. Now it took a lot of experimentation to find a wax that made the skis slide more reluctantly, and I used this with some success for the duration of the course.

The evenings were no less hectic. Norwegians take their drinking as seriously as they do their ski-ing. Consequently the licensing laws forbid the sale of spirits after 6 p.m. Not that this causes much inconvenience: it is common practice to buy spirit from the nearest chemist and flavour to taste. Every family takes a pride in its *Hjemmebrent*. It is dispatched on its mission of havoc with a hoarse shout of *skol!*—one local word with which we were all familiar.

I prefer the phonetic "ski-ing" to the more correct "she-ing". The latter leads to confusion with an entirely different sport—a sport which was practised with enthusiasm by most of my fellow-Marines. The local hotel housed sixty Swedish girls, who were also on a ski-ing course: it was well patronised in the evenings, and many a jaded skier found a new Valhalla.

Our antics on ski were a source of some amusement to the local toddlers. They would have been better occupied at school, had they not been under age; the yells of derision as they flashed across our ski tips tended to interrupt our concentration.

After a week's *langlauf* practice we were ready for the 10-kilometre race—the "passing-out parade". Sixty-five minutes was the maximum time allotted—fifty minutes earned a silver medal and forty minutes a gold medal or, conversely, a visit to the hospital. The route had been planned with Machiavellian cunning; every straight run terminated in an abrupt bend to avoid a pond or ditch. The instructors skied gravely alongside, occasionally doubling back to round up a straggler and reappearing in time to thrust a glucose drink into our hands as we crossed the finishing line. The track was a ribbon of ice and once committed to the deeply rutted tramlines, it was only necessary to lean forward in the prescribed fashion and leave the rest to gravity. Negotiating the "points" was much more difficult and inevitably ended in disaster. I had, however, evolved a formula for success, which stood me in good stead. A smoothly executed fall at each bend saved one from over-shooting the track like many more fancied competitors and wasted less time. Progress was spasmodic, but I qualified with a few seconds to spare and upset the form books.

Fortified by my unexpected success, it occurred to me that I had now earned a brief respite, and laid plans for Romsdal accordingly. Sam Bemrose, the gay Lothario, joined the expedition for a different reason, although he too was in search of "fresh fields and pastures new". Henry Berg, one of the instructors, completed the trio. He was a member of the Norwegian team who reached the summit of Tirich Mir in 1950—a determined-looking individual with a craggy profile which might have been hewn from his native Romsdal.

We covered the sixty miles from Dombås to Aandalsnes in Henry's ancient box car, which we named the Thin Wall Special. It was held together by bits of rope and the hand of Odin, but as the journey was downhill all the way we made quite good time.

Aandalsnes, a thriving fishing port, is at the head of a long fiord and surrounded by some of the finest scenery north of the Alps. The Romsdal Alps rise sheer from the sea to a height of 5,000 to 6,000 feet. The gorge carrying the road and rail link to Dombås cleaves the heart of the range and is hemmed in by mighty precipices. On one side is the famous Romsdalshorn, on the other the Trolltinder Wall, claimed to be the greatest face in Europe. There are only two routes on the 5,000-foot Wall, both led by the local guide Randers Heen—of whom, more anon.

For Sam's introduction to mountaineering Henry Berg had selected the Vengetind (6,000 feet). We left at 7 a.m. and motored for some miles along the side of the fiord. A short distance up a side valley the snow plough appeared to have given up the struggle, and all tracks ended. Here Henry announced, with evident relish, that we should proceed henceforth on ski. This was a cruel blow, reference to the map indicating plainly that six miles and 2,000 feet of ascent lay between us and the start of our route. We toiled up through the forest, letting our guide break trail in the soft snow. Fortunately he knew no English, and to each wrathful inquiry "How far now?" he smiled impressively and replied "*ja ja*."

After 2 hours we entered a steep gully where an ice-axe would have been more useful than a ski stick. Here without regret we abandoned the skis, though only after I had slithered back some distance in what is probably termed "reverse snow plough position".

After our poor showing on the boards I was determined to vindicate our climbing ability. Consequently Henry and I ploughed parallel troughs in the snow as far as the head of the gully, when I was still in the lead by a short head. Here it became necessary for Sam to rope up, and by the time I had tied his bowline Henry had forged ahead and I found myself second on the rope.

We followed a graceful snow *arête* which swept serenely upwards for 1,000 feet to terminate in the beautifully symmetrical summit cone. The climbing was interesting if not very exciting, and the exposure on either side quite remarkable.

At 2 p.m. we duly arrived on the top and were greeted with a view extending from Snöhetta to the Jotunheimen. It was ample reward for the long tiring slog, 6,000 feet in all. The descent passed without incident, a long glissade followed by the now familiar spasmodic ski-run down to the valley.

After supper Henry proposed that we should pay a call on Herr Arne Randers Heen, perhaps Norway's most celebrated climber. Later in the evening we would adjourn to a nearby dance hall and so justify Sam's week-end. Unhappily for Sam the fates and Randers Heen willed it otherwise.

Our host was a dynamic personality. Adam Watson senior had already told me a lot about him, and it was apparent that his approval of our plans would be tantamount to a papal blessing. His humble abode was a shrine to the memory of every Norwegian climber, alive or dead. Every wall was festooned with portraits and relics. The broken stump of Slingsby's ice-axe was there, so too was a sardine tin from which Carl Hall had once supped— each item neatly tabulated. The most recent exhibit was a piton "used on the Trolltinder Wall by Heen on the occasion of his memorable ascent". Most of the climbing books in his vast library were inscribed by the authors to "A.R.H." In order to digest every iota of available climbing literature he had taught himself four different languages.

During the Occupation it was Arne who organised the local resistance movements. When the British landings at Aandalsnes failed, Nazi bombers devastated the town and obliterated his home with its already formidable library. All that remained was the charred stump of Slingsby's axe, which he unearthed triumphantly from the debris.

Nothing could quench his flow of anecdote. Held as a hostage by the Nazis and waiting possible execution, he had written a book of poems to while away the time. This book he now produced and undertook the considerable task of translating all the poems into English for the benefit of his audience, appealing to Sam when a phrase slipped his memory. The sounds of revelry across the street faded in intensity and finally ceased altogether. At 1 a.m. Arne poured the last libation and announced that I would shortly be accompanying him on a winter ascent of his favourite mountain, the Romsdalshorn. We would leave early, he explained, in order to overtake the rest of the party who were already sleeping in a small hut at the foot of the mountain. Henry promised to have me up and ready for the road at 6 a.m.

In fact it was 5 a.m. when we set out, as Norwegian Summer Time had been in operation since midnight. As we followed the previous day's tracks up the valley Arne discoursed at some length on his favourite topic, the Romsdalshorn. It was, of course, Norway's finest peak—he had climbed it 125 times, so he ought to know. In winter it was a much sterner problem and had only yielded on seven occasions, six of these ascents led by himself. Today was a special occasion, for I was the first alien to attempt the climb in winter.

At the hut we discovered the rest of the party still in their beds. They refused to adjust their watches to the new time and were in no mood to respond to Arne's impetuosity. We were off again almost immediately, leaving the others to pursue us at their own discretion.

Only one of them accepted the challenge and overtook us at the foot of the face. Arne introduced him as the "Pupil", and I never learned his name. He was a tigerish-looking individual, bursting with suppressed energy, and appeared to merit a fairly tight rein.

We cramponned briskly up a 50-degree slope for several hundred feet until Arne announced that we had climbed far enough for a fall to have fatal consequences and should therefore rope up. The Pupil was to lead, and so further his education.

It is difficult to recall the salient features of the route: I was more concerned in watching my companions. The Pupil was climbing with such fire that Arne seldom had time to find a belay before the rope ran out and he had to start off again. Naturally my rope received scant attention; I would have accepted this as a compliment had the route been easier. It was no worse than Observatory Ridge in foul conditions, but I thought it merited a token respect.

The Pupil had now learned two words of English and bellowed "Kom Toom!" whenever he noticed any hesitation on my part. Eventually, in desperation, I slung caution to the winds and surrendered to the impetus of the party. We climbed in line abreast, yards of loose rope snagging on every projection.

Presently came a hoarse shout from Arne, our middle man on the rope. A mischievous coil of nylon rope had encircled his throat, and gone taut. The classic tableau of Laocoön and his sons trapped in the python's coils seemed commonplace by comparison.

"What are we using this rope for, anyway?" I demanded suddenly. The elder statesman considered the question seriously.

"Because one of us might fall," he replied cautiously.

"That's what I'm afraid of," I confessed, "perhaps it would be safer without the rope?"

For a second he looked blank and then roared with laughter, translating "the joke" for the Pupil's benefit. "Most amusing," they agreed, "but with the rope we are safe." I sighed—there was no point in pursuing the argument.

Two hours later we had overcome the icy lower ramparts and entered a long snow gully—the Hall's Rinne—running up towards a notch on the skyline, close to the actual summit of the peak. I now found myself, quite inexplicably, in the middle of the procession. Two taut ropes disappearing into the mist exerted equal and opposite pulls, threatening to tear me apart. One came from the Pupil who had spurted ahead on reaching easier ground, the other led back to Arne, who had chosen the wrong route and wished to descend. There was only one solution, as all my shouts were answered by redoubled tugs from both ropes; I applied a firm tension to the Pupil's rope, and breathed again. Fortunately he was not on difficult ground.

Somewhere over to the left was the route by which the Romsdalshorn was first climbed in 1826. The pioneers were a local blacksmith and farmer, and the feat was the result of a wager made during "a merry drinking bout". They proved the authenticity of their ascent by leaving a large cairn on the top, and there it remained "to the wonder and amazement of beholders" till Hall's party made the second ascent in 1881—a sequel to at least a dozen unsuccessful attempts by noted mountaineers of the day.

Two hundred feet below the notch the gully narrowed to a vertical glazed chimney, which the Pupil overcame in fine style; Arne and I pulled ourselves up the fixed rope to save time. It was attached to one of his bolts, which had been cemented into position at strategic points on the tourist route and had, no doubt, averted several catastrophes. He had the right to safeguard his own mountain, he maintained stoutly, and I saw no reason to doubt his judgement.

At three in the afternoon we emerged on the summit, a lofty acre of wind-swept scree, cut off on every side by plunging precipices. It was our first halt since leaving the car. We dined in the summit hut, an excellent house capable of sheltering three dwarfs in comparative comfort. There was even a stove and chimney—no firewood was supplied, but this could be obtained by descending 3,000 feet to the valley. When I asked whose hands had wrought the miracle the oracle smiled broadly.

"Need you ask? But I am more proud of the garden."

He dug energetically in the snowfield for several minutes and, finally reassured, straightened up.

"Look there," he pointed triumphantly.

At the bottom of the hole was a tiny frozen blob.

"One of my Alpine rock plants," he announced, "soon it will bloom again."

I was more impressed by the fine array of summit cairns. There was only one to which he laid no claim; this was the original cairn of 1826. One commemorated his hundredth ascent of the Romsdalshorn, another the centenary of the Norske Tindeklub.

It seems the latter occasion was celebrated with all necessary respect. Arne had insisted on a climber of every nationality attending, so all the nearby hotels were combed for potential ambassadors. Thus it was that Adam Watson senior found himself representing Scotland at the dinner, and also on top of the Romsdalshorn; the ascent of the peak completing the night's festivities.

Before leaving the top we signed our names in the Visitors' Book, or rather Arne did, since it was his property, adding "First non-Norwegian winter ascent of the Romsdalshorn." "This must be a great moment for you," he said. I nodded weakly.

The descent was fast, frantic, and furious. I leapt from one *rappel* into the next, struggling to keep abreast of the field. Many of the abseils were superfluous, but Arne wished to test some of the more recently fixed bolts, to determine whether the cement had set properly.

Once off the mountain they allowed me half an hour's start on ski, arranging a rendezvous in the valley. One ski arrived punctually—the other ski and its owner some minutes later. By this time Arne had phoned for a vehicle to collect us, and an excellent meal awaited us in Aandalsnes on our return.

As I relaxed in the train *en route* for Dombås it occurred to me that my week-end's respite from ski-ing had turned into something of a busman's holiday. I opened my pristine copy of the "Romsdal" Guide, edited by a certain A. R. Heen. In it I read as follows: "The Romsdalshorn—undoubtedly the finest peak in Norway. Even by the tourist route it is an entertaining scramble, beset with amusing little problems."

"Amusing little problems. . . ." By comparison, the winter ascent is positively hilarious!

THE TROLLS WERE ANGRY

From The Climbers' Club Journal, 1966

(An attempted first winter ascent of the Trolltinder Wall—the highest mountain face in Norway, March 1960)

I FIRST SAW the Trolltinder Wall in March 1959. For a few minutes, I was scarcely able to believe my eyes. The legend propagated by the Norwegian Tourist Board of a "gigantic precipice perhaps the biggest in Europe" tucked away in remote Romsdal had seemed, on the face of it, rather unlikely. Nobody seemed to have heard of it.

Consequently the impact of that first encounter was shattering in the extreme. Here was a face approximately 5,000 feet in vertical height, six miles in length and containing only three lines of weakness, if such they might be called, which appeared to offer the slightest chance of success. Two of them had been climbed by the local guide, Arne Randers Heen: both were first ascents.

Arne it was, who told me the history of the wall. In 1933, when the Eigerwand and the North Face of the Grandes Jorasses were under almost constant siege, the unclimbed North Wall of the Trolltind was virtually unknown outside Norway. Yet in point of fact there was little to choose between these three great bastions, superficially at any event. All three sport 5,000 feet of live rock, most of it distinctly hostile.

N. E. Odell, of Everest fame, was a visitor about this time and the first to make a serious attempt. Opposite the old country house of Fiva in the Romsdal valley an ill-defined slanting rake cuts diagonally up the Wall towards a notch on the ridge below the summit of the Store Trolltind. It is a long tenuous line, almost devoid of ramification, but eminently practicable. Odell mentions his early attempt in a preface to Heen's account of the first ascent in the *Alpine Journal*, writing "I did not get much over a third of the way up, being troubled at the time with a strained leg."

Arne Randers Heen lives at Aandalsnes. From his home to the

foot of the Trolltinder Wall is not much more than an hour's walk and he had often examined the Wall for a hidden flaw, until eventually, like Odell, he settled on the Fiva Route as offering the best prospects.

His first ascent with his cousin Erik Heen had been the sensation of the season, and proved to be a landmark in the history of Norwegian mountaineering. It was not only the hardest recorded rock climb in Norway: it was also the first route in Norway to rival the big Alpine *nordwands*, for length and continuity. Inevitably its reputation for fierceness has declined with the advances in skill and technique, and although only five parties have repeated the climb, its neglect would not appear to be due to any intrinsic difficulty. The first British party to complete the route estimated it as no more than A.D. sup. on the Vallot Scale, or Mild Severe by British standards—although they recall "that an air of tension was prevalent throughout".

In 1958, thirteen years after his first success, Arne Randers Heen, now aged 54, accompanied by the expert young climber Per Hoybakk of Oslo made a second route on the wall. It was a remarkable feat for a man of his age for once again Heen's climb was significantly more difficult than anything previously attempted by Norwegian climbers. The Trolltinder Wall, as already mentioned, extends for six miles along the Romsdal valley. It culminates above in a fantastic array of weird pinnacles of all shapes and sizes, these being the petrified "trolls" or gnomes from which the mountain gets its name. The Fiva Route finished at the notch below the highest point, the Store Trolltind, at the seaward extremity of the ridge. One and a half miles along the ridge is another major peak, the culminating point of the greatest buttress in all Norway—the Trollryggen, the mighty centrepiece of the Trolltinder Wall. This was the line chosen by Heen for his second ascent. Unlike the nearby Fiva Route, there is here no obvious line of weakness. The first party took only fifteen hours, a remarkable *tour de force*, considering the difficult route-finding involved. In 1959 two German climbers, Gottman and Obst, were on the route for three days and used 150 pitons. Arne's triumph was further enhanced by the failure of his old rival Professor Arne

Naess of Oslo to repeat the feat. Arne likes to recall that when
the Professor was fighting for his life on the wall, a local Romsdal
cow, no doubt fired with patriotic zeal, consumed the professorial
tent and provisions. The story is perpetuated by a framed water-
colour in Arne's study, depicting the Trollryggen, the Professor,
the cow and the tent. The original tent, now restored, is also on
show. Arne is a tailor to trade, and he it was who sought out the
chewed up fragments of canvas and stitched them together with
painstaking accuracy. He reckons it was well worth the effort, if
only to witness his old adversary's discomfiture when confronted with the tent. It will be one of the principal exhibits in
Arne's climbing museum which he hopes one day to present to the
Norwegian Alpine Club.

As my only opportunity of visiting Norway occurred at Easter
(by courtesy of H.M. Forces), I was content to admire the Trollryggen from a distance. Even that first brief glimpse of the
Trolltinder Wall, was, however, enough to convince me that the
Fiva Route would one day, perhaps in the not too distant future,
yield to a winter assault.

So a dream was born. But another year passed before there was
any chance of realising that dream. In the meantime I discussed
my plans with Sam Bemrose and Vyvyan Stevenson, and the
grubby postcard I had bought in Aandalsnes was the basis of
much improbable theorising and premature jubilation. The photo
had been taken in early spring and showed the Fiva Route as a
straight snow gully, apparently without pitches, and well suited
to a long fast glissade. (It has since occurred to me that the North
Face of the Matterhorn, seen from certain angles, looks very
similar in winter. Nobody has yet glissaded it—voluntarily.)

In March 1960 the long-awaited opportunity arrived. The three
of us were again in Norway with a detachment of Marines,
learning the rudiments of ski warfare. All we needed was a
week-end of settled weather and a satisfactory alibi. We explained
to our host, the Norwegian Commandant, that we had selected
the Trolltinder face as offering suitable terrain for advanced
snow warfare training and intended to carry out a preliminary

reconnaissance. He was quite definitely taken aback at this, but apart from doubting our sanity, was not disposed to argue.

Five thousand and three hundred feet of snow climbing is a long way. We had already labelled it the longest snow climb in Europe, and as such decided that it ought to be accorded all due respect, even a formal reconnaissance. For this purpose I set off a day ahead of the others, equipped with field-glasses and a watch to time the frequency of falling stones. Sam and Steve remained behind to accumulate food and ironmongery.

In the Romsdal valley, spring was in the air. Birds sang in the trees, butterflies flitted through the meadows. Unlike the English pastoral scene there was not a courting couple in sight, hence no need to tread carefully. It was all very quiet and peaceful.

I spent most of the day soaking up the sunshine. It had been suggested I might make a short trip up the wall to bring back some first-hand information. In the circumstances I settled for a long-range reconnaissance.

Through the binoculars I was looking at a very different landscape: a sombre curtain of smooth grey granite interlaced with strands of glistening ice. Here and there a little snow clung tenaciously to tiny ledges, serving to alleviate, though only to a small degree, the almost Stygian gloom of the vast amphitheatre. Only on the Fiva Route was there any obvious continuity of snow, but the enormous scale of that route was only now coming into true perspective. That tiny isthmus must be a 200 foot ice pitch. Nor was there only one hiatus—I could count at least a dozen and perhaps there would be even more ice than was apparent from below. That insignificant snow-field half-way up the cliff was in reality a hanging glacier, more than a quarter of a mile wide. Above was the upper gully, 2,000 feet of it at a rough guess. There lay the crux of our enterprise. Four hundred feet below the skyline notch, the thin thread of snow terminated abruptly to reappear, after 200 feet. What lay in between? Nothing very hospitable—that was certain. It would be appalling to be thwarted so near the top and have to face a 5,000 foot descent. I thought of the White Spider on the Eiger and shivered involuntarily.

I might still have yielded to my better judgement if I had not paid my customary call on the "Trollmannen", as he has been called in the local press, the famous Arne Randers Heen. His first reaction to my plan was startled incredulity but it then transpired that he had mistaken our objective for the Trollryggen, so this was quite understandable. Regarding Fiva Route, he was by contrast, almost optimistic.

"What about the difficult bit near the top?" I queried. He smiled enigmatically, as if I had chanced upon a closely guarded secret.

"It looks difficult—yes, but it is not difficult at all. You will find a big hole in the rock, I remember it well."

I was impressed, so much so that I forgot to press him further on the exact location of the hole. This was indeed a pity, as events proved. The "big hole" became in effect a magic formula for success, and so completely captivated our imagination that we confidently expected to find a great tunnel cleaving its way miraculously through the bowels of the mountain, a sort of emergency exit when things got too mixed-up in the gully. How could we possibly fail?

Sam and Steve arrived in the evening, accompanied by our Norwegian ally Henry Berg. Henry lived within sight of the Trolltinder but although he had climbed as far afield as Tirich Mir in the Himalayas he had never set foot on the Wall and affirmed he had no wish to do so. He had dropped in merely to pay a social call. It was one o'clock in the morning when he left, by which time he had reached two important decisions; firstly that he had a natural taste for Scotch whisky—this we could corroborate—and secondly that he was duty bound to accompany us upon what was after all his native mountain. From our point of view it was an ideal arrangement as we would now be able to climb in two pairs, Sam and Henry on one rope, Steve and I on the other. We were optimistic enough to assume that the consequent saving in time would enable us to dispense with bivouac equipment, the argument being that if you plan and provide for a bivouac you seldom avoid one. It is a dangerous line of reasoning which we would have done better to reject.

We left Henry's car outside the deserted lodge at Fiva and set off through the birch woods. It was 7 a.m., late enough by any standards, and the first rays of the sun were already tipping the topmost spires of the Trolltinder. On the credit side it was a mere twenty-minute walk to the start of the climb and there was no Alpine *bergschrund* to delay us at the outset.

Steve and I led off, anxious not to waste time waiting for the other two who were still blundering through the forest. The first pitch was on rather holdless rock of hard very difficult standard. Then we traversed leftwards into a long snow runnel which courses down the lower slabs. These look exceedingly steep from the road and probably deterred the earlier Norwegian climbers from closer inspection which reveals the average angle to be not in excess of 50 degrees. The runnel was lined with good hard snow ideally suited to step kicking. If this was a foretaste of what was to follow we were in luck. After four or five rope-lengths we were held up by a vicious little ice pitch. It was water ice of an almost metallic consistency and although only forty feet in height exacted half an hour of our valuable time. I thought it was worth V.S. This took us out on to a large ledge at the top of the introductory slabs where we found a few stunted birch trees, a last link with the sylvan meadows we had left behind us.

Somewhere down below a piton was being driven in and from the direction of the noise we guessed the others had taken a different line up the slabs. We decided not to wait for them as we had previously agreed to climb independently in order to save time.

They overtook us some 500 feet higher as I was already finding it necessary to cut steps. I had acquired twelve-point crampons in Oslo but they had not been fitted with bindings and could only be lashed on with string, a most unsatisfactory arrangement. Consequently I had accepted Henry's offer of nailed boots and refrained from offering any criticism as I did not wish to hurt his feelings. The boots were in fact quite useless—too long in the toe, too narrow in the instep and minus most of the hob-nails on the sole. Hence I now had to cut steps on comparatively easy snow, thus holding up the rest of the party who were sensibly shod in crampons. I consoled myself that at least we would have a useful ladder of steps in the event of retreat.

We seemed to be making remarkably good progress. Only three hours had gone past and already we were more than a third of the way up the face. Behind us lay 2,000 feet of relatively easy, albeit exposed snow-fields, each one interlocking with the next with seemingly miraculous precision. Heen's guide book was less encouraging. It was a slim volume full of terse epigrammatic sentences which did little to inspire the weary climber with renewed confidence. Our progress to date was summed up in a single sentence: "Up across easy slabs and grassy slopes until reaching corner."

The sun had discovered us again and it was unbearably hot and stuffy. The brooding silence was almost uncanny: no clatter of falling stones or rumbling avalanche broke the stillness. The huge cauldron between our perch and the Trollryggen was still in shadow. It was indeed a fearsome place hemmed in by the grimmest of grim precipices. This part of the wall is reputed to be exactly vertical for all of 3,000 feet; the steepest wall of its size in Europe, Heen claimed. It was certainly too steep to carry any snow despite a recent heavy fall.

Not long afterwards we turned the prominent corner of the face and finding no obvious continuation to the diagonal rake we had been following we had recourse again to the guide book. "Up through the main gorge to a snowdrift half-way up the wall," it announced. Allowing for the free English translation of Heen's manuscript, the snowdrift was obviously the large hanging glacier which now could not be far above us. "Gorge" presumably referred to "gully" of which there were several, none of them very accommodating. Heen had suggested that we might experience difficulty getting on to the glacier if there was much ice on the rocks. We found them everywhere to be thickly plastered and as the next testing pitch was reputed to be severe in summer it became all the more important to hit off the right line the first time. The others had a flattering faith in my route-finding ability and as they offered no alternative suggestions I transferred to a higher snow terrace leading round towards a blind corner.

Much to my delight, in the shallow cave beyond the corner I found a beer bottle—admittedly empty but material proof that I had not lost the scent (referring of course to my route-finding ability).

Above the cave was one of the key pitches of the climb, a ninety-foot *dièdre* streaked with rivulets of clear ice. The right wall was overhanging, the left wall a smooth slab from which some frozen tufts of grass extruded offering a few toe scrapes to maintain balance. I progressed laboriously up the crack in the angle jamming my right arm behind the icicle colonnades. It must be a messy place in the summertime: now it was cleaner but the coeffcient of friction was correspondingly less.

From the top of the *dièdre* I had to climb a further thirty feet through deep floury snow to find a belay on the left-hand *arête*. On the far side of the *arête* was a considerable abyss, possibly the "gorge" mentioned in the guide book. It was too far for us to rope down into the bed of the gully, but we would have to cross it at some point if we were to get on to the hanging glacier. Fortunately the gully steepened a little way above before ending in an enclosed *cirque* below a cordon of overhangs. At this point we would be able to *rappel* down from the *arête* and subsequently continue from the other end of the snow *cirque* up one of the icy channels which issue from the lower rim of the glacier.

The short *rappel* landed us on a fine eyrie below the overhangs where we made our first and only halt of the day, munching some glucose tablets for much needed energy. One hundred and fifty feet of snow-ice at an angle of 65 degrees separated us from the glacier. The snow had partially split away from the wall on the right and by jamming up the cleft we were able to dispense with ice-axes. At one point the cleft widened to form an ice cave. It occurred to me in passing that it was an ideal spot for a bivouac.

The hanging glacier was wide and spacious though somewhat steeper than we had anticipated. As we moved from the warm sunlight into the shadow of the upper precipice so the atmosphere became at once more hostile and menacing. Mighty walls hemmed in the head of the glacier but over in the top left-hand corner was the narrow chasm which marked the start of the 2,000-foot upper gully. Our fortunes hung in the balance. It was two o'clock in the afternoon and we were only a little over half-way up the face. Everything depended on our finding sufficient hard snow in the floor of the gully to bank up a succession of chockstone pitches which had proved to be impassable in summertime. Heen's route went up the buttress on the left side of the gully: it was festooned with clear ice and did not even bear thinking of as an alternative.

A continuous stream of fine powder snow was pouring down the gully as we hammered the first belay piton into the side wall: there did not appear to be any genuine avalanche risk but we could not afford to take too much for granted in such a confined channel. The spindrift itself was indirectly to our advantage for it had helped consolidate the snow by carving out a central trough. The sun never penetrates into this gully so the absence of a surface crust was not unexpected. The slope varied in steepness from 50 to 65 degrees in places and we had often to pull up on the shafts of our axes as the snow was insufficiently hard packed for cutting handholds. Occasionally we sank in above the knees. All the time the gully twisted leftwards, effectively limiting our horizon to the top of the next pitch ahead.

At 4 p.m. we passed what Hollywood scriptwriters call "the point of no return". Now we had to win through or spend the night on the face, a harrowing prospect without any bivouac gear.

Progress was slow and the fast pace we had set earlier on was beginning to tell: in fact we had been kicking or cutting steps for nine hours with only a single ten-minute break for lunch. A thinly covered bulging chockstone held us up for another half-hour and then the gully, hitherto tightly confined, began to open out towards the left. Surely nothing could stop us now, only 600 feet from victory?

"What does it look like up there?" Steve shouted impatiently. He had been asking the same question for at least an hour. This time I was at last in a position to give him an answer.

"Ghastly, I'm afraid. Come up and see for yourself." I sensed the profound gloom that my reply produced; even Henry, who could only converse in sign language, was shaking his head mournfully with a woebegone expression which betokened impending disaster.

The four of us were strung out on a large 65-degree angled snow-field to the left of the true gully which had just lost itself in a giant frieze of icicles. Below our feet the snow-field plunged down dramatically towards the top of Heen's buttress allowing us an uninterrupted view of the Romsdal valley. Overhead a lofty spur of granite reared its ugly head, sealing off the only path to salvation as securely as a cork jammed in the neck of a champagne bottle. Beyond the spur we assumed must lie the col. Only 600 feet of hard climbing remained, but measured in hours of daylight that left us in an unenviable position.

What about "the big hole", our promised passport to safety? The problem was where to look for it. We had first to decide whether to go left or right of the spur as there was not enough time remaining to try both sides. We certainly did not intend to split the party: at the moment we could not muster one proper belay between the four of us but there was at least some psychological strength in numbers.

The rest of us voted for the right-hand traverse but Henry pointed confidently up to the left. Now Henry spoke very little English but such was his apparent familiarity with the route we had been following that we had formed the impression (mistakenly) that he had already been up here in the summertime. So without more ado we headed up towards a fearsome looking chimney on the left of the spur.

A twenty-foot rock step with no appreciable holds and protected only by a doubtful axe belay was a bad omen. One slip here would have meant a complete write-off: it seemed as if we were beginning to climb with more desperation than hope.

Two further run-outs of eighty feet saw me up to the base of the chimney where I realised with sickening certainty that we had reached the end of the line. Far from chancing upon a hidden subterranean passage-way I could not even find a reasonable belay stance. The chimney above was overhanging for one hundred feet and any cracks which might have taken pitons were obscured by ice. A tight spot, as the saying goes.

It was 6 p.m. If we chose to continue we were only 300 feet from a comfortable bivouac. On the other hand we had only two and a half hours of daylight in which to work out our salvation. I retraced my steps cautiously and rejoined the others. Sam and Steve supported my plea that the only sane course open to us now was to retreat to the nearest bivouac site rather than risk spending the night out without bivouac gear, the four of us strung out along the face without any appreciable security or proper liaison. Henry wanted to push on regardless and emphasised this by producing a thick cluster of pitons from his rucksack. He was overruled though not without dissension.

Speed was once more all important. Already our wet clothes were starting to freeze and what it would be like when the sun went down God alone knew. At all costs we would have to find somewhere a snow cave large enough to hold the four of us.

Negotiating the pitch we had just ascended was a tricky problem. As there was nothing to anchor a doubled rope we left my spare ice-axe behind as an emergency stanchion. Even so we could only use the rope to steady our descent as the axe was buried in dangerously loose snow. On the exposed ice-field below we moved as a party of four, Henry holding the responsible position in the rear: once in the gully we split into two pairs and moved together.

The shadows lengthened. It was a beautiful evening and the crimson glow tipping the Romsdalshorn would no doubt have lent inspiration to Rebuffat's pen. We took a more material view of the situation. In another half-hour the light would start to fail and to further complicate the situation there was not going to be a moon. Down in the valley the evening train from Aandalsnes, all lit up, rattled merrily through the birch woods finally disappearing into a tunnel with a long mournful whine.

After our skirmish with the ice slope, the gully was relatively easy going. The ladder of steps we had made earlier on was invaluable and we lost height rapidly. Ice caves were, however, conspicuously absent.

At 9 p.m. I reached the top of the chockstone pitch half-way down the gully and began to look for a piton crack. Eventually I found one that satisfied me and slid down the pitch on my stomach, double rope in one hand, ice-axe held ready in the other just in case the piton came out: undue pessimism perhaps but in this case it was a worthwhile precaution.

"O.K. Steve, I'm down—the piton's quite safe."

A pregnant silence, then a volley of oaths, "Safe by . . . the blasted thing has come out in my hand". It seemed rather amusing at the time, why I don't know.

"Put it back and stop shouting," I said consolingly. The others could see no humour in the situation and produced torches to search for another suitable crack. It was well after dark when they finally succeeded.

What now? Keep moving it would seem: we still had a ladder of steps to guide us and even if we could not see them very distinctly we had only to tread carefully. Sam was cheerfully confident.

"The light is quite adequate, I don't know why you're all complaining."

I thought he must have eyes like a bat, no doubt because he's normally more active during the night than he is during the day. At the next stance I fell into a confused reverie concerning cats on the tiles, night fighter pilots and the beneficial effects of vitamin A. I woke up with my full weight on the belay rope. This would never do, better to carry on chain-smoking. At least that would make it less easy to drop off . . . (What am I saying!?)

In the confined part of the gully there was no light at all and the steps were partly filled in. "Blow this," I thought, "It's time to dig in." My snow hole turned out to be pretty futile, affording about as much protection as the ostrich gets when it pokes its head into the sand.

Sam arrived with a rush. I had forgotten to warn him about the hole and he had been alarmed to suddenly find himself treading space. "What the hell did you dig in here for, anyway?"

I felt immediately ashamed of my defeatist attitude. "Just trying to keep warm," I muttered.

The gully opened at last on to the hanging glacier and the tension eased in consequence. It was much lighter in the open and we had little difficulty in avoiding the *séracs*. Nor was it quite so important now to find a bivouac-site inasmuch that the later we climbed the easier would be our task in the morning and the shorter our vigil with the stars.

Sometime after midnight, however, I stumbled on the same ice grotto I had noticed on the way up. To the four of us in our exhausted state it was a ready-made haven of rest. The snow tongue of the glacier had split away from its containing rock wall to form a natural chamber entered from above through a narrow aperture. It was draught-free and up against one wall was a bank of snow in which seats could be cut. What more could you ask for? Steve supplied the answer—"food, drink and dry clothes". We had enough spare gloves and socks to go round, but that was the extent of our reserve clothing. I thought of an Aberdonian friend whose oft-repeated remark on a climb "I'd like fine to have a woman up here", was his only concession to formal conversation. He would have found much to say. It was cold enough to freeze the proverbial brass monkey.

A feeble attempt to raise our morale in the Munich tradition by singing patriotic songs died an early death. Soon only the monotonous pizzicato of chattering teeth broke the icy silence.

Once during the night someone heard a faint cry in the outer darkness, but was accused of over-dramatising the situation. Little did we know but at that moment our faithful henchman Rod Tuck was searching for corpses at the foot of the wall. His first reaction on finding our headquarters deserted had been to locate the whisky bottle. As the night wore on his finer instincts prevailed and he was filled with remorse. The three empty sleeping bags became in his disordered imagination three long white shrouds, mute witnesses to his treachery. He rose unsteadily to his feet and armed only with a torch and a tin of Elastoplast set out upon his mission of mercy.

At 6 a.m. a grey dawn ushered in another day, and Tuck gave up the search to return to bed. Meanwhile in a small ice cave 2,000 feet up the face the vital spark was not yet extinguished. Encased in their icy armour, the Four Men of Fiva Route were engaged in heated argument. Sam complained that I had fidgeted all night. I maintained that he had pushed me off the rucksack on to the ice. Steve complained that our mutual grievances had lost him his night's sleep. Henry just complained. Nobody understood what he was trying to say, so nobody particularly cared. Three days later when his toes turned black it was our turn to apologise.

His frostbite was fortunately not serious—merely a nine-days' wonder which excited some admiration and which was the only tangible souvenir of our night on the mountain. We had escaped lightly, because the night temperatures in Norway during March are much lower than one normally meets in an average Alpine season. We would undoubtedly have fared worse in less sheltered surroundings.

The rest of the descent passed off uneventfully. On three occasions the spare rope had to be rigged for an *abseil* and it was not until noon that we were able to uprope at the foot of the face. Twenty-nine hours had passed since we left the valley and this total included twenty-two hours of actual climbing. It was good to be back.

An old man, probably the caretaker of the lodge, awaited our return. He greeted us with thinly concealed amusement.

"You have made a mistake I think. On the other side the mountain is less steep and you can drive your car half-way to the top."

We sighed wearily and explained that far from wishing to climb the Trolltind our sole remaining ambition was to climb into bed. When he heard how we had spent the night he shook his head knowingly.

"I think perhaps Mr. Troll is angry with you. It is very bad when Mr. Troll is angry. I am happy you are still alive."

We agreed wholeheartedly. Mr. Troll when roused could be a thoroughly nasty customer.

A fortnight later, Steve and Henry Berg took the old man's advice and climbed Store Trolltind by the easy route from Stegfoss. In thick mist they located the notch in the ridge where the Fiva Route ends and with extreme caution descended a few rope lengths towards the Romsdal valley. Their intention was to descend, roping down if necessary, to the highest point we had reached and then climb back up to the ridge. In this roundabout way they hoped to complete—to their own if no one else's satisfaction—the first winter ascent of Fiva Route. There was of course the obvious hazard that if they made an error of judgement and overstepped the mark they would be faced with another 5,000 feet descent. Our recent escapade had made headlines in the local press and earned for us some ephemeral notoriety: a Repeat Performance would certainly have brought the house down.

Bearing this in mind they chose to abandon the attempt when only 100 feet short of their objective. They did not encounter any great difficulty in the top 300 feet, but said that the crucial chimney which had defeated us looked frankly impossible from above. If we had taken the right-hand traverse then we might have succeeded although the climb would still have been very borderline.

A few feet below the notch they found Arne's "big hole". It proved to be just an ordinary hole behind a chockstone. With a little effort you could crawl through the hole and emerge on top of the chockstone, although it was probably easier to scramble round the side. So much for speculation!

The Trolls looked on in stony contempt. This time they had fooled us. Maybe next time it would be our turn. . . .

A SHORT WALK WITH WHILLANS

1963

"DID YOU SPOT that great long streak of blood on the road over from Chamonix? Twenty yards long, I'd say."

The speaker was Don Whillans. We were seated in the little inn at Alpiglen and Don's aggressive profile was framed against an awe-inspiring backdrop of the Eiger-Norwand. I reflected that the conversation had become attuned to the environment.

"Probably some unfortunate animal," I ventured without much conviction.

Whillans' eyes narrowed. "Human blood," he said. "Remember—lass?" (appealing to his wife Audrey), "I told you to stop the car for a better look. Really turned her stomach, it did. Just when she was getting over the funeral."

I felt an urge to inquire whose funeral they had attended. There had been several. Every time we went up on the Montenvers train we passed a corpse going down. I let the question go. It seemed irrelevant, possibly even irreverent.

"Ay, it's a good life," he mused, "providing you don't weaken."

"What happens if you do?"

"They bury you," he growled, and finished his pint.

Don has that rarest of gifts, the ability to condense a whole paragraph into a single, terse, uncompromising sentence. But there are also occasions when he can become almost lyrical in a macabre sort of way. It depends on the environment.

We occupied a window table in the inn. There were several other tables, and hunched round each of these were groups of shadowy men draped in black cagoules—lean-jawed, grim, uncommunicative characters who spoke in guttural monosyllables and gazed steadfastly towards the window. You only had to glimpse their earnest faces to realise that these men were Eiger Candidates—martyrs for the "Mordwand".*

* Eiger pseudonym coined by German Press—literally "Murder Wall".

"Look at that big black bastard up there," Whillans chuckled dryly, gesturing with his thumb. "Just waiting to get its claws into you. And think of all the young lads who've sat just where you're sitting now, and come back all tied up in sacks. It makes you think."

It certainly did. I was beginning to wish I had stayed at Chamonix, funerals or no funerals.

"Take that young blonde over there," he pointed towards the sturdy Aryan barmaid, who had just replenished his glass. "I wonder how many dead men she's danced with? All the same," he concluded after a minute's reflection, "t'wouldn't be a bad way to spend your last night."

I licked my lips nervously. Don's philosophic discourses are not for the faint hearted.

One of the Eiger Candidates detached himself from a neighbouring group and approached us with obvious intent. He was red haired, small and compact and he looked like a Neanderthal man. This likeness derived from his hunched shoulders, and the way he craned his head forwards like a man who had been struck repeatedly on the crown by a heavy hammer, and through time developed a protective over-growth of skull. His name proved to be Eckhart, and he was a German. Most of them still are.

The odd thing about him was his laugh. It had an uncanny hollow quality. He laughed quite a lot without generating a great deal of warmth, and he wore a twisted grin which seemed to be permanently frozen onto his face. Even Whillans was moved.

"You—going—up?" he inquired.

"Nein," said Eckhart. "Nix gutt! . . . You wait here little time, I think. . . . Now there is much vatter." He turned up his coat collar ruefully and laughed. "Many, many stein fall. . . . All day, all night. . . . Stein, stein." He tapped his head significantly and laughed uproariously. "Two nights we wait at *Tod Bivouac*." He repeated the name as if relishing its sinister undertones. ("It means Dead Man," I said to Whillans in a hushed whisper.) "Always it is nix gutt. . . . Vatter, stein. . . . Stein, vatter . . . so we go down. It is very funny."

We nodded sympathetically. It was all a huge joke.

"Our two Kameraden, they go on. They are saying at the telescopes, one man he has fallen fifty metres. Me? I do not believe this." (Loud and prolonged laughter from the company.)

"You have looked through the telescope?" I inquired anxiously.

"Nein," he grinned, "Not necessary . . . tonight they gain summit . . . tomorrow they descend. And now we will have another beer."

Eckhart was nineteen. He had already accounted for the North Face of the Matterhorn as a training climb and he intended to camp at the foot of the Eigerwand until the right conditions prevailed. If necessary, he could wait until October. Like most of his countrymen he was nothing if not thorough, and finding his bivouac-tent did not measure up to his expectations he had hitchhiked all the way back to Munich to secure another one. As a result of this, he had missed the settled spell of weather that had allowed several rivals to complete the route, including the second successful British team, Baillie and Haston, and also the lone Swiss climber, Darbellay, who had thus made the first solo ascent.

"Made of the right stuff, that youngster," observed Don.

"If you ask me I think he was trying to scare us off," I suggested. "Psychological warfare that's all it is."

"Wait till we get on the face tomorrow," said Whillans. "We'll hear your piece then."

Shortly after noon the next day we left Audrey behind at Alpiglen, and the two of us set off up the green meadows which girdle the foot of the Eigerwand. Before leaving, Don had disposed of his Last Will and Testament. "You've got the car-key, lass, and you know where to find the house-key. That's all you need to know. Ta, for now."

Audrey smiled wanly. She had my profound sympathy.

The heat was oppressive, the atmosphere heavy with menace. How many Munich Bergsteigers had trod this very turf on their upward path never to return to their native Klettergarten? I was humming Wagner's *Valkyrie* theme music as we reached the lowest rocks of the Face.

Then a most unexpected thing happened. From an alcove in the wall emerged a very ordinary Swiss tourist, followed by his very ordinary wife, five small children and a poodle dog. I stopped humming immediately. I had read of tearful farewells with wives and sweethearts calling plaintively, but this was ridiculous. What an undignified send-off! The five children accompanied us up the first snow slope scrambling happily in our wake, and prodding our rucksacks with inquisitive fingers. "Go away," said Whillans irritably, but ineffectively. We were quite relieved when, ultimately, they were recalled to base and we stopped playing Pied Pipers. The dog held on a bit longer until some well directed stones sent it on its way. "Charming, I must say," remarked Don. I wondered whether Hermann Buhl would have given up on the spot—a most irregular start to an Eiger Epic and probably a bad omen.

We started climbing up the left side of the shattered pillar, a variant of the normal route which had been perfected by Don in the course of several earlier attempts. He was well on his way to becoming the Grand Old Man of Grindelwald, though not through any fault of his own. This was his fourth attempt at the climb and on every previous occasion he had been turned back by bad weather or by having to rescue his rivals. As a result of this he must have spent more hours on the Face than any other British climber.

Don's preparations for the Eiger—meticulous in every other respect—had not included unnecessary physical exertion. While I dragged my weary muscles from Breuil to Zermatt via the Matterhorn he whiled away the days at Chamonix sun bathing at the Plage until opening time. At the Bar Nationale he nightly sank five or six pints of "heavy", smoked forty cigarettes, persuaded other layabouts to feed the juke box with their last few francs and amassed a considerable reputation as an exponent of "Baby Foot", the table football game which is the national sport of France. One day the heat had been sufficiently intense to cause a rush of blood to the head because he had walked four miles up to the Montenvers following the railway track, and had acquired such enormous blisters that he had to make the return journey by train. He was nevertheless just as fit as he wanted to be, or indeed needed to be.

First impressions of the Eigerwand belied its evil reputation. This was good climbing rock with excellent friction and lots of small incuts. We climbed unroped, making height rapidly. In fact I was just starting to enjoy myself, when I found the boot. . . .

"Somebody's left a boot here," I shouted to Don.

He pricked up his ears. "Look and see if there's a foot in it," he said.

I had picked it up: I put it down again hurriedly.

"Ha! Here's something else—a torn rucksack," he hissed. "And here's his waterbottle—squashed flat."

I had lost my new-found enthusiasm and decided to ignore future foreign bodies. (I even ignored the pun.)

"You might as well start getting used to them now," advised Whillans. "This is where they usually glance off, before they hit the bottom."

He's a cheery character I thought to myself. To Don, a spade is just a spade—a simple trenching tool used by gravediggers.

At the top of the Pillar we donned our safety helmets. "One thing to remember on the Eiger," said Don, "never look up, or you may need a plastic surgeon."

His advice seemed superfluous that evening, as we did not hear a single ricochet. We climbed on up, past the Second Pillar and roped up for the traverse across to the Difficult Crack. At this late hour the Crack was streaming with water so we decided to bivouac while we were still dry. There was an excellent bivouac cave near the foot of the crack.

"I'll have one of your cigarettes," said Don. "I've only brought Gauloises." This was a statement of fact, not a question. There is something about Don's proverbial bluntness that arouses one's admiration. Of such stuff are generals made. We had a short discussion about bivouacking, but eventually I had to agree with his arguments and occupy the outer berth. It would be less likely to induce claustrophobia, or so I gathered.

I was even more aware of the sudden fall in temperature. My ultra-warm Terray *duvet* failed by a single critical inch to meet the convertible bivvy-rucksack which I had borrowed from Joe Brown. It had been designed, so the manufacturers announced, to Joe's personal specifications, and as far as I could judge, to his personal dimensions as well.

Insidiously and from nowhere it seemed, a mighty thunderstorm built up in the valley less than a mile away. Flashes of lightning lit up the whole Face and grey tentacles of mist crept out of the dusk threatening to envelop our lofty eyrie.

"The girl in the Tourist Office said that a ridge of high pressure occupying the whole of central Europe would last for at least another three days."

"Charming," growled Whillans. "I could give you a better forecast without raising my head."

"We should be singing Bavarian drinking songs to keep our spirits up," I suggested. "How about some Austrian yodelling."

"They're too fond of dipping in glacier streams . . . that's what does it," he muttered sleepily.

"Does what"?

"Makes them yodel. All the same, these bloody Austrians."

The day dawned clear. For once it seemed that a miracle had happened and a major thunderstorm had cleared the Eiger, without lodging on the Face. Don remained inscrutable and cautious as ever. Although we were sheltered from any prevailing wind we would have no advance warning of the weather, as our horizons were limited by the Face itself.

There was still a trickle of water coming down the Difficult Crack as Don launched himself stiffly at the first obstacle. Because of our uncertainty about the weather and an argument about who should make breakfast, we had started late. It was 6.30 a.m. and we would have to hurry. He made a bad start by clipping both strands of the double rope to each of the three pitons he found in position. The rope jammed continuously and this was even more disconcerting for me, when I followed carrying both rucksacks. Hanging down the middle of the pitch was an old frayed rope, said to have been abandoned by Mlle Loulou Boulaz, and this kept getting entangled with the ice-axes. By the time I had joined Don at this stance I was breathing heavily and more than usually irritated. We used the excuse to unrope and get back into normal rhythm before tackling the Hinterstoisser. It was easy to find the route hereabouts: you merely followed the pitons. They were planted everywhere with rotting rope loops (apparently used for *abseils*) attached to most of them. It is a significant insight into human psychology that nobody ever stops to remove superfluous pegs on the Eiger. If nothing else they help to alleviate the sense of utter isolation that fills this vast Face, but they also act as constant reminders of man's ultimate destiny and the pageant of history written into the rock. Other reminders were there in plenty—gloves, socks, ropes, crampons and boots. None of them appeared to have been abandoned with the owners' consent.

The Hinterstoisser Traverse, despite the illustrations of pre-war heroes traversing "a la Dulfer", is nothing to get excited about. With two fixed ropes of unknown vintage as an emergency handrail, you can walk across it in three minutes. Stripped of scaffolding, it would probably qualify as Severe by contemporary British standards. The fixed ropes continued without a break as far as the Swallow's Nest—another bivouac site hallowed by tradition. Thus far I could well have been climbing the Italian Ridge of the Matterhorn.

We skirted the first ice-field on the right, scrambling up easy rubble where we had expected to find black ice. It was certainly abnormally warm, but if the weather held we had definite grounds for assuming that we could complete the climb in one day—our original intention. The Ice Hose which breaches the rocky barrier between the First and Second Ice-fields no longer merited the name because the ice had all gone. It seemed to offer an easy alley but Don preferred to stick to known alternatives and advanced upon an improbable looking wall some distance across to the left. By the time I had confirmed our position on Hiebeler's route description, he had completed the pitch and was shouting for me to come on. He was well into his stride, but still did not seem to share my optimism.

His doubts were well founded. Ten minutes later, we were crossing the waterworn slabs leading on to the Second Ice-field when we saw the first falling stones. To be exact we did not see the stones, but merely the puff of smoke each one left behind at the point of impact. They did not come bouncing down the cliff with a noisy clatter as stones usually do. In fact they were only audible after they had gone past—WROUFF!—a nasty sort of sound half-way between a suck and a blow.

"It's the small ones that make that sort of noise," explained Whillans, "Wait till you hear the really big ones!"

The blue print for a successful Eiger ascent seems to involve being at the right place at the right time. According to our calculations the Face should have been immune to stonefall at this hour of the morning.

Unfortunately the Eiger makes its own rules. An enormous black cloud had taken shape out of what ought to have been a clear blue sky, and had come to rest on the summit ice-field. It reminded me of a gigantic black vulture spreading its wings before dropping like lightning on unsuspecting prey.

Down there at the foot of the Second Ice-field, it was suddenly very cold and lonely. Away across to the left was the Ramp; a possible hideaway to sit out the storm. It seemed little more than a stone's throw, but I knew as well as Don did, that we had almost 1,500 feet of steep snow-ice to cross before we could get any sort of shelter from stones.

There was no question of finding adequate cover in the immediate vicinity. On either side of us steep ice slopes, peppered with fallen debris, dropped away into the void. Simultaneously with Whillans' arrival at the stance the first flash of lightning struck the White Spider.

"That settles it," said he, clipping the spare rope through my belay karabiner.

"What's going on?" I demanded, finding it hard to credit that such a crucial decision could be reached on the spur of the moment.

"I'm going down," he said, "That's what's going on."

"Wait a minute! Let's discuss the whole situation calmly."
I stretched out one hand to flick the ash off my cigarette. Then a
most unusual thing happened. There was a higher pitched
"WROUFF" than usual and the end of my cigarette disappeared!
It was the sort of subtle touch that Hollywood film directors dream
about.

"I see what you mean," I said. "I'm going down too."

I cannot recall coming off a climb so quickly. As a result of a
long acquaintance Don knew the location of every *abseil* point
and this enabled us to bypass the complete section of the climb
which includes the Hinterstoisser Traverse and the Chimney
leading up to the Swallow's Nest. To do this, you merely
rappel directly downwards from the last abseil point above the
Swallow's Nest and so reach a key piton at the top of the wall
overlooking the start of the Hinterstoisser Traverse. From here a
straightforward *rappel* of 140 feet goes vertically down the wall
to the large ledge at the start of the Traverse. If Hinterstoisser
had realised that he would probably not now have a Traverse
named after him, and the Eigerwand would not enjoy one half
its present notoriety. The idea of "a Point of No Return" always
captures the imagination, and until very recent times, it was still
the fashion to abandon a fixed rope at the Hinterstoisser in order to
safeguard a possible retreat.

The unrelenting bombardment, which had kept us hopping
from one *abseil* to the next like demented fleas, began to slacken
off as we came into the lee of the "Rote Fluh". The weather had
obviously broken down completely and it was raining heavily.
We followed separate ways down the easy lower section of the
Face, sending down volleys of loose scree in front of us. Every
now and again we heard strange noises, like a series of muffled
yelps, but since we appeared to have the mountain to ourselves,
this did not provoke comment. Whillans had just disappeared
round a nearby corner when I heard a loud ejaculation.

"God Almighty," he said (or words to that effect) "Japs!
Come and see for yourself!"

Sure enough, there they were. Two identical little men in

identical climbing uniforms, sitting side by side underneath an overhang. They had been crouching there for an hour, waiting for the bombardment to slacken. I estimated that we must have scored several near misses.

"You—Japs?" grunted Don. It seemed an unnecessary question.

"Yes, yes," they grinned happily, displaying a full set of teeth. "We are Japanese."

"Going—up," queried Whillans. He pointed meaningfully at the grey holocaust sweeping down from the White Spider.

"Yes, yes," they chorused in unison. "Up. Always upwards. First Japanese Ascent."

"You-may-be-going-up-Mate," said Whillans, giving every syllable unnecessary emphasis, "but-a-lot-'igher-than-you-think!"

They did not know what to make of this, so they wrung his hand several times, and thanked him profusely for the advice.

"'Appy little pair!" said Don. "I don't imagine we'll ever see them again."

He was mistaken. They came back seven days later after several feet of new snow had fallen. They had survived a full-scale Eiger blizzard and had reached our highest point on the Second Ice-field, If they did not receive a medal for valour they had certainly earned one. They were the forerunners of the climbing élite of Japan, whose members now climb Mount Everest for the purpose of ski-ing back down again.

We got back to the Alpiglen in time for late lunch. The telescope stood forlorn and deserted in the rain. The Eiger had retired into its misty oblivion, as Don Whillans retired to his favourite corner seat by the window.

PART III
Satire

THE GREATEST SHOW ON EARTH*

From The Climbers' Club Journal, 1966

> We do not court publicity, but we know how to use it.
> AMERICAN PROVERB

THERE WAS A time when I used to deprecate the activities of our professional brethren. When their familiar faces scowled at me, I switched off the television set. When they invaded the Daily Press columns with their frank, forthright and financially remunerative views, I wrote angry letters to the Editor of the *Alpine Journal* (later forgetting to post them). When they subscribed their names to a new article of climbing equipment, I tested it to destruction, and returned it to the manufacturers.

Ever since its Immaculate Conception in 18??, the Alpine Club had politely but firmly refused membership to applicants bearing the taint of professionalism. Smythe was O.K.—he wrote philosophic books and published photographs but this was merely a lucrative sideline. Then came Bonington and Crew and they had to think again. It was obvious that as Committee members their deviationary activities would come under scrutiny and prove to be a source of acute embarrassment.

Thus it was that we suddenly heard the shattering Renunciation of Amateurism, or "Shamateurism" as we now prefer to call it. The measures adopted were swift and ruthless. Henceforth professional climbers would be treated as our brother-members.

*C.C.J. Editor's Note

(1) The events referred to in this Article took place on the Red Wall of the South Stack—a 400-foot high sea cliff near Holyhead, Anglesey. They occurred during the preparation and filming of the "Cliff Hangers", a programme that was televised "live" on B.B.C. TV on Easter Saturday 1966.

(2) The following climbers appeared by kind permission of B.B.C. Outside Broadcasts: Joe Brown, Ian McNaught-Davis, Royal Robbins, Tom Patey, John Cleare, Rusty Baillie, Dennis Gray, Roy Smith, Eric Beard and John Amatt.

Even Gaston Rebuffat. A few piping voices raised their quavering chorus of dissent, but were instantly silenced. Club members might take female pupils for climbing instruction and be paid in cash instead of in kind. They might appear on the Telly under their own names instead of being introduced as "A member of the British Alpine Club who wishes to remain anonymous". An era of Bonington Cagoules and Crew Duvets was in sight. Some said the club had prescribed for itself "a transfusion of new blood, which would enrich, sustain, and inspire." Others said that the Club funds must have been in a poor way. Everyone was optimistic.

Tradition, however, dies hard. To set the issue on a sporting basis—you might favour occasional exchanges between leading amateur or professional tennis players, yet deplore the invasion of Wimbledon's sacred turf by the Jack Kramer professional circus.

This last example is not without its mountaineering parallel. We now have our own Travelling Circus of highly paid performers. Their names are household words—Brown, Bonington, McNaught-Davis, Crew, Ingle, Cleare. Any schoolboy can regurgitate the catalogue of credits—the Kilnsey Overhang, the Eiffel Tower, the Cheddar Gorge, the Centenary Matterhorn climb—and now the *dreaded Red Wall of the South Stack*. . . .

It is extraordinary how money talks—especially if one keeps an open mind about these matters. "If I am ever involved in one of those extravaganzas," I once proudly proclaimed, "I will donate my entire share of the proceeds to charity, or the MacInnes Alsatian Dog Fund—assuming that I agree to participate," I added hurriedly. Little did I expect that one day I would be forced to swallow my words.

It all began with a letter from John Cleare. (Incidentally—if you should cherish any secret hopes of breaking into the Big Time, waste no time on Brown or Crew. These men are underlings. The Supremo who pulls the strings is John Cleare—the silent man with the Midas touch.) He wrote with his usual air of authority: "The climb will 'go over live' on Easter Saturday, thus reaching the largest possible audience. It will prove to be an enormous success and will undoubtedly set new standards of visual entertainment. Nothing can now interfere with agreed plans, apart from a General Election—which would be tedious but could only result in a temporary postponement. I am counting on you to lead the second rope. Rusty and I will be climbing alongside you with TV cameras and the actual climbing party will consist of four members—Chris Bonington, Mac Davis, yourself and—a bird. The bird will be selected not only on her ability to lead V.S. but also her ability to look well in a bikini—which she will be required to wear. I have taken upon myself the responsibility of selecting a suitable candidate and have already pruned my list of possibles down to four."

"Why this bird of yours?" I asked him on the phone. He coughed discreetly. "Sex," he replied, "is all important. The average viewer must identify himself with the climbers. We find that this helps."

"She'll be pretty blue if it snows," I suggested.

"I have no doubt that she will be very cold indeed," replied Cleare with some indifference. "This, however, will be her problem and not mine."

It so happened neither Bonington nor the elusive "bird" were included in the production cast. Bonington was still resting in hospital while the "bird" was unexpectedly discarded to make way for the well known American climber—Royal Robbins. Royal was a legendary figure in his own country, but would be making his maiden appearance on B.B.C. TV. His participation would also strengthen the likelihood of a replay on the American TV network. Cleare is usually one step ahead of his rivals in these matters. "This is Big Business, man," he says, steely eyes glinting through horn-rimmed spectacles. "To act big, you must think big."

John had named the Red Wall of the South Stack as the location of the forthcoming epic. I should explain that the Red Wall is on the Anglesey sea cliffs, near Holyhead and about a quarter of a mile south of the South Stack Lighthouse. It was a name that had been coined by John himself. No previous pioneer had ventured upon it and there were several good reasons for this. It was vertical, accessible only by boat, and apparently composed of repulsively loose rock—(an impression which was later confirmed). On either side were fine unclimbed cliffs of impeccable granite which were more attractive propositions in every respect save one—they did not measure up to B.B.C. Outside Broadcast specifications. The first problem in telly-mountaineering is not how to lead Mahomet to the mountain but how to bring the mountain to Mahomet. This is often quite perplexing.

I was curious to see the area in which I would perform, before I signed the written contract. In fact I even drove down to Anglesey one week-end for an unofficial reconnaissance. It was a vile day and the gigantic breakers from the Irish Sea were surging half-way up the 400-foot wall, drenching the cliff top with spray. I came away with vivid impressions of dripping disintegrating granite set at a thought-provoking angle. As soon as I got home I phoned John and I suggested that he might offer my part to some more deserving candidate. He was at first astounded, then disarmingly reassuring. "I understand what has happened," he said soothingly, "you have been to the wrong cliff. In the circumstances you have every right to be gripped. I would have been too." Much later on I discovered I had been to the right cliff after all, but by that time I was inextricably committed. . . .

It was T-Day minus six, when I next returned to South Stack. I had been unable to fit in any practice climbing on my local crags and a brief work-out with Hiebeler Prussikers had resulted in a fall of twelve feet—the distance between the landing and the hall floor. I landed on the crown of my head, so earning the admiration of my small son and his friends who had gathered to watch the event. This incident confirmed my distrust of these new-fangled gadgets, which I had disliked on sight. It was also a bad omen.

There was a lot of activity at the cliff top. A group of B.B.C. mechanics and workmen were erecting scaffolding on the very edge of the precipice, at what was judged to be a good vantage point for photography. They did not seem very happy in their work, pausing frequently to cast fearful glances over their shoulders.

"Better you than me, mate!" they shouted, as I passed.

The climbing team had set up their quarters in a huge mess tent near the top of the climb. We had each been allotted a generous living-out allowance which would have covered board and lodging at the Dorchester, but for reasons other than thrift we elected to live on the site. During the next few days a lot of rope and attractive ironmongery would be on 24-hour display and there are a few among the climbing fraternity whose distaste for commercialisation might activate a demonstration of protest.

The red-bearded figure of Rusty Baillie dominated the near foreground. He was festooned in multi-coloured rope, *étriers* and slings that radiated around him in a complicated network, the interstices secured with Tom Frost Knots. Could this be the mysterious Tiger's Web of which we had heard so much? With the notable exception of Rusty, few climbers are able to recognise a Tiger's Web when they see one, and fewer still understand what to do with it, once found. This is why so many climbers are buying Tiger's Webs.

As well as the publicised principals, several other shadowy figures hovered in the wings, each with a dual role as understudy and prop-man. Dennis Gray—the Yorkshire "Scot"—bubbling like a mountain brook (in spate). His constant companion—John Amatt—taciturn and remote like the mighty Trolltinder Wall whose secrets he had been the first to penetrate: Roy Smith— a P.T. sergeant of proportionate build whose physique approximated most closely to the popular conception of "the Mountaineer"—a sort of cross between Tarzan and Garth. Roy had been granted C.O.'s leave in order to attend. ("How are you, Sergeant? Mr. Gray, the Himalayan Explorer, has been in touch with me again. He asked for you personally, so of course I agreed immediately that you must be released. It seems they want you for some Top Level stunt on television.")

Eric Beard made up the complement of the Reserve Team. One of the Camera Units was to operate from the far end of an exposed knife-edge ridge. The lives of these unfortunate men would be

"Beardie's" personal responsibility. On a preliminary reconnaissance, Baillie and Cleare had abseiled down on to this ridge,
lowering a B.B.C. cameraman in front of them. This unsung
hero had no previous mountaineering experience and his return
to the cliff top involved prussiking up a rope that hung clear of the
rock for almost sixty feet. To quote John Cleare's words it had
been "a particularly stout effort". His colleagues were to have the
advantage of a steel ladder on the vertical section. From the foot
of the ladder a series of bucket steps, hewn out with ice axes,
crossed a slippery mud slope to the little eyrie that housed the
camera. "Beardie" and I worked on this project for two days although work was occasionally interrupted by the sporadic
attempts of small boys to scale the mud slope below our feet.
Every other alleyway of intrusion was covered by a constable on
duty at the cliff top. (As the producer thoughtfully suggested, it
would be ironic to interrupt the programme for the death of a
spectator.)

Meanwhile Messrs. Baillie, Gray, Smith, and Amatt were
pegging up the Red Wall. As they twisted and thrashed at the
end of their 150-foot life-lines, pitons and hammers pounding out
a staccato bass, they invoked nostalgic memories of pre-war
Munich Spider-men.

Although the Red Wall was to be the setting for the last act of
our forthcoming melodrama, none of the principal actors
participated in the early rehearsals. They were not even permitted
to examine their scripts in advance. The producer explained that
this was necessary to conserve an atmosphere of tension and lend
verisimilitude to the live recording. I was not really sure what he
meant, but whatever it was, I didn't agree with it. I knew for a
fact that Rusty was deliberately spacing the pegs and bolts so as
to combine maximum economy with minimum security. He
obviously relished the prospect of viewing the coming attraction
from an excellent seat in the gods, and when any of us questioned
him about the technical difficulties he licked his lips in a suggestive
fashion. "There are a few ten foot gaps between pitons," he
admitted, "but we imagine you want to show the public a little
rock climbing if only to justify your selection."

The few holds that Nature had provided proved to be loose and needed prising off. In the process one of the abseil ropes was damaged and almost completely severed. It was a chance discovery, which could equally easily have been overlooked. . . .

As the hours passed, so the excitement mounted. It transpired that the fixed rope for the Tyrolean Traverse (Act 2, Scene 2) was fifty feet too short. "We require 300 feet of new full-weight Terylene rope," demanded Cleare. "We require it immediately. Therefore it is imperative that it should be dispatched from London this morning."

"Item—300 feet of Terylene rope," said the Producer. "Someone make a note please."

"I'm not even happy about the dinghy," Cleare mused. "The shape of it irritates me—I don't know why."

"State shape required and quote dimensions," said the Producer. "We will supply."

This power-play induced an awestruck silence among the newcomers. Here was a new John Cleare—a human computer like Peter Crew, with circuits whirring soundlessly in highly tuned machinery.

"I like my camera position," he confided in one of his rare relaxed moments. "I feel it has excellent potential." In as far as one could apply this property to several cubic feet of air suspended half-way between Heaven and Hell, he was right. He intended to film the proceedings from the end of a 100 foot rope, man and machine inseparably welded together—a miniature space satellite.

As the crowds started to collect at the cliff top, so the principal actors arrived. First to appear was Royal Robbins, outwardly serious and thoughtful, but with an occasional disarming smile that betrayed his keen sense of humour. Royal had shorn off his beard since our last meeting and thus lost some of his Sphinx-like inscrutability. One now wondered how often the man behind the beard had enjoyed a secluded laugh.

At first he picked his way along the cliff top with what looked like unnecessary caution, pausing to peer carefully over the edge. For a time, I really convinced myself that he was just as apprehensive as I was. As Royal's potential partner, that gave me some encouragement. It was short lived. About an hour later somebody spotted him dangling from his jumars, half-way down one of the fixed ropes. He was quietly ruminating in his rope harness, tapping an odd suspect peg with his C.M.I. hammer or making a few minor adjustments to the spacing of the pitons. After six hours leisurely inspection, he returned to the cliff top and pronounced himself well satisfied with the arrangements.

Next on the set was Ian McNaught-Davis, who was on jocular back-slapping terms with producer, cameramen, engineers, and climbers alike.

"Well Mac, are we going to be gripped this time?" asked the Producer. As a TV personality, this was what set Mac on a higher pedestal than the rest of us. It was difficult even for climbing companions to tell whether Mac was seriously involved on a route or merely adding a dash of colour to the proceedings. Such ambiguity is the hallmark of greatness.

Like the Poor Man's "Bluff King Hal", Mac adamantly refused to treat any situation with appropriate gravity. The climbing arena now bore a vague resemblance to a Naval Dockyard, full of busy little men alternately hammering, shouting and swearing. "There are too many people here," he said, "all getting in each other's way. How about some boulder practice?" I accepted the invitation gladly, with nostalgic memories of the Mustagh Tower and days spent trundling large boulders down Himalayan precipices under Mac's eager direction. It is a sport that combines maximum entertainment and destruction with minimum effort and is thus a very satisfying hobby for a healthy, fun loving Anglo-Saxon—which Mac is. It was heartwarming to see the flames of boyish enthusiasm light up his features as deafening crescendos of splintering granite shook the ground underfoot, filling the air with the heavy poignant stench of sulphur. Occasional shouts from the pitoneers on the Red Wall told us that traditional British "sang froid" was running thin. It only encouraged Mac to redouble his efforts. "This is the real drama," he roared, hooting with delight at each muffled outcry of protest.

Only one place remained to be filled: the leading rope, which had been left vacant with Bonington's abdication. Where in Snowdonia could we unearth a man who could step into Bonington's boots? Right on the doorstep, as it happened. Who would have foreseen that this very month, none other than Joe Brown—the Old Master—would be opening a new sports shop in Llanberis. "Just the Place for the Human Fly", said the local headlines (thus provoking Dennis Gray to mail a letter addressed to "The Human Fly, Llanberis, North Wales", which apparently reached its destination).

No one was better fitted to stamp the seal of success on our brave new venture than the man whose epic conquests of the Aiguille du Midi and Clogwyn du'r Arddu had first captured the public interest and whetted the appetite for real life drama on the heights. I was dispatched forthwith to Llanberis with orders to enlist Joe Brown's assistance regardless of cost.

We pulled up at the cliff top late in the morning of T-Day Minus Two. One could sense the importance of the occasion. Cameramen and sound engineers had been standing idly at their posts since 10 a.m., the hour when preliminary run-throughs had been scheduled to start. All recriminations were forgotten as the old maestro ambled happily on to the set to take up his accustomed position on the rostrum.

"Well done, Joe!" said the Producer. "Glad to have you back."

Nothing could go wrong now: the mere presence of this man was sufficient to ensure success. Unlike every other newcomer he did not rush immediately to the cliff top in order to satisfy his curiosity. He sat down in the tent, drank a cup of tea, and slowly and deliberately laced up his climbing boots. Joe is not easily ruffled.

The dress-rehearsal for the dress-rehearsal was almost lost to view in a clinging off-shore mist. To make matters worse the acoustics suffered from an unexpected source of interference—the fog-horn of the South Stack Lighthouse, a mere 300 yards away. Every twenty seconds or so everything was swallowed up in a deafening blast from the hooter. This was really annoying. There was even talk of bringing pressure to bear on the Lighthouse Keeper, but nothing came of it. We could not have competed on any terms whatsoever with the spectacle of the Dublin Steamer running aground on the rocks below the television cameras.

By now I was thoroughly immersed in the rituals of Tele-climbing. Even the evening "de-briefing session" had become part of an accepted pattern of existence and was no longer a butt for cynical amusement.

B.B.C. Outside Broadcasts Producer, Dennis Monger, took the chair on these occasions. "Now chaps. Has everybody got a drink? Right. I have noted down here a few hints and suggestions. Item One, the Climbing Party. Too much back-chat. The usual climbing calls, of course," he gestured expansively, "are in. Very necessary. Topical, in fact. Everything else—out. We tune you in when we need you. We fade you out when we don't need you. Unfortunately, there have been occasions when we did not fade you out quickly enough. Which brings me to another point. Language. Tone it down chaps. Every Welsh fishing vessel can pick us up on their short wave to say nothing of the onlookers at the cliff top who have a loudspeaker. Mac, for instance. I'm sure you had no idea we were listening when . . .? No, of course not. Not to worry. Item Two. Climbing Action—the Red Wall. . . . Untidy. Not enough to maintain interest. In fact at one point I'm sure I noticed that all four climbers were completely stationary. This won't do. We must speed things up but we must not—of course—sacrifice safety. O.K.? Incidentally, Mac, that was a nice personal touch dropping your helmet into the sea. Gave us excellent scale perspective. Intentional, of course? Oh . . . I see. Never mind we'll get you a new one. Item Three. Our Climbing Cameraman. Come in, John Cleare. I'm sure you've got a few comments to make?"

John clears his throat portentously. "My interpretation is this," he begins, speaking with computer-like precision, "as soon as I get the O.K. from the Icky Gammy* my intention is to *zoom* in the leading pair, capture some action close-ups and lead up to the big moment when Joe steps out at the top. Then I switch and *zoom* down on Royal. . . ."

John succeeds in investing his job with a certain dynamic appeal by liberal use of such energetic words as "zooming in". His was a

* This is what it sounded like. Apparently some special Master Camera?

performance that should not have required glamourising. He had
all the attributes. Tarzan and Armstrong Jones in collaboration
could not have earned more profound public respect. My personal
grouse was that he should be consistently introduced as "Our
B.B.C. Cameraman John Cleare"—thus inferring that John was
a sporting type B.B.C. technician, game to have a go at anything,
including mountaineering. The fact that his climbing ability was
obviously no whit inferior to ours created an inferiority complex
which was not improved by chance remarks overheard in the crowd.

"Cor, look at him. He's better than any of them stars. Ruddy
great camera and all. What's his name? It isn't even in the programme!"

So to the Day of Decision. Anyone whose curiosity or cynicism
has spurred him to read this far must also have been sufficiently
amused to watch the live recording. (There are also, of course, a
moronic minority who are incapable of switching off what they
do not wish to hear.) Hence it may be taken for granted that
readers do not wish to be reminded of the details of the live
performance. For that matter, neither do I.

There are of course several things that deserve fuller explanation. For example, I am not deaf, contrary to the opinion now
held by most viewers. To identify oneself with the role that
has been allotted, it is at least necessary that one's ear-piece should
emit occasional snatches of commentary. Even an odd crackle
helps to relieve the isolation and the utter frustration that results
from complete silence. From the moment that I leapt over the
cliff edge, uttering some inconsequential cliché about my Cliff
Assault training with the Royal Marine Commandos, I lost all
contact with the broadcasting unit. I knew with absolute certainty
that this would happen. As the final count down began, a cheerful
optimist was still fiddling with my radio set. "Can you hear that?"
he said, twiddling a knob, somewhere. "Very faintly," I answered,
"it sounds like coarse sand being scraped over glass."

"Temporary atmospherics—you'll get used to it," he chuckled.
"Nothing can go wrong, providing that you remain absolutely
motionless for the next three hours." He was gone before I could
register a protest.

I have always distrusted mechanical and electrical gadgets. They don't like me and I don't like them. In my experience there are only two types of machine, one of which works and the other doesn't. I used to own a 1932 B.S.A. motor cycle. When it broke down, which was frequently, I kicked it until it sprang to life. I always kicked it at the same spot, whose vulnerability I had originally located by trial and error. To this day, I do not know what part of its anatomy I was stimulating. Nevertheless I was invariably successful.

As far as the radio set was concerned these punitive measures proved a complete failure. I shook it, turned it upside down, banged it—all to no avail. Unknown to me, the Transmitting Component continued to work perfectly, so that a large part of my three-hour soliloquy was relayed to the listening populace. (We had been ordered that in the unlikely event of a breakdown in reception we were to continue speaking until told to stop. They would tune us in whenever they wanted us.)

Secondly, there was the controversial matter of the pitons and bolts on the Red Wall, of which we all took liberal advantage. It must have been patently obvious to most people that whoever fixed them there it was not the climbing party. And here I must pay my tribute to the honesty of our veteran leader—"Baron" Brown. It was my suggestion that we should add insult to illusion by simulating the actions of piton insertion and extraction. Several taps of the hammer alongside a pre-inserted piton would satisfy all but the most keen-sighted of viewers. Sleight of hand would be required to put across the imaginary transfer of piton from waist-loop to the cliff-face, but that was merely a question of practice. It was left to Joe to polish the tarnished honour of British mountaineering. "Sorry, old chap," he said gravely, "I'm afraid that would not be playing the game."

From my own point of view the most exciting part of the programme was the final instalment—the epic of the Red Wall— punctuated by pitons, bolts, *étriers* and everything that I normally deplore and don't know how to use. It was, in fact, my first major excursion into the unknown hinterland of leepers, rurps and bong-bongs. Although I had been intrigued by their names I had not wished to press the acquaintanceship further. It proved to be an initiation by fire which had many bewildering moments.

"We all enjoyed the pirouette in *étriers*," observed Paul Ross when I called at his Lamplighter Café on the way home. This was one of those best-forgotten incidents which are invariably remembered in vivid detail. I had in fact assumed that the end of the transmission had intervened in time for me to elude detection. Unfortunately this was far from being the case, and the commentator had been so impressed that he promised viewers "They would be returning instantly to South Stack *should anything unforeseen occur*."

What happened was very simple. When Royal took in the slack a mischievous coil of rope dropped over my head, thereby causing the climbing rope to take one complete turn round the *étrier*. Only when all the slack had been snatched away beyond recall came the discovery that I was being pulled tightly up against the *étrier*. The *étrier* was my only sure means of support. It was a long multi-rung affair so the obvious solution was to revolve in space and thus untwist the coil. Of course, I realised that this was not an accepted manœuvre in Artificial Climbing so I had to delay the fateful moment until (as I fancied) transmission had ended. All the time I had to shield the tell-tale tangle from the searching inspection of Cleare, aggressively poised in space like a hovering kestrel. He had spotted that I was hiding something and was squinting through his view-finders.

When I emerged breathlessly on to the cliff top, draped in *étriers*, slings, hammers and prussikers, Royal glanced inquiringly at my hands. They were criss-crossed with cuts and covered in blood. "Back home in the States," he remarked, "they say you can always distinguish a good Aid Man by his hands."

"Lots of scars?" I suggested hopefully.

Royal shook his head gently. "No scars," he said.

Any remorse I might have felt was quickly dispelled by a rush of small boys waving autograph books. They had waited a long time to collect the signature of the fourth member of the distinguished rope. The role of a TV star has its unexpected compensations.

My fellow climbers had been less patient. In the mess-tent there was a flurry of activity. Like conquering heroes of old, they now disputed among themselves for a share in the booty. The spoils of war—a vast heap of glittering "chrome-molly"—disappeared as if by magic, swallowed up in a dozen rucksacks. Some of the star-studded cast had already ensured tenancy by making good their departure. Others were on the point of leaving.

"Here's a useful length of fine nylon," said Rusty, offering me a chewed-up boot-lace, which his dog had regurgitated. "Better luck next time," he added sympathetically.

Doubtless there will be a next time. Tele-climbing is a powerful drug and the number of known addicts is increasing. However, there is a limited supply and the circle keeps a careful check on membership. The "circus" as they are now commonly known, have their own code of rules, which newcomers must learn to respect. Within these limitations I see no reason why teleclimbing should not continue to flourish. It is a way of life that brings its own rewards. These are often considerable.

A GLOSSARY OF COMMONLY USED CLIMBING TERMS AND PHRASES

or

The TV Armchair Guide to Mountaineering—(with special reference to the Red Wall of the South Stack)

Climbing Rope—fulfils many functions, e.g. it may be used for lassooing projecting spikes, crossing impassable gorges or for pulling up climbers who have lost their nerve.

A solo climber—One man falling alone.

A roped party—Several men falling simultaneously.

Hemp (rope)—A rope that breaks.

Nylon (rope)—A rope that melts.

Ice-axe or "Pick"—An implement for chopping holds in mud or soft rock.

Piton or "Spike"—An implement for opening tin cans (various other uses).

Knife—Indispensable. Should be instantly attainable. One of these saved several lives on the Matterhorn.

Snap-link—A Link that Snaps.

Safety Helmet—A safety device for climbers falling head first. If the fall is a long one the climber may become completely impacted in his helmet and be telescoped into a small globular mass which can be easily stowed in a rucksack (cf. mountain rescue).

A Tiger's Web—A hopeless tangle of rope or ropes.

A Pied d'Elephant—A special short climbing boot for climbers who have had all their toes amputated.

Leepers—Small jumping insects encountered on Welsh sea cliffs.

Krabs—Another unusual hazard encountered on Welsh sea cliffs. (If this last hazard is a considerable one, Lobster Claw Crampons are worn.)

A Cow's Tail—The frayed end of an old climbing-rope.

A Lay-back—An unusually comfortable bivouac.

A Hand-Jam—A climber with one hand caught in a crack.

A Foot-Jam—A climber with one boot caught in a crack.

A Good Jam—A climber who is permanently stuck in a crack.

A "Joe Brown"—A climber with large hands who gets stuck in cracks.

Whillans—An orange-coloured rucksack.

A Novice—Someone (often dead) who should be kept off the mountains at all costs.

An Experienced Climber—Someone whose death was unavoidable.

An Alpine Club Member (syn. Veteran)—Someone who never dies but slowly fades away.

(Contrast:) An Alpine Veteran—Someone who has been to the Alps.

Steeplejacks, Munich Fanatics, Dangle and Whack Merchants, or Masters of the Sophisticated Modern Techniques—Alternative terms (of different vintage) for a Piton Climber.

A careful climber—A slow climber.

A cautious climber—A very slow climber.

A climbing-nut—A reckless climber.

A running Belay—A cowardly second.

A Thread Belay—An asphyxiated second (due to a slow third man and a very fast leader).

A "Descendeur" (French)—A Term of derision. The opposite of a climber.

A "Super Charlet" (French)—A proper Charlie.

A psychological belay—(Alt. usage) (1) A female second; (2) Looks like a belay but isn't. . . .

A Classic Route—Much loose rock and grass.

A Direttissima—A very long free fall or "Plunge".

A long Run-out—A very long arrested fall.

"One of Nature's Last Strongholds" or "The Last Great Problem"—
A B.B.C. Outside Broadcasts Production.

Overhanging—Vertical.

Vertical—Steep.

Scrambling—Fairly Steep.

Interesting—Nerve-racking.

Thin—Non-existent.

Amusing—Die Laughing.

Gripping—McNaught-Davis at the Crux.

The Crux—Where everyone else unties to watch the leader.

"Fissure" (French)—A dirty, unpleasant crack.

Backing up, Straddling, Back and Knee, Back and Foot, Foot and
Mouth—Various postures adopted in Chimneys (?Derivation—
Kama Sutra).

Considerable Exposure—No Privacy.

Free Climbing—No charge for Spectators.

A Rurp—A strenuous grunt. (A combination of a rift and a burp.)

Abseiling—Showing off, Pretending to Fall.

Committed (to the Route)—Under Suspended Sentence of Death.

Peeling off—Undressing.

Climbing Calls (cf. Blackshaw—The Penguin's Guide to Mountaineering)

"Tight Rope, Please"—"HELP!!!"

"A Little Slack"—"Lower away gently".

"Below"—Leader announcing that he is dropping a rock on his
second's head (cf. Safety Helmets, Further Uses of).

Bong—One hit.

Bong-Bong—Two hits.

Two tugs on the Rope—Second must be securely belayed from above
before proceeding. If two forcible tugs fail to dislodge the leader
he may assume all is well.

*Phrases which are frequently overheard on TV Mountaineering Broadcasts
(now explained)*

"He seems to be experiencing some difficulty"—"He is about to fall off".

"These chaps climb for Pleasure!"—These men are very well paid.

. . . Zooming in . . .—John Cleare focusing his camera.

"Master of the Ice Glazed Rock"—Not very experienced on Welsh
sea cliffs.

"I think we've cracked it" (Quote—Joe Brown)—I am starting the last Grade VI pitch.

Overheard indistinctly: "Get stuffed . . ."—there is distortion in sound. Please do not adjust your set.

"Just look at our TV Cameraman John Cleare, showing these experts how to do a Fast Abseil—there is a temporary distortion in vision."

(Splash)

We apologise for the loss of vision due to circumstances beyond our control.

"Whew! Oh! I see . . . how terribly unfortunate. Were we insured?"

We are interrupting this programme to return you to the Studio. . . .

APES OR BALLERINAS?

From Mountain, May 1969

Man with all his noble qualities . . . still bears in his bodily
frame the indelible stamp of his lowly origin.

DARWIN

IF EVERYONE MADE a point of remembering that, we might be
spared a lot of mountain philosophy and psychoanalysis. And
Mallory would have been better informed. "Why do you
climb?" The answer should be apparent to the veriest moron.
"*Because it is the natural thing to do.*" Climbers are the only genuine
primordial humanoids, heirs to a family tradition inherited from
hairy arboreal ancestors.

Recently, of course, the scene has altered. All the interesting
trees have been cut down by the Forestry Commission and replaced with elementary stereotyped firs, which any fool can
climb. Bird's-nesting is illegal. That removes the only obvious
reason for climbing trees. Nowadays, if you decided to take up
residence in a tree, somebody would immediately call out the
fire brigade. Admittedly the Queen lives in a Treetops Hotel
when she goes to Kenya to unwind, but then the Queen, as
someone remarked, is a special case. As far as the average citizen
is concerned, a man up a tree is assuredly up to no good, and he
must be speedily charged or certified.

So what other outlet is there? Mountains are the obvious choice.
We can discount university types who climb College buildings,
because you need a pretty elastic imagination to be satisfied
with a substitute twice removed. As regards potholers, they are
mere troglodytes . . . pale, anaemic offspring of the Cave Age.

This then is the reason . . . pure and simple . . . why we climb
mountains. But what I am leading up to is this business of "style",
by which every mountaineer seems to set great store. Nothing
annoys me quite so much as to hear someone described as a

"stylist" climber (largely because my own climbing technique has never been noticeably so graced).

Everyone knows what is meant by a "stylist" climber. He features in all the best climbing obituaries, viz: "I never saw X . . . make a false or hurried move. He would stand motionless, sometimes for half an hour or more, on the tiniest of rugosities, lightly caressing the rock with sensitive finger-tips as he deliberated his next move. Movement, when it came, was a fluid ripple of conscious style executed with the lithe grace of a ballet dancer". History usually fails to record how he met his end.

The French, as might be expected, are the supreme stylists. If you don't know what I mean, have a look at the illustrations in Rebuffat's book, *On Snow and Rock*. Every picture shows the author examining himself in some graceful and quite unbelievable posture . . . like something out of *Swan Lake*. Even the captions carry a note of smug satisfaction: "Climbing means the pleasure of communicating with the mountain as a craftsman communicates with the wood or the stone or the iron upon which he is working" (portrait of Rebuffat, standing on air, studiously regarding his left forearm, hands caressing smooth granite). "On monte comme une echelle" (inset photograph of Rebuffat self-consciously climbing a ladder).

It all looks so effortless. In fact, by the time you've finished the book and found a smooth 70 degree slab to practise on, you're feeling light as thistledown and lithe as Nureyev.

Now to the test. Open the book of instructions and begin. The finger-tips brush the rock like sensitive antennae; the arms are not above shoulder level; the knees are retracted to avoid possible contact with the rock; the stomach is tucked in, the head held high; the features are composed, relaxed and earnest . . . you are prepared to "communicate".

Stage One: with infinite delicacy the right foot is elevated eighteen inches and the boot tip placed deliberately on a tiny wrinkle.

Stage Two: the left boot is aligned with the right boot by stepping up smoothly and deliberately. Any effort is imperceptible. . . .

Strange! You're lying flat on the ground with a squashed nose.

Another attempt; another failure. Time passes, along with your faith in Rebuffat.

Suddenly and inexplicably you succeed.

Why?

Simple really. You lost your temper and became uninhibited. Ancient primitive reflexes took over. The old jungle juice started throbbing through your veins. If you had two hands to spare, you would beat your chest with pride. Intellectually you may have retreated a couple of million years . . . physically you're thriving.

Heave, clutch, thrutch, grunt! Up you go, defying gravity with your own impetus. So what, if it looks ungraceful? Joe Brown doesn't look much like a ballet dancer. Primeval? . . . possibly.

Now you can appreciate why the chimpanzees are the happiest-looking animals in the zoo . . . hurling themselves about and swinging joyfully from bar to bar. Who ever heard of a maladjusted chimpanzee?

Stripped down to fundamentals, this is is what mountaineering is all about. A regressive metamorphosis, if you like. Nobody should have to learn how to climb. In fact most people spend a lifetime unlearning. The most competent climbers I ever saw were some city kids on a bomb-site. They were swarming all over the place like monkeys. They were masters of every technique known to man or Rebuffat . . . chimneying, straddling, hand traversing, and many other manœuvres quite outside the scope of the average climbing manual.

It all proves that no one needs to be taught to climb; one merely needs reminding of something one knew even before going to school.

Reverting to nature is generally satisfying . . . physically and psychologically. It may not be ethical, it may not be moral, but it is usually agreeable. Normally you draw the line, if only for social reasons. In the mountains you can afford to be completely uninhibited. Here, man can act in the manner born, using whatever physical talents nature has bestowed on him. He needs no instruction manuals, no rules and no regulations.

Where does style come into this? Every climber has his own natural "style", to use the word in its proper context. He inherits it. Climbing instruction, to be of any value, must foster natural style. Try to curb it and you land up in trouble. Try to impose your own style on a "learner" and you double his difficulties.

The sort of climber I like to watch is the man who knows where he's going, and wastes no time getting there. A latent power and driving force carries him up pitches where no amount of dynamic posturing would do any good.

An efficient mountaineer, by this reckoning, need fulfil only three criteria. He must not fall off. He must not lose the route. He must not waste time. Time may be endless on an English outcrop; in the Alps it can mean the difference between life and death.

These are accomplishments to be learnt neither from books nor from other climbers. Although we are all differently proportioned, we all have some natural ability derived from our primitive ancestors, and that's what we need to develop.

Which takes us back to the apes. Climbers are conceited characters when you pause to think about it. They liken themselves in prints to Gods, Goddesses, and Gladiators; tigers, eagles, and chamois; craftsmen, gardeners and ballet dancers; and even, in one case at least, to computers! One seldom reads of climbers who resemble apes, chimps, or orang-outangs. Comparisons are only odious when too near the bone.

You don't teach children to walk . . . they teach themselves. Why, then, teach the descendants of the apes to climb? They can also be left to teach themselves. But don't expect them to resemble ballet dancers.

So, next time you see a jaded climber at the foot of a cliff, dangle a bunch of bananas from the top. You may be surprised at the energetic response. Why? Because it's there, of course. . . .

THE PROFESSIONALS

From Mountain, July and September 1969

There is a tide in the affairs of men, which, taken at the flood...
SHAKESPEARE

THE ALPINE CLUB of South Audley Street has at last been submerged in the ever-rising flood of professionalism. No less an authority than Eric Shipton, past President of the Club, has announced his intention of organising conducted tours to the Western Cwm of Everest. Three hearty cheers! If the winds of change were reversed, you would not be reading an excellent publication like *Mountain*, and I would not be recompensed for my contributions. Writing for money no longer makes me feel that I am sacrificing my principles; I am merely waiving them.

Five years ago, it was a different story. At that time, I was an immaculate amateur, steeped in the traditions of the British gentleman-climber who climbed strictly for pleasure because he could well afford to do so. I had been nurtured on tales of sweat and high endeavour: "The right men high at the right time"; "all the porters pulled their weight"; "the first man up Everest gets there over the head and shoulders of everybody in front of him"; etc.

Even in that sterile, arid plain, the springs of professionalism were seeping through. It is easy now to appreciate that the primary objective of every previous British Everest Expedition was to write the Expedition Book on getting home. Whether the expedition succeeded or not, book sales were unaffected: the British always admire a gallant loser ("giving the mountain a chance").

Nowadays, among those pleasure-seeking sportsmen, we discern certain shadowy scientific figures—the anthropologist, physiologist, and geologist. Their presence gave the party an air of Scientific Respectability—and ensured adequate financial support. The experts' qualifications were seldom tested, and a good time was had by all.

It would have been bad form to congratulate those blue-blooded pioneers on their professional acumen and foresight. Today, we can recognise it as the thin end of the wedge which has been driven in so hard by subsequent expeditions that it now forms a permanent belay for impoverished climbers. This is why organising a Himalayan expedition no longer calls for a large capital outlay, but for highly-geared salesmanship.

It was clearly only a matter of time before the Alpine Club opened its big front door to the professionals it once ostracised. In doing so, it swallowed its principles for the umpteenth time in its history. On this occasion, there was little of the usual burbulent dyspepsia and rhetorical diarrhoea: many of the sitting committee were themselves already firmly established on the bandwagon. When Faust yielded to the persuasions of Mephistopheles, the unfortunate wretch was rewarded with eternal torment. I envisaged the same fate when I signed on with Chris Brasher for his vintage spectacular "The Old Man of Hoy". Unlike Faust, I was not consumed by hell-fire; I enjoyed a pleasant holiday in Norway at the expense of my ill-gotten gains. Nobody is going to carry a banner for Telly climbing, but one has to admit that the rewards—although hardly spiritual, mystical, aesthetic or even ethical—are quite substantial.

Of course there are still minor undercurrents of dissatisfaction. The climbing rank and file are never slow to declaim when their more prominent fellows are seen making a public meal of the fruits of office. At the same time, criticism is guarded: nobody is going to dismiss the grapes as sour, when he still has an outside chance of climbing the tree.

The layman's reaction is much more enthusiastic. For more than a decade, he has been waiting impatiently for mountaineering heroes to replace Hunt, Hillary, Tensing and the Abominable Snowman. Once upon a time, you had to go all the way to Everest to earn public acclaim. Now, you need only appear on television hanging upside down from the end of a rope. In more ancient times, the same sort of enthusiasm was aroused by public hangings. Chris Bonington took a rather dramatic photo of me on the first ascent of the Old Man of Hoy. I was trying unsuccessfully to extract pitons he had inserted. Feet treading air, three parts hanging on the rope, hands clawing for holds that didn't exist, I was gripped—terrified. The cigarette clenched aggressively between my teeth was slowly burning my lips because I could not chuck it away; the apparently exultant grimace on my face was indicative of impending suffocation. Some months later, to my great displeasure, I saw the photograph reproduced in a children's weekly *The Commando*. By courtesy of Bonington, I had been featured as Number Ten in the series "Men who Dare". The caption read: "Any of these pegs could come out at the twitch of a finger. To be respected . . . you've got to be able to tackle sheer cliffs like this and enjoy it. Anybody want to have a go?" (Several local five-year olds did, and had to be rescued.) In every house I was besieged by youthful readers of *The Commando*, and I enjoyed temporary fame as a sort of homespun Tarzan—an unusual role for a country G.P. Then came the news that the Old Man of Hoy had been climbed by a lad of their own age—a seven-year-old primary school boy! Now, I was totally ignored. Small boys passed me in the street. Nobody asked for autographs any more.

The efforts of the Boningtons, Brashers, and Gillmans of the climbing world have certainly borne fruit in one direction. The public are at last realising that accidents are not the only interesting feature of mountaineering. Previously one could scarcely blame them for assuming that a "solo climber" was a "single man falling unaccompanied", and a "roped party" consisted of "two or more men falling simultaneously". The only difference between "hemp" and "nylon" climbing ropes was that one broke and the other melted. Ropes that did not either break or melt were assumed to have been cut in the interests of self-preservation. This was why climbers always carried pocket knives.

In the Press, any non-fatal climbing event was allocated to the most junior reporter. He was left to embellish it as best he could. For example:

"The Mustagh Tower is 90,000 feet high. The last 89,000 feet are either vertical or overhanging." (*The Times 1956*)

"'Safety Helmets are very useful indeed,' declared Lord Hunt, 'especially for climbers who fall head first.'" (*Daily Express?*)

"Brian Robertson's parting message as he leaves for the 'Robertson Direttissima' on the West Face of the Dru (still unclimbed!): 'This is without doubt the Last of the Last Great Problems. We anticipate climbing for day after day without ever making contact with the cliff face.'" (*Daily Express*).

"'I like leading,' says Hoy-hero Peter Crew. 'It means that I can fall further.'" (*source forgotten*).

These random samples are not exceptional. It is little wonder that climbers are regarded as a race apart. The self-appointed ambassadors of our sport are now bridging the gap themselves and establishing a new rapport with the reading public. Good luck to them, if they make a little in the process—they deserve it!

"It's all very well for you, Tom," said the well-known professional Mr. X. "You can climb whenever you want to. I have to consider my readers."

Opportunists like Mr. X cut their cloth to suit the market, even though the finished article is not always acceptable to the dyed-in-the-wool amateur (if you will excuse the extended metaphor). Personally, I admire Mr. X for his honesty. I do not envy him his job. He has to work hard. But I like someone who proclaims blatantly what others whisper furtively. "Shamateurism" is the true trademark of hypocrisy.

A professional climber may be defined as one who gains financially from participation in the sport of mountaineering. This is a general definition, and we have to itemise, because professionals are men of many colours—"Forty Shades of Grey", to misquote the song.

One thing must not be forgotten: professionals have been known to climb for pleasure! In my humble, biased opinion, the man who sacrifices a sunny day transporting some inadequate fellow up a climb (which he, the incompetent, selects) deserves every penny he earns.

One final point: any characters named hereafter are as nearly fictitious as we could make them. Any resemblance to others is unfortunate.

1. Instructors and guides

There are important differences between the duties of an instructor and those of a guide. The function of an *instructor* is to instil sufficient confidence in his clients to enable them to qualify for next year's Advanced Course. Anyone with initiative, headed notepaper and an illustrated brochure, can set himself up as an instructor. The B.M.C. issues "Guides' Certificates", but most clients consult the adverts and select their instructor on the strength of his climbing reputation. This is regrettable, but inevitable. So far, there have been remarkably few accidents.

The function of a *guide* is to elevate a specific client by unspecified methods to the top of a specific mountain. Hence the "special kind of guide–client relationship", which was so beloved of Victorian mountaineers that it formed the basis of all early British explorations in the Alps. In recent years, the aesthetic aspects of guided ascents have been questioned. A prize bull which is dragged to market by the ring in its nose gets little opportunity to appreciate the scenery along the wayside. What can we say about the guided gentleman-client? He is roused at 2 a.m. to the numbing horror of a Traditional Alpine Start, frogmarched up and down the Hörnli Ridge in the grey half-light of dawn, and restored to the hut in time for a late breakfast. Because of the commotion, intense cold, physical exhaustion, indigestion and insomnia, his recollection of events is hazy—to say the least. Retrospectively, he records in his guide's "Führerbuch": "A hard but satisfying day was enjoyed by all. Emil, that stouthearted fellow, was in cracking form!"

So much for the Golden Age. Of the two groups, the Instructors probably do the least harm.

2. The equipment patron (or Eponymous Nomenclator—ref. Oxford English Dictionary)

This man deserves pride of place in any list of professionals. He has discovered the ideal source of wealth. His income is earned by lending his name to a pair of boots, a pair of long underpants, or a new rucksack. There is only one necessary qualification:

he must bear an illustrious name. (How to acquire this will be discussed in some future issue.) An Equipment Patron should be addressed as "Technical Advisor"; if sponsored by one of the better firms, the term "Technical Consultant" may be preferred.

Joe Soap Proudly Announces
(by Courtesy of Humpalot Ltd.)
THE NEW JOE SOAP EXPENDABLE
A Sac To Break Your Back!
(It's way out behind!)

3. The equipment vendor

His interests are wholly commercial. With regard to his equipment, one thing goes without saying: nothing but the best is good enough for the dedicated climber. Every equipment vendor is agreed on this. That is why they all stock the best. One novel feature is the emergence of symbiotic alliances, designed to further joint sales ("If I give you a shoulder, you give me a pull").

Example:

Mayhem Tojo, the Well Known Equipment Expert,
Used
A Joe Soap Expendable—On His Greenland Campaign 1968. He is proud to associate his name (and picture) with this remarkable and useful product.

4. The circuit lecturer

Lecture venues are widely scattered. This is a great comfort to the Circuit Lecturer who suffers from an occupational phobia of being followed around the country by enthusiastic fans: they would be puzzled by the almost identical features the lecturer encountered on his ascents of the North Face of the Eiger and the South Face of Everest. The similarities are not entirely coincidental, but arise from the lecturer's practice of using the same set of slides to illustrate several different climbs. Variety can be introduced by reversing the slides in the projector. The lecturer has probably forgotten that he borrowed the slides from a friend who took the original photographs on Kinder Downfall. The comings and goings of Circuit Lecturers are well publicised:

TONIGHT ! ! !
(In the Town Hall)
"OVER THE HILL AND UP THE POLE"
My Climbing Adventures in Eight Continents
by
CRISPIN BONAFIDE

(1) After the lecture, autographed copies of the lecturer's book will be sold by public auction.
(2) Persons who suffer from a morbid fear of heights are advised *not* to attend this performance.

Comments: "Hundreds fainted in the aisles"   *Daily Blurb*
            ". . . I too was gripped . . ."   *Lord Hunt*
            "A golden message to every Award winning
            schoolboy"   *Duke of Edinburgh*
            ". . . Such rugged uncompromising
            masculinity . . ."   *Women's Page*
            "Not since the immortal Whymper . . ."
                                              Alpine Club Spokesman

5. *The feminine angle*

This has been pretty well cornered by the comely authoress of *Space between My Toes*. Viz:

"'Come off it, MUFFET,' he growled. 'Get up that crux and stop arguing.'

"I purred ferociously like a great cat, and flowed silkily up the overhang. Sometimes I really hated him."

6. *The mountain photographer*

"There is a bit more to mountain photography than merely taking snapshots with a camera," remarked a famous mountain photographer. The television millions who marvelled at John Dimm of Delta Group hanging upside down by his heels also witnessed the birth of a new art form. Its concepts are faintly Freudian. "I do not think of my camera as a camera," writes John Dimm, "I regard it as a *mechanical appendage* [sic] to my body."

The mountain photographer earns his bread and butter by mass-producing postcards of classic rock climbs, which look more difficult on the postcards than they actually are. These are the sort of pictures that Nig and Nog will buy to take home to Mum for her family snapshot album.

"Our Nig was up there on his holidays. It makes me sick to even look at it . . .", etc.

7. *The expedition opportunist*

Dear Sirs,

I have the honour to inform you that the Joint Anglo-International Physio-Sociological Expedition to the Western Alps 1969 has selected your firm's boots/ropes/tinned foods/watches/toilet paper to accompany them on their great enterprise. In token appreciation of your generous assistance, we shall report in due course on how your product reacted/tasted/felt under extreme climatic conditions/high altitude.

Yours faithfully, Acting Equipment Secretary,
London Headquarters, J.A.I.P.S.E.

8. *The Pressman incognito*

This rare migratory bird of prey is a casual visitor. His special talents lie in dishing up the "Low Down from Up High", suitably flavoured for popular consumption:

"Our Man in Kleine Scheidegg, Peter Hillman reports:
'Tonight an uneasy silence hangs like a pall over the brooding North Wall as the two rival parties prepare to spend their 135th successive night on the Face. Despite strenuous efforts by both teams to pull apart, guides and local experts suggest that there is a very real danger that the two routes may now in fact *merge*. This would create a most unpleasant situation without precedent in Alpine history. International complications would be inevitable. Tonight, leaders of both teams held urgent radio consultations with legal experts at base camp. Fortunately, these threatened developments have at least revived flagging public interest in the climb. Programme popularity figures are rising steadily. This helps to dispel earlier rumours that the B.B.C. had considered taking the show off the air because it was lacking in real-life human drama. The rumours came at the end of a fourth accident-free week.' "

9. The mountain rescue team spokesman

This public-spirited citizen receives no cash rewards for his services, although more deserving than most. We include him in the survey, because he receives free equipment and free licence to influence public opinion through the media of Press and Television.

Viz: *Daily Blurb*—Stop Press

"Albert Clod, 66-year-old Birmingham botanist was today severely injured in an incident on Mount Buachaille ('The Big Shepherd') in Glencoe ('The Glen of Weeping'), when avalanche dogs interrupted their training to dash to his assistance. A local rescue team spokesman said later:

'This lamentable affair illustrates only too clearly the utter folly of allowing Englishmen unlimited access to the Scottish Hills in winter.'

Hospital authorities confirmed that Mr. Clod was still too shaken by his recent experiences to comment fully. 'I owe it all to those dogs,' he said briefly.

Chief Constable McHooter issued the following statement: 'The lives of valuable canine auxiliaries were unnecessarily hazarded by this inconsiderate and ill-advised escapade.' "

Being a rescue team organiser brings its day-to-day irritations. The following letter purports to be a true copy of one received by Hamish MacInnes. Hamish has the mixed fortune to occupy one of the few houses in Glencoe, and his voluntary duties include the evacuation of all fallen and generally incapacitated climbers who might otherwise clutter up the landscape of the National Park. To avoid identifying a well-known English public school, the names have been changed. Otherwise, this is an exact facsimile:

Dear Sir,

I write to inform you that I shall be visiting your area with 26 boys from my school, accompanied by two masters, Mr. H. E. Fell and Mr. Y. Sexton. We intend to tackle some of the harder routes as described in the old edition of the Mountaineering Club Guidebook. I would be grateful if *you could warn your Team of our arrival on the 20th inst.* and ask them to stand by for the duration of our visit.

Enclosed is a S.A. envelope for your reply to the following questions:
(*a*) The name and address of the nearest Doctor/or hospital.
(*b*) The number of casualties your Team can cope with at any one time.
(*c*) The name of your local Church of England minister.

Yours faithfully, (Rev.) C. O. Finn (Principal)

10. *The Telstars*

The Telstars (or television rock-climbing entertainers) are multiplying rapidly. In many respects they are the brightest stars in the professional firmament, as they earn the most money for the least work in the shortest time. That aside, one has to point out that neither the B.B.C. nor I.T.V. offers a retainer, and employment is on a casual basis.

I have some slight experience in this field, as I have been type-cast as a climbing clown. Instead of a cap and bells, the B.B.C. supplied me with faulty earphones which only functioned when I tilted my head 45 degrees to the left and shook it vigorously. Viewers got the impression that I was either a deaf mute or suffering from St Vitus' Dance.

Telly-climbing calls for some knowledge of elementary stage craft. Although the climb looks terrifying, you have to persuade yourself that it is quite easy and at the same time persuade viewers that it is even more terrifying than it looks. Good telly-climbers should always appear "gripped". This comes easily to me—I usually am gripped. Characters like Brown and Crew have to pretend to be, and nobody knows whether McNaught-Davis is really gripped or not. That is the measure of his artistry.

Another of the minor conceits of telly-climbing is that the climbing team should appear to be unaware of the microphones nestling against their windpipes, the spotlights of the giant television cameras, the sixty assorted sound mechanics, electricians and prop-men, and the policemen restraining the crowds at the cliff top. It is, after all, an *informal* occasion:

"B.B.C. Outside Broadcasting Cameras are now going to *drop in* on a group of typical British climbers who are getting away from it all by taking part in a typical Saturday afternoon climb on a typical British crag. And, as we join them, we find them singing that old climbers' favourite—'Clementine'. Well, well! Hello there chaps! Sorry to interrupt the song. Would you care to tell us a little about what you're doing, why you do this sort of thing, and—to put it in a nutshell—what makes the Modern Climber tick?"

The major star in this twinkling constellation is of course the well-known impresario—producer/commentator to boot—Mr Lucifer Basher. Basher pulls the strings that control the tiny puppets on the rock face. He also strings clichés together tighter than they have ever been strung before.

"The *Old* Man of Hoy! 450 feet of towering, tottering Sandstone soaring above the blue waters of the Pentland Firth. And here today (!)—come to do battle (!!)—the *young* men (!!!), the tiny pin-sized climbers plastered like human flies to his gritty sides. And here too (!)—eager to take up this fantastic challenge—Britain's own master technician himself. What a confrontation!   Once-in-the-space-of-a-lifetime-comes-a-man such-as-this!!!" (We are shown an unidentifiable figure being vomited upon by a fulmar petrel.)

"How's it going, Joe?"

(Silence.)

"Well—Joe can't hear us for the moment, so we'll quickly move down the rope to anchor man Ian McNaught-Davis." (A lone climber is seen idly flicking pebbles off a ledge with his boot.)

"Come in Mac!"

(Vague splutters.)

"Well, Mac can't speak to us just now, because of a mechanical fault . . . I know!—let's nip across and see what Chris is doing..."

The giant cameras swing obediently as the duffle-coated figure at the cliff top gestures expansively.

I rather liked the telegram that American Outside Broadcasts sent to their British counterparts:

"Great viewing! This is what television is all about."

It sure is, buddy! Stick around and we'll show you more . . .

11. Guide book editors

These characters have a thankless job. Most people imagine that the aim of every guide book editor is either to make a fortune or to bolster his reputation by giving his own routes extra prominence. In fact, they earn very little money and a lot of vitriolic abuse. Ironically, their bitterest critics probably earn more by criticizing them: (Ref. Obsessional Correspondents—No. 14; and Pressman Incognito—No. 8.)

Dear Sir,

I write out of a sense of public duty. Last Sunday, armed with the new guide book, I made the ascent of Hooligan's Wall and confirmed what some of us have suspected all along. *The climb is frankly impossible by all normal human standards.* It took me *all of 15 hours* to get up.

Let the editor of the guide book now come forward and vindicate himself by repeating the route in the presence of a Watchdog Committee appointed by some responsible body such as the *Sunday Times.* I would like to think that he could. It is his public duty to try.

Yours responsibly, "Hill-Man"

Author's Note
We congratulate "Hill-Man" on his vigilance.
All future claims to first ascents should be submitted to the *Sunday Times* in the first instance, for ratification. In all cases, *Lord Thomson's decision will be final.*

12. The mountaineering scientist

Have you ever seen a rock climber with a climbing rope marked in inches, a pencil in one hand and a slide rule in the other? Have you noticed how he consults his slide rule and scribbles hurriedly on his anorak cuff before committing himself to a hard move? The climber was probably Dr Malcolm Slesser, the well-known Scottish Scientific Technologist, a man with an equal head for heights and figures. Slesser was the first to point out that:

$$\frac{p^2}{W} - 2p = \frac{20T}{EN} \quad (S.M.C. \; Journal \; 1958)$$

How comforting it is to know that "Nylon mountaineering rope can absorb an impact kinetic energy of 0.235 ft.lb./foot length per lb. tensile strength"!!! In a tight spot, a cool-headed leader will consult his Slesserian Tables to calculate the chances of the rope parting under the impact of a falling climber. Many leaders have probably fallen with their calculations incomplete. If that were the case, it would be doubly unfortunate, because the Tables generally confirm what is already feared: *the rope will break*. It is impossible to argue with a mathematical equation.

Mountaineering scientists are much in demand for Himalayan expeditions. If they cannot be found, they must be created. When asked to join the Rakaposhi Expedition, I was awarded the extra status of Physiologist. Our leader, Mike Banks, insisted upon this.

"I know nothing about Physiology," I told him.

"There are many excellent books on the subject," he replied pointedly.

One recent expedition included a Psychologist, whose job was to study the reaction of fellow members to stress and high altitude. Many interesting data came to light. I still feel it would have been better to study the various individual reactions to sharing Camp Six with a snow-goggled psychologist. It is difficult to imagine a situation more loaded with potential emotional trauma.

13. *The compulsive autobiographer*

Most climbers nurse secret ambitions to write a book. Invariably, the story begins in the nursery, where seemingly minor events are found to contain special significance:

"From my very earliest days, I was aware of an irresistible urge to climb out of my cot. This clearly indicated to me that I was destined for mountaineering greatness."

The text is liberally illustrated with full-page close-ups of the author's face which tell their own graphic tale.

(*a*) The Author as a Youth (arrogant, hirsute)
(*b*) The Author before the Eiger (anxious expression,
   receding hairline)

(c) The Author after the Eiger (happy smile, rapidly receding hairline)
(d) The Author after the Last Citadel (happy smile, total baldness)

14. The obsessional correspondent

A small but significant income is earned by the compulsive
or obsessional correspondent who contributes letters to the
Editors of popular climbing magazines. The literary output
of these gentlemen is prolific, and they can write about practically
anything or nothing, and be paid for it. One distressingly common
example is the Lonely Heart Correspondent:

Sir,

I am 48 and would like to meet another climber, not of the same
age group or sex, but with similar interests. Please put me in touch
with the female climber featured on page 38 of your excellent January
Issue—"The Big Bag that goes on all the Expeditions".

Yours hopefully, (Mr.) P. A. D'Elephant

15. The international cement mixer

Traditional British insularity is exemplified by one of Mike
Banks' off-the-record remarks during a protest strike among our
Expedition porters. "The English language is understood all over
the World," he declared impressively, "providing one shouts
loudly enough."

Present-day diplomatic trends are directed towards cultural
exchange, as a better medium for getting across the British point
of view. Under this heading, we find mountaineering included.
These goodwill missions can be a source of deep satisfaction to the
mountaineering ambassador concerned, whose expenses are
usually fully covered.

Viz: *Daily Blurb*

Addressing a London Press Conference, Sir Oliver Branch
said: "I take leave of my Outer Mongolian friends with a keen
sense of personal loss, and return to these green Island shores with
vivid memories of a Nation firmly entrenched in its environment
and thoroughly steeped in its traditions. In a simple but moving

ceremony to mark my departure, they presented me with a plastic bust of Mao-Tse-Tung and decorated me with the Grand Order of Lenin (First Class). These I shall always treasure. Replying, I asked them to accept a tiny fragment of rock, hewn from the summit of our highest mountain, Ben Nevis, as a small token of our esteem. I also reminded them of the peculiar affection that we in this country hold for the Mountains of Outer Mongolia, and of the close ties that have always existed between our respective Alpine Clubs. Because of language barriers my remarks were improperly understood, although greeted with great enthusiasm and loud applause. Next month, we in Britain play host to 146 Outer Mongolian mountaineers and their families. I appeal to any climber with available floor space and some knowledge of Oriental customs to get in touch with me as quickly as possible. Unfortunately, I myself shall be unable to extend a personal welcome, as I have a long standing engagement in Baluchistan to open a new Polo playing field."

Postscript

This list is by no means complete. Various categories remain, such as Fell and Rock Club Hut Wardens, Yeti Hunters and those privileged Peeping Toms—the Mountain Ornithologists. Space is limited . . .

If I appear to occupy an uncommitted position between amateur and professional ranks, this is not the case. I have some professional experience in categories 1, 4, 6, 7, 9, 10 and 11. My experience has not so far proved profitable, otherwise I would not be writing for this excellent publication! (Mr Editor please note).

In conclusion, I must crave the indulgence of various friends and acquaintances by reminding them that "Caricature is the highest form of Compliment". It also constitutes a free advertisement! Better to be misrepresented or misquoted, than to be missed out!

THE ART OF CLIMBING DOWN GRACEFULLY

A Symposium of commonly used Ploys. . . .

MODERN CLIMBING IS becoming fiercely competitive. Every year marks the fall of another Last Great Problem, or the fall of the Last Great Problem Climber. Amid this seething anthill, one must not overlook the importance of Staying Alive.

This is why I propose to devote a few lines to "The Art of Climbing Down Gracefully"—the long, dedicated Decline to Dignified Decrepitude.

I have had another title suggested, viz: "How to be a top climber without actually climbing". This is not only misleading—it makes a travesty of this article. One must assume that respect has been earned honourably on the field of battle and not by mere subterfuge. It is in order to maintain this respect, that one employs certain little subtleties that would ill befit a brash impostor.

In short, this is a symposium for Mountaineers—not mountebanks!

1. The "Off-Form" ploy

This one is as old as the hills but still widely used. Few climbers will admit to being "on form". Everyone would feel uneasy if they did.

Again, a climber who was "on form" during the morning can be feeling "off-form" by early afternoon. If an interval of forty-eight hours or so has elapsed between climbs, he may talk of being "out of condition". If the interval is a month or longer, he may justifiably consider himself to be "out of training". Unfortunately so many climbers take their training seriously nowadays (with press-ups, dumb-bells, running up the down-escalators in tube stations, etc.)—that it is unwise to be out of training when in the company of dedicated mountaineers. A friendly invitation to Bowles Mountaineering Gymnasium can be the natural outcome of such a remark.

2. The "Too Much Like Hard Work" ploy

This is the Englishman's favourite gambit when climbing (or not climbing) North of the Border. Many Scottish cliffs are admittedly remote by comparison with Shepherd's Crag, but I have heard this sort of generalisation directed at Glencoe, where you can scarcely leave the main road without bumping your head against an overhang. No, this simply will not do! Far more effective is the Sassenach Second Choice Gambit, viz.:

3. The "Chossy Climb" ploy

"Poxy", "Chossy", "Spastic" and "Rubbish" are all terms characteristically used by English and Welsh climbers to denigrate Scottish routes which they have either failed to climb or failed to find (without searching too minutely).

Eyewitness reports could in fact reveal that Spiderman made repeated attempts to overcome the crux, before he was ignominiously repulsed and left hanging in a tangle of slings and *étriers*, but this is completely at variance with the official Party Line, which stresses Spiderman's disgust on finding the initial holds cloaked in greenery. His aesthetic senses had been so offended that he had instantly abandoned the climb and spent the day more profitably in a nearby hostelry.

Spiderman's reputation remains untarnished. It is the luckless pioneers who are singled out for derision just as they were preparing to crow over his downfall—a neat demonstration of how to convert defeat into a moral triumph. A really selective "route gourmet" like Spiderman can sometimes spend years in a fruitless quest for perfection without ever finding a climb to which he can justifiably or morally commit himself.

4. The "Ice-Man" ploy

This is the exiled Scotsman's counter-ploy when lured on to English outcrops. "I'm a Snow and Ice Man myself!" is a fairly safe assertion at Harrison's where it is highly unlikely that you will be given the opportunity to demonstrate your skills.

Oddly enough the first time I heard this line it was spoken by an Englishman. The scene was an Alpine hut, at that time (1952) almost entirely populated by Oxbridge types—pleasant fellows, although all unmistakably tarred with the same brush, and handicapped by their common background. Amid this select group one particular rank outsider stuck out like a sore thumb. I was captivated by his facility for saying the wrong thing at the wrong time. ("I say! You two lads have got definite promise. If one of you gets himself killed would the other please look me up? I'm looking for a partner for the Brenva.")

This man had swallowed Smythe and Murray piecemeal and could regurgitate selected phrases from either author with gay abandon. His impact on the Establishment was shattering: "All this talk of VIs and A3s bores me to tears," he would announce in a loud voice, addressing no one in particular. "Show me the Englishman—Yes; show me the Englishman, I say—who can stand upright in his steps, square set to the slope, and hit home hard and true, striking from the shoulder! There must be very few of us Ice-Men left around. Ice-Manship may be a forgotten craft but it's still the Cornerstone of Mountaineering. Never forget that! Any fool can monkey about on rock overhangs but *it takes craft and cunning to beat the Brenva!*"

He got away with it too. The "Great Mixed Routes" are so seldom in condition that a dedicated Ice-man can remain in semi-permanent cold storage without much fear of exposure.

5. The "Secret Cliff" ploy

This dark horse is seldom seen in the Pass, but makes a belated appearance at closing time. He speaks slowly and reluctantly with a far-away look in his eyes. "We've been sizing up a new crag," he eventually admits after much probing, "amazing why nobody ever spotted it before, but then climbers don't get around much nowadays. . . . We're not giving away any details of course until we've worked it out. . . . Should be good for at least twenty more top-grade routes. . . ." etcetera.

None of these routes ever appear in print, but this too can be explained away at a later day by the Anti-Guide-Book ploy: "Why deprive others of the joys of original exploration? We don't want such a superb crag to suffer the fate of Cloggy, and become vulgarised by meaningless variations."

Evasiveness can be finely pointed.

"What route did you climb today then?"

"Dunno, we haven't named it yet!"—is perhaps one of the most spectacular.

All these ploys find their ideal medium in the "Solo Man Gambit".

6. The "Solo Man" gambit

The subtlety of this ploy is that no one, apart from Solo Man, knows how he spent the day. From the moment he disappears at the double over the first convenient hillock his movements are shrouded in mystery. He needs no accomplice, and he holds all the aces.

"Had a look at Vector today. . . . Quite thin. . . ." (Solo Man had indeed looked at Vector. He did not like what he saw.) *Or:* "Forgot the Guide Book. . . . No idea where I was . . . damn'd good route all the same! . . . Yes, it probably was a first ascent, but I won't be entering it. You can't expect me to remember details: one route is just the same as another as far as I'm concerned." *Or:* "Found the Tension Traverse pretty tricky . . . a rope would have been quite useful. . . ."

7. The "Responsible Family Man" ploy

This is the most stereotyped of all the non-climbing ploys. How often has the marriage altar (halter?) proved the graveyard of a mountaineer's ambitions? The little camp-follower who cooked the meals and darned everybody's socks is suddenly transformed into an all-demanding, insatiable virago whose grim disapproval makes strong men wilt in their *kletterschühe*. Climbing weekends become less and less frequent and, despite well-meant advice from climbing friends on the benefits of "the Pill", it is only a year before the union is blessed with child. In many cases this is the natural end of all things, but a few diehards still put in an annual appearance—pale shrunken ghosts, who glance nervously over their shoulders before they speak.

"Don't seem to get away much nowadays," they mutter despondently. "Can't take the same risks—unfair on the kids." So saying, they leap into their Volvos or Mini-Coopers and become power-crazy charioteers, mowing down crash-barriers and terrorising the walking populace. Back home they scream to a halt in a cloud of dust and shrink back into normal dimensions.

"Sorry you had to wait up for me, Dear—just dropped in for a quick one with the lads and got a bit carried away."

This is very effective because it contains an element of pathos, and brings a lump to the throat of the most hardened of Hard-Men. Some ageing climbers, no longer able to make the grade on the crags, have been known to contemplate matrimony as the only honourable way out.

8. The "Wrong Gear" ploy

With a little foresight it is always an easy matter to bring the wrong equipment for the day, and then allow everyone to share your vexation. Such a man will turn up for a winter assault on Point Five Gully, wearing brand new P.A.'s.

"Great God! I didn't expect to find snow on the Ben this late. Just my luck. . . ."

For a week-end's climbing at Harrison's he will have borrowed a pair of High Altitude Everest Boots.

"Just breaking them in for the Real Thing. Not much use on the small hold stuff but jolly good for the South Col."

I remember an American climber who survived an entire summer at Chamonix by means of this ploy.

"You're missing all the fine weather," we told him.

"I'm an Aid-man," he explained, "and I'm stuck here till my hardwear arrives. It was crated up in New York three weeks ago and the last I heard it was in Paris."

The elusive crate, in fact, never reached its destination. First it was in Cherbourg, then Paris, finally Chamonix. From Chamonix it was redirected to Paris, before the owner could stake his claim. We left him a month later still propping up the Juke Box in the Bar National.

"Some guys have all the goddammed luck," he complained bitterly.

9. The "Gammy Leg" ploy

A permanent physical disability can be a useful handicap, but before it can be turned to advantage it must be something immediately obvious. A wooden leg, for example. (Winthrop Young climbed the Grépon with a wooden leg, but he was unusual.)

Any lesser incapacity is scarcely worth the discomfort it entails. Everyone knows by now that Don Whillans used to perform with a whimsical knee-joint that was so unstable it dislocated every time he turned in his bed, but the same knee-joint carried him to Gaurisankar and back, with only occasional halts for realignment. Joe Brown, when not putting up new Extremes at Gogarth, slipped a disc in his back garden. Raymond Lambert, the Swiss Guide, climbed even better when all his toes had been amputated. This brought his centre of gravity nearer the footholds. There are many more tales of courage or triumph over adversity. Too many, in fact. Extracting sympathy from the present younger generation is like wringing blood from a stone. So if you still sport an old War Wound from the Dardenelles, your best bet is to suffer in silence.

10. The "Faulty Alarm-clock" ploy

Somebody ought to manufacture Faulty Alarm-clocks for weekend climbers. Far better to blame an inanimate object for your misfortunes, than to inculpate your companions. . . .

One acquaintance of mine, a Mr. X., always made a point of discussing the next morning's breakfast before turning in for the night. Companions, who assumed that he intended to rise and breakfast himself, were dismayed to waken at 10 a.m. to the sight of an irate Mr. X. pointing accusingly towards an alarm-clock which had mysteriously appeared at their bedside overnight.

"You promised to waken me when the alarm went off!" he thundered, "And here I've been, lying awake, not knowing the time, and now it's too late to attempt anything worthwhile! Really, this is too bad!" etcetera.

11. The "Föhn Wind" and other Bad Weather ploys

Writes René Desmaison with spine-chilling candour, "I have heard it said that it takes more courage to retreat than to advance. I cannot share these sentiments!" M. Desmaison is of course a Frenchman writing for Frenchmen, but he would scarcely get away with this sort of remark in the British *Alpine Journal*. Not by a long chalk. It strikes at the very foundations of British Alpinism and undermines our most deep-rooted traditional ploy— "Giving the Mountain Best".

It was during my first Alpine season that I came into contact with the ever popular Zermatt gambit. An elderly gentleman, wearing knickerbockers and armed with alpenstock, would totter out on to his hotel balcony, raising aloft one pre-moistened, trembling index finger.

"Aha!—I thought as much," he would chuckle grimly. "The Föhn Wind is in the offing! No climbing for you young fellow, for a week at least!"

I was a bit frustrated by this and the next time I went up to a hut I determined to follow the advice of local Alpine Guides. If they don't know, who does? Thirty-two Guides slept at the Couvercle Hut that night, and they all got up at 2 a.m. like a major volcanic eruption. One Guide, with an attractive female client in tow, walked out, prodded the snow with an ice-axe, sniffed the night air, and without a word retired to his bed. It later transpired that this was the celebrated X. X. Thirty-one silent Guides looked at each other, shook their heads, and retired likewise. We woke at 8 a.m. to find brilliant sunshine.

"Pourquoi?" I demanded wrathfully of one, "Pourquoi?" (It was one of the few French words at my disposal, so I used it twice.)

"X. X. a dit!" he said reverently, mentally crossing himself, "C'est trop dangereux!"

"Pourquoi?" I demanded again, not without reason.

"X. X. a dit!" he repeated, waving his arms towards a cloudless horizon, "Tempête de neige, qui va venir bientôt sans doubt."

The last time I saw X. X. he was heading for the valley with the attractive blonde in close attendance. It was the first day of what proved to be a ten-day record heat wave. I remembered the time-honoured Victorian advice, "Follow the Old Guide—he knows best!" There was more than a grain of truth in that statement. . . .

In the hands of a reliable weather-lore expert the Bad Weather ploy can be practically infallible. Such a man can spend an entire Alpine season without setting boot to rock, simply by following the bad weather around, and consistently turning up in the wrong place at the wrong time.

12. The "Greater Ranges" ploy

Historians tell us that Frank Smythe only began to function properly above 20,000 feet. This adds up to a pretty considerable handicap, when you consider how much of his life must have been spent at lower altitudes. It is all part of the mystique which surrounds The Men who are expected to Go High.

For this ploy some previous Himalayan experience is essential; it may involve a tourist weekend in Katmandu, a transcendental meditation with the Maharishi. Once the aura has formed, you can hardly go wrong. You can patrol the foot of Stanage with all the invested authority of an Everester. No one expects you to climb. It is enough that you retain a soft spot for your humble origins.

"This is all very different from the South Col!" you can remark crisply, as you watch bikini-clad girls swarming over the rocks like chameleons. Any off-the-cuff comment of this nature goes down well, and gives them something to talk about after you have moved on. As I said before, nobody really expects a man who has survived the South Col to risk his neck on a paltry outcrop.

"I'm a Gritstone Man myself!" you can admit with pride, and then proceed to qualify the statement, "But let us keep our sense of proportion, and remember that British crags are not an end in themselves but a Springboard to the Greater Ranges. The Battle of Waterloo was won on the playing-fields of Eton! That is something we must all remember. . . . "

Old Winthrop Young summed it all up in his Valedictory

Address to the Alpine Club, "These armies of young boys and girls practising their wholesome open-air callisthenics, flooding the valleys in hale and hearty chase of pins-and-needles upon which to thread their athletic limbs upside down. . . . What was their love to ours? . . . the pursuit of the distant white Domes . . . etc. . . . etc. . . . etc."

13. The "Base Camp Martyr" ploy

This philanthropic character always contrives to be the Odd Man Out.

"Look here, chaps! Let's be sensible about this. A rope of two makes much faster time than a threesome, and I'm only going to hold you back. It's the team effort that counts, after all. If we get Two Men to the Top we will not have failed! I may be kicking my heels at base camp but I'll be with you in spirit: you both know that. Good Luck and Good Hunting!"

14. The "Old Man of the Mountains" ploy

The essence of this ploy is that you cannot teach an Old Dog new tricks, viz:

"Play up, and play the game—but learn the rules first. Ignore the rules, and the game is no longer worth playing. Present-day rock acrobats don't accept exposure as part of the game. They protect themselves every yard of the way with ridiculous little gadgets of all shapes and sizes. The designations are unimportant —they are un-British in name and un-British in nature! Gone are the days of Kirkus and Edwards, when a leader had sufficient moral conviction to run out 150 feet of lightweight hemp before taking a hitch! Who wants to join the clanking Slab-queues to witness the crucifixion of a long-loved friend. I found *this* at Abraham's Ledge on the Crowberry last week!" (unwrapping a rusty piton which he carries around for this purpose). "Covet it young man at your peril! My race may be run, but never let it be said that I helped beget a generation of Cream-Puff climbers."

To qualify for the Hob-Nail Brigade the speaker need not have reached the allotted three-score-and-ten, but he should at least cultivate an aura of venerability and familiarise himself with the appropriate vocabulary, viz.:

Acrobats, monkeys, engineers, technicians, and steeple-jacks	the Modern Generation
hare-brained escapade	a new route
Munich mechanisation	artificial climbing
Death-or-Glory fanatics	Hard-men
Dangle-and-Whack merchants	Aid-men
The Golden Age	pre-1930
The Iron Age	post-1930
A sound climber	an old climber
A cautious climber	a very slow climber
A mature climber	an ageing incompetent
A die-hard traditionalist	a rude old man
Unjustifiable	perhaps quite hard
Utterly unjustifiable	quite hard
A great mixed route	a snow plod
A courageous decision	chickening out
An Alpine Start	the time to leave the Bar National

THE SHAPE OF THINGS TO COME

EXPLANATORY NOTE

A recent issue of *Mountain* provides the startling information that 1 per cent of the population are now active climbers—a threefold increase in less than a decade. If this trend is continued we expect that by the year A.D. 2000 the majority of the British public will be active climbers. Mountaineering will have supplanted Association Football as the most popular national pastime. There will be an acute shortage of climbable rock. And climbing journalism will have geared itself to keep pace with popular demand. The impact that these developments will make on our everyday lives can be best appreciated from examining the bi-millenary issue of *Mountain*—or *Wilson's Weekly* (as it will then be known). . . .

WILSON'S WEEKLY
(incorporating *Mountain*)

KEN WILSON
(The Voice of Mountaineering)

BRINGS YOU
THE LATEST WITH THE GREATEST

★   ★   ★

WHETHER YOU ARE . . .

AN ARMCHAIR MOUNTAINEER . . .

OR A NORTH WALL VIRTUOSO . . .

YOU CANNOT AFFORD TO IGNORE

WILSON'S WEEKLY
THE PAPER THAT EVERY CLIMBER IS SEETHING ABOUT!

EQUIPMENT NOTES

A critical analysis by Our Technical Expert Peter Crewant of a New Product

This month's most enlightened product comes from the Flog workshop. It is an interesting device comprising 17 separate high tensile chrome molybdenum components matched together with incredible cunning to form an intricate interlocking many-faceted, ingenious device of quite extraordinary complexity.

Its function is not as yet fully understood but research continues. A prototype model is on display at the Demolen showrooms and Flog experts have invited distinguished climbing visitors to put a name to the new device, or to list the various uses to which it might be put. A prototype model is offered free of charge to the climber with the most original suggestions. It weighs (approximately) 35 lbs. 7 ozs. and will be marketed for 99 N.C.

Obviously this is going to be an important addition to the armamentarium and an essential investment for every informed young climber.

BOOK CORNER

Recommended Reading:

EVEREST ON BOARDS. This is a "must" for all skiers. A colourful history of skiing on Mount Everest. The author is a three times winner of the South Col Grand Slalom.

THE UPPER SIXTH VS. THE WHITE SPIDER. Good Yuletide entertainment for the very young. The stunning adventures of one hundred school boys with their popular Gym master on the North Wall of the Eiger.

THE MARRIAGE ART IN ETRIERS. Complete and unabridged. A frank fearless guide for the young climbing couple. The book is clearly and concisely illustrated by John Cleare, who has portrayed his subjects with dignity and sincerity.

THE FEMININE VIEWPOINT

We predict that this year's Baudrier will be more flesh hugging than ever before and Tiger's Webs will reveal all, or nearly all, for the first time. We also predict that Joe Brown, whose Autumn collection comes out next week, will slash 6 inches off the hemline.

THE WORLD OF WILSON
(*A weekly chronicle of World Events*)

Hoy Outrage! New Development

The sensational collapse of Scotland's far-famed sea stack, the Old Man of Hoy, was described yesterday at Scottish Mountaineering Club Headquarters as an "irreplaceable loss".

Police authorities, although understandably cautious, trace a possible link between the latest disaster and the recent Napes Needle explosions. "We have not yet ruled out the possibility of sabotage by a retaliatory activist group," commented a uniformed official.

Police wish to interview two young climbers, speaking with a marked Southern accent, who were seen unloading gelignite from a boat shortly before the disaster and who, it is thought, may be able to help them in their inquiries. "If as we suspect they have nothing to hide, let them come forward and say so. They have nothing to fear," said Chief Constable MacHooter.

Meanwhile the search continues, and Police are leaving no stone unturned.

Explorer Flies in to Tumultuous Welcome: Dennis Mobbed

Wildly cheering crowds mobbed explorer, Dennis Gray, when the star flew in to London Airport yesterday at the end of his successful Andean campaign. Delirious fans, including many Helly Hansened, long-gartered schoolgirls, screamed and sighed ecstatically as their hero was hustled into a waiting helicopter by two rows of riot squad Police, armed with truncheons. "I guess the kids remember me," commented the weather-beaten, sun-scorched veteran. He had escaped recognition for a brief instant because of the dark glasses, which he wears following his recent snow blindness.

What had he missed most at the high camps on Apoplectica?

"My favourite Yorkshire pudding, of course," quipped the gnarled explorer.

"What happened up there when the going got tough?" shouted one reporter. "Buy Dennis's next disc and find out," snapped his agent. "Dennis will not be pulling punches, I can assure you."

Casualties Soar

Casualty figures for last month reached a new peak it was revealed yesterday in a BMC press release. "This is a very welcome trend," said a spokesman. "It shows that ever-increasing numbers of young people are being attracted to our National sport. Thanks are due in part to the BBC. Intensive coverage of recent climbs has had a lot to do with the current upsurge of enthusiasm.

Highlanders' Anger Mounts

With the introduction of Giant Snow Making Machines at all major English outcrops, Scottish Highlands hoteliers face another lean winter. "We are not dismayed," a well-known climbing publican told me. "Artificial snow is not the same as the real thing, as any Scots mountaineer will tell you. And where, pray, can you enjoy a real Cairngorm blizzard except in our beloved Cairngorms? That is something your English snowmakers have not yet considered!"

"*Save the Alpine Club*" *Campaign*

"Any climber with a sense of history, or who can still remember the Golden Age of Mountaineering, has a bounden duty to support this worthy cause," declared Lord Hunt launching a £100,000 fund-raising campaign to save the Alpine Club, former nursery of such all-time greats as Ed "Matterhorn" Whymper. The proposed dissolution comes as no surprise. Beset by financial difficulties and badgered by relegation problems the South Audley Street combine had seemed bound for downstairs for some weeks now. Their Chairman told our reporter, "The loss of several key players to the professional ranks has seriously weakened our playing strength. It's a sad fact but the crowds don't seem to turn out for us any more. Only a handful of spectators gathered to cheer on the 'Amateurs' at Llwedd last weekend and this was always one of our happy hunting grounds. The old lads all played their hearts out (literally, in one case I regret to say). If I have to single out anyone for praise it must be our stouthearted anchorman Major Bollard, who took the brunt of several long falls, stopping all but one, but nevertheless stuck to his onerous task with commendable fortitude."

SPORTS ROUND-UP
MacPiton wants away £100,000 Price Tag

Veteran Scots striker Hamish MacPiton will almost certainly sign for Sestogrado Milan this week. That is my confident prediction, writes our roving columnist *Ken Wilson*. As part of the player-cash deal the Italian Club have offered the Creag Dhu ten Cortina Squirrels in addition to the £100,000 already quoted.

"I feel my style is more suited to Continental Climbing Grounds and that my future lies with Sestogrado," the tartan Tiger told me as he relaxed in his luxury Glencoe swimming pool. "It is true that I was a little upset to be dropped last year," he admitted ruefully. MacPiton has only recently resumed with the Reserves following a lengthy spell in hospital with injuries he sustained on impact.

Give up now, Joe! Veteran Cragsman's Inept Display

When will ageing grey-haired veteran Joe Brown hang up his climbing boots? That is the question thousands of Rock and Ice supporters are asking following last Saturday's crushing defeat by visiting Alpha. Looking all of his sixty years, the former Llanberis Idol saved his worst display of the season for this vital "needle" fixture. The Human Fly appeared to be short of pace and could scarcely raise a gallop at the finish. Daniel Boone never gave up trying, but was too often left to plough a lone furrow in the middle of the pitch. The remaining members seem to be infected with their General's apathy, and found difficulty in keeping their footing on the slippery surface.

For Alpha the towering Boysen was outstanding, but McHardy was booked for showing dissent, and will be expelled.

The "Lost Outcrop" of Helsby: A Tragedy of our Times

"It's P.A.s only" from now on for all sandstone devotees. This drastic ruling follows the news that the former sandstone outcrop at Helsby has been completely eroded into the hillside by "jack booted buckeroos, who strut across the Mountain Stage like Nazi Gauleiters". These hard hitting words aimed at climbers who still favour Composition Soles, formed part of the moving funeral oration delivered over the crumbling remains of one of Britain's earliest climbing grounds, where this week-end over a thousand "Friends of Helsby" made a sad pilgrimage to pay their last respects.

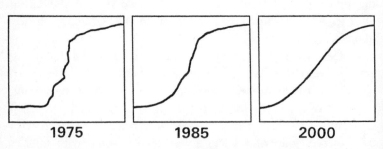

1975   **1985**   **2000**

Profile of a Dying Crag   A classic example of Hold Erosion

by our lobby correspondent Ken Wilson

"Access" Bill gets Second Reading

Welsh Farmers and Peasants who seek to impede climbers in the lawful pursuit of their legitimate pastime by means of concealed ditches, electric fences and unchained sheepdogs will in future face severe penalties. This is the substance of a new Bill which empowers climbing officials and stewards "to take all necessary steps" to ensure unrestricted access at all times to areas of live rock, wherever they may exist.

Quarry Overlords Face Summit Confrontation; Sports Minister promises Showdown

If returned at the next Election the Liberal Party intend to re-nationalize the Quarries.

"There is a shortage of good rock in Britain today," said Sports Minister Mike Banks, hinting at lack of co-operation from the Quarry Owners Association. "All over the country, every week-end long-suffering climbers are queueing up on grossly overcrowded outcrops while, behind their barbed-wire barricades, the Quarry Overlords plot the destruction of complex ridges and *arêtes*, whose ephemeral delights the average climber-in-the-street may not savour." He suggests the appointment of a Watchdog Committee of the BMC to vet all future planned excavations so that these may be carried out in such a way as to conform with accepted mountaineering aesthetic standards.

"We must take action to safeguard our Heritage," he told a frantically cheering crowd.

S.N.P. leaders see this as a belated effort to capture the Floating Climber Vote. They have put forward alternative proposals aimed at further extending pre-existing cliffs, in order to provide a greater scope and variety of climbs for all categories of climber. "We see this as the only realistic solution to the problem," declared Shadow Minister Malcolm Slesser, ridiculing Lord Banks' suggestions. "Do not forget," he added, "that it was an S.N.P. administration which provided Climbing Walls in every school playground and created a Chair of Mountaineering at each of our major universities. Some of us are old enough to remember the days when our mountain arenas were empty wastelands where you might search vainly for hours without encountering a single fellow human-being. We've put an end to all that, Thank God, but our work is not yet done. May I remind many climbing friends that we in S.N.P. are pledged to meet the rising costs of Mountain Rescue by taxing the non-climbing Public, who can well afford to pay. Why should *we* the climbers finance a service which we provide. The situation is wholly absurd."

THIS WEEK'S MAIN FEATURE: FACE TO FACE (Number 6)
KEN WILSON, *The Voice of Mountaineering meets* GRIFF FIFI!
(*A Recorded Interview*):

WILSON: Introducing this week's Man of the Mountains—Griff Fifi. Griff, I bring you felicitations from the readers of *Wilson's Weekly*, the paper every climber is seething about.

FIFI: The pleasure is mine.

WILSON: Last year, you—Griff Fifi—carried off the supreme accolade when you were awarded the coveted Golden Bong of Grindelwald. Can we describe this as the most thrilling moment of your star-studded career?

FIFI: You can*not*. The most thrilling moment of my star-studded career was watching Ken Skyhook plummet off the Corner. That punk deserved all he got.

WILSON: Very understandable. You and Ken were always re-nowned rivals. Your close friends tell me this was the only occasion you have been known to smile. Is that so?

FIFI: Let's just say that the moment had its lighter aspects.

WILSON: Anyway let us now turn back the pages to the day when you made your début as humble Feed Man for the Pied Elephant second string. Do you still remember that far back?

FIFI: Yes. Mind I'm not saying that you got to be cultured to be a good Feed Man. You don't. The Feed Man's job is to keep the ammunition moving up the pipeline. He spends most of the game either squatting in his *étriers* or slipping jumars up the feed-line. But he ain't cultured.

WILSON: Anyway—with your quite amazing versatility it wasn't long before you earned a reputation as an all-round general purpose utility player. Is it true that you often *got in* as Anchor Man during your spell with Nordwand Munich, the crack Teuton combine?

FIFI: This is quite correct. In fact I lost count of the falling lead men I've stopped. They tell me I got the horniest hands in the game. Never wore gloves of course, guess that's my secret!

WILSON: And then, of course, you finally carved your personal niche in the Halls of Fame when you took over as No. 1 Lead Man for the Rockhoppers, a position that you quickly made your own. To what special training do you attribute your incredible successes?

FIFI: I graduated from the School of Hard Knocks, man. You either got it or you ain't got it and there's always some young punk breathing down your short neck and waiting to try your boots for size. Right now I got more metal plating in my skull than you have bone, man, but I can't afford to let up my standards. I got a sense of duty to my fans, I guess. One of these days I'm bound for the Long Ride through Space, but till that comes I aim to keep on betting in the iron and reaching towards those distant goddamned clouds.

WILSON: And on that stirring note of high endeavour, we must bring this interesting discussion to a close. In conclusion I would like you to accept this handsome volume entitled

This is your life, Griff Fifi

(*Fanfare of trumpets and unprecedented enthusiasm*)

PART IV
Verse

CAIRNGORM TIGER

Away up North
In Kincorth
Garthdee or Kaimhill*
Tricouni tricksters—they top the bill
Joe Brown
Look Down
From your pillar of fame
Cairngorm Tiger is my name.

Tune: When the Midnight Choo Choo leaves for Alabam

When the Climbers' Special pulls out for Braemar
At three fifteen from Aberdeen†
They'll be heading for the crags of Lochnagar
There'll be V.S. climbers, grey old timers, anyone, anyone
For the cliffs of Skye are very seldom dry
    And that's the reason why
    Everyone has gone . . . on . . .
    Ben a'Bhùird and Lochnagar
    That's where all the good routes are
    All Aboard, all aboard, all aboard the Three Fifteen.

* The three main cantonments of Aberdeen which gave birth to the Pioneers of the Golden Age (1950–60).

† In those bad old days when climbers were forced to work for a living and nobody owned a motor car everybody went to the hills in a special bus supplied by Strachans Ltd, which left Bon Accord Square, Aberdeen, at 3.15 p.m. every Saturday.

AIGUILLES DES CAIRNGORMS

(*The Alps: 1954*)

Tune: The Mountains of Mourne

Oh Chamonix's really a wonderful sight
There's the cafés by day and the pictures at night
They're all wearin' duvets, they look awful neat
And everyone laughed as I walked down the street
"For Blicks Old Tricounis are all very well
But quite out of place here" remarked Monsieur Schnell
So I told him his Friends were no use to me
Where the Aiguilles des Cairngorms sweep down to the Dee.

I purchased a duvet and a cagoule as well
On the earnest advice of my friend Monsieur Schnell
He said "Now your outfit is très elegant—
Yet it lacks one essential—a pied d'elephant."
But later when I was alone in the tent
I counted up all the money I'd spent
And thought of my creditors waiting for me
Where the Aiguilles des Cairngorms sweep down to the Dee.

I met Armand Charlet he said with a frown
"I think if you're British you climb with Joe Brown?
So tell me how many North Faces you've done?"
He sighed with dismay when I answered him "None".
"I climb in the Cairngorms you'll know of their fame?"
He said "I-have-*not*-even-heard-of-the-name".
Back home in the Cairngorms they all would agree
What an ignorant bastard old Charlet must be.

The bloated aristocrats sip their champagne
As the corpses come down in the Montenvers train
A telescope stands at the head of a queue
"Ten francs a time for a peep at the Dru".

They tell me that I should be hiring a guide
But then it's not only a question of pride
For he's only a poor Aberdonian you see
Where the Aiguilles des Cairngorms sweep down to the Dee.

I stopped at the Briolay I asked for advice
Lord Wrangham remarked that the Walker was "nice"
They told me the Grépon was much overdone
They talked of the Brenva but only in fun.
But I think the Midi's a far finer peak
It's only one hour in the téléphérique
But after all that you'll find that you might as well be
Where the Aiguilles des Cairngorms roll down to the Dee.

I've drunk all their wine and it's gone to my head
Now all that I want is to die in my bed
The gendarmes were kind when they saw me in pain
They said they'd return when I'm sober again
I dreamt that I followed a bright shining star
To the friends who are drinking tonight in Braemar
So I'll wait for the whisky that's waiting for me
Where the Aiguilles des Cairngorms roll down to the Dee.

So it's back to the Cairngorms, the Friends who are true
And the lassies who speak the same language as you
To hell with the gauloises and garlic and wine
Its bradies and chips in the old Brauchdryne
To the mountains where Smith is a time honoured name
And a handshake from Brooker the passport to fame
Wherever I wander, my heart it will be
Where the Aigulles des Cairngorms sweep down to the Dee.

THE CAIRNGORM CLUB MEET'S CIRCULAR CALYPSO

Any appropriate calypso tune: the original was the Cricket Calypso "Ramadhin and Valentine"

At 6.30 in Golden Square
All the Cairngorm Veterans will be there
And the hazardous approach
Will be made by motor coach
With expert mountaineers indeed—
Perkins, Smithy and Birnie Reid.

All communications
Regarding meets and excursions
Must be addressed only
To the Meets Secretary
And it is requested on no pretence
To ring him at his residence.

During the return journey
Arrangements will be made for tea
Members are asked to see
That guests are suitably
Equipped for any emergency
By order of the Secretary.

Of all the climbs on Lochnagar
The Black Spout is the best by far
While from The Ballochbuie
You can always climb the Stuic
But the pitch to make the expert blanch
Is the Chockstone in the Left Hand Branch.

EXCELSIOR
(*A Braemar Ballad*)

The shades of night were falling fast
As from the Fife a man was cast
He lay forgotten on the snow
His friends had left an hour ago.

"A taxi to the Derry Gate
The night is cold, the hour is late"
The woman shook her aged head
"The taxi driver's gone to bed."

But suddenly to his surprise
A maiden stood before his eyes
She said to him "'Tis cold you be
You won't be cold in bed with me."

He said "My comrades wait for me
I cannot stay the night with thee."
And as he answered with a sigh
A tear stood in his bright blue eye.

The cold north wind blew down the glen
The mist lay low upon the Ben
His footsteps lost in drifting snow
He staggered blindly to and fro.

They found the corpse beneath the ice
They left a stone with this device:
"He died Alone—It came to pass
From mixing whiskies with his Bass."

ACH, MEIN GROSSEN BOTEN

*(A spurious Teutonic version of the S.M.C. perennial "My Big
Hobnailers")*

Oh the *Marteau-Piolet* it hangs on the wall,
The hammers and the slings and the drills and all,
But we'll scrape off all the mud, and we'll polish off the blood
And go up to the mountains in the snow!
Let the pitons rattle, as we go to battle,
Sound the ever-ringing peal of steel on steel!
Let the happy chink of the old snaplink
Echo o'er the mountains and the snow!

    Ach! Mein Grossen Boten!
    (Auf! Mein Kletterschühen)
    Ach! Mein Grossen Boten!
    How they speak of frozen feet, and lengthy stride o'er
      Bergschrund wide—
    Ach! Mein Grossen Boten!
    Ach! Mein Grossen Boten!
    Memories raise of hellish days upon the Eigerwand.

Then our V.S. men will assault the Ben,
Profanities will echo up and down the glen,
And every little Tiger will be training for the Eiger
When we go up to the mountains in the snow.
Then our cragsmen bold will swarm down the shoots
And avalanche the tourists on the tourists' routes,
While others, never flagging, Munro-baggers are debagging
When we go up to the mountains in the snow!

In the grim grey dawn, we struggle ever on
Though the nights are long in the *Pied d'Elephant*,
Though the heartbeat quickens, and the stonefall sickens
When we go up to the mountains in the snow.

And when the grim day's done, and the victory's won,
We drink a *Tutti Frutti* to Giusto Gervasutti,
  All the Bergkameraden will return to Inverarnan
Descending from the mountains through the snow!

Salvationists who amble up an entertaining scramble
Or quietly disappear upon a solitary ramble
Should be made to sweat with fear on an Amiable Severe
When we go up to the mountains in the snow
We'll slacken off the chockstones for the vital thread belay
Every Thank God Hold will be prised away
We'll block off all their through routes, make their old routes
  into new routes
When we go up to the mountains in the snow.

  Ach! Mein Grossen Boten
  Ach! Mein Grossen Boten
  How they tell of days of Hell with Tommy Weir or
    Doktor Bell
(*or,* Dreams arose of the old Kinghaus, and ringing cries of
    "Rauss, Rauss, Rauss!" (*shouted or screamed*))
  Ach! Mein Grossen Boten
  Ach! Mein Grossen Boten
  Throes disclose of toes that froze upon the Eigerwand.

THE S.M.C. VETERANS' SONG

(H. MacInnes—slightly amended T. W. P.)

Tune: The Admiral's Song from "Pinafore"

On Saturday I leave the town
And I head for the hills with a serious frown
I've a steady head and sturdy legs
And I scorn the city and its drunken dregs
I am so tough and fit you see
They made me a member of the S.M.C. } × 2

On Buchaille's cliffs I climb all day
And you'll hear my grunts of ecstasy
I hew big steps with mighty blows
High up in the gully where the Raven goes
Because I climb so daringly
They made me a member of the S.M.C. } × 2

And then at last a woman came
Heard down south of my climbing fame
She cooked my meals, she kept me warm
Belayed me well in the fiercest storm
She was so young and so shapely
She couldn't be a member of the L.A.C. } × 2

But now I climb my hills from afar
And totter into the nearest bar
And when I've downed some whisky neat
The tales that I tell are not discreet
I shoot the bull so convincingly
I'm an Honorary member of the S.M.C. } × 2

MACINNES'S MOUNTAIN PATROL

Inspired by a Press cutting which quoted Hamish as saying:
"The time is not far distant when Dogs will replace Policemen
as Mountain Rescuers."

Dedicated to Scotland's leading philanthropist and his gallant
pack of Avalanche Dogs.

Tune: Verse "Anthony Clarke"
Chorus "*The Four Legged Friend*", or anything else that
comes to mind

Ghillies and shepherds are shouting Bravo
For Hamish MacInnes, the Pride of Glencoe
There'll be no mercy missions, no marathon slog
Just lift your receiver and ask them for DOG

Chorus: That four legged friend, that four legged friend
He'll never let you down
When the Heat is on, you have only to send
For that wonderful one two three four legged
friend.

Deceased on the piste, or deranged on the schist,
Maimed in the mountains, marooned in the mist,
Dead or dismembered, the victim is found
By Hamish MacInnes's Merciful Hound.

Chorus: That four legged friend, etc.

Occasional mischief is wrought by the dogs
On Englishmen, Irishmen, Welshmen and Wogs
Their only concern is to further the lot
Of the blue blooded true blooded patriot Scot.

They come from their Kennels to answer the call
Cool, calm and courageous the Canine Patrol
Sniffing the boulders and scratching the snow
They've left their mark on each crag in the Coe.

Chorus: Those four legged friends, etc.

RED PIQUE

(*The Alpine Club Song*)

What did you learn at the Alpine Club
The Alpine Club, The Alpine Club
What did you learn at the Alpine Club
Three cheers for the old A.C.

I learned "Red Peak" was most unfair
'Cos McNaught-Davis doesn't swear
We must not be too hard on Ted
Ted's well fed but he's well bred
I learned Wraith Jones was hurt to the core
He swore he'd take his case to law
Wraith has a novel alibi:
"Tape Recorders *always* lie".

I learned George Lowe was very blue
He didn't leave because of Sue
George was a conscientious lad
And felt he should go home with Dad.
What did you learn about Derek Bull
The gay young blade of the Oxford School
Everyone says that he was there
But no one knows exactly where.

The Scottish bunch were rather dour
Their attitude was pretty poor
They won't be asked on another stunt
By the Alpine Club or Colonel Hunt
The moral is—we can't afford
To lose George Band or Michael Ward
Our proudest victories have been won
By chaps like Anthony Rawlinson.

Customs change and so alas
We now include the working class
So we invited Good Old Joe
To come along and join the show
He played his part, he fitted in
He justified our faith in him
We want the climbing world to know—
That the chaps all got on well with Joe.

I learned that the Russians are my friends
It's up to us to make amends
They trust Sir John 'cos he's a Knight
He's never wrong, he's always right
The flags are down, Sir John's in tears
No more trips to the High Pamirs
No more permits for the chaps . . .
Because of Malcolm Slesser's lapse.

The Noble Blood of an English Peer
Adapts to a rarefied atmosphere
And that is why the Old School Tie
May be expected to Go High.
Up they go! DAMN good show!
Stamping steps in the Virgin Snow
Hey nonny No! Fol dol dol!
Jolly John Hunt and the Old South Col.

Credo: Our climbing leaders are no fools
They went to the very best Public Schools
You'll never go wrong with Everest Men
So we select them again and again
Again and again and again and again
You won't go wrong with Everest Men
They went to the very best Public Schools
They play the game, they know the rules.

*So let's all join the Alpine Club
The Alpine Club, the Alpine Club
Let's all join the Alpine Club
Huzzah for the old A.C.!

One last question for Sir John
Where have all the hard men gone?
Good Old Joe! Why not Don?
Where was Christian Bonington?
Sir John replied "The mountaineers
Who showed the flag in the High Pamirs
Were men of charm and tact and skill
Overflowing with goodwill!"

Chorus: That's what I learned at the Alpine Club, etc.

* As an optional extra the choruses may be performed by Morris dancers wearing traditional costume.

ANNAPURNA

Tune: Twenty Tiny Fingers

Twenty frozen fingers, twenty frozen toes
Two blistered faces, frostbite on the nose
One looks like Herzog, who dropped his gloves on top
And Lachenal tripped and fell, thought he'd never stop.
    Bop bop bop bop bop bop bop bop bop.

"Take me down to Oudot" was all that he would say
"He'll know what to do now", said Lionel Terray
"Your blood is like black pudding" said Oudot, with his
  knife
"It is not too late to amputate if I can save your life".
Chop chop chop chop chop chop chop chop chop.

No tiny fingers, No tiny toes
The memory lingers but the digit goes
In an Eastern Railway carriage, where the River Ganges
  flows
There are Twenty Tiny Fingers and Twenty Tiny Toes.
Chop chop chop chop chop chop chop chop chop.

TWO TINY FIGURES

Tune: The Eigerwand

Two tiny figures on the ghastly north wall;
And a hungry great bergschrund, just right for a fall;
The avalanches roar, and the thunder-clouds boom,
And the black shiny rocks are like walls of a tomb.

There's a crack in the distance and an ominous roar,
The leader looked up and he silently swore
As a hail of large boulders, all jagged and red
And his blood-crusted fingers were clasped on his head.

With his last dying seconds he hung grimly on,
And he thought of the glory that was then all gone,
While his second still anchored to a piton below
Saw a bloody red circle appear in the snow.

With fingers all crippled and cramped with the ice,
He scraped at the knot clamped tight like a vice.
A cold perspiration broke out on his face,
As the ghastly cadaver came ripping through space.

A sickening jerk tore the rope from his grip—
Out sprang the piton, away flew the clip.
Out in a giant parabola he flew—
A small hurtling object outlined in the blue.

A thousand feet down he wedged in a crack,
With the spike of his ice axe lodged in his back.
His second still hanging on an unbroken line
With a constant velocity revolved on his spine.

For two desperate days and a terrible night
They spurred themselves on in their desperate fight;
Let the Valkyries howl in the pitiless sky—
But the Führer has ordered: You will conquer or die.

A climber has fallen, but why let us mourn?
For each one that dies, there are two to be born.
Ready to rise at the Führer's command,
To conquer or die on the grim Eigerwand.

BALLAD OF BILL MURRAY
Tune: Ballad of Jesse James

Bill Murray was a lad, who climbed on many crags
In the years before the war
For it was the Golden Age when he strode across the stage
In those grand old days of yore
    With Mackenzie and MacAlpine and Tom Mackinnon
      too
    That philosophic, philanthropic crew,
  They shattered the spell of the mighty Doctor Bell
  They were all good men and true.

'Twas in the Clachaig Gully that young Murray rose to fame
On the slabs of the Great Cave Pitch
Where other men had failed, his experience prevailed
And he crossed that fateful ditch—
On the Wall of Jericho, they shouted "Will it go?"
As he hung on a hair-trigger hold
He answered not a word and he rose like a bird
Through the mud and the slime and the cold.
    With Mackenzie . . . etc.

In the gullies of Glencoe they trod the virgin snow
With Mackenzie to lead in the van
With hawk nose distended and blue eyes flashing fire
He was more like a God than a man
They plied the ashen shaft, applied their native craft
Standing square, hitting home, hard and true
And they climbed their hardest routes in tricouni-studded boots
There was nothing that those heroes wouldn't do.
    With Mackenzie . . . etc.

In that Tournament on Ice, Death or Glory was the price
For those knights in shining armour long ago—
You must forage for yourself on that ghastly Garicks Shelf
With every handhold buried deep in snow.

Murray did his Devil's Dance on each microscopic stance
Recording his impressions of the view,
There was green ice in the chimneys and black ice at the crux
And not a single piton or a screw—
    With Mackenzie . . . etc.

THE JOE BROWN SONG
Tune: North to Alaska

Many tales are told of climbers bold
Who perished in the snow
But this is a rhyme of the rise to fame
Of a working lad named Joe.
He came from good old Manchester
That quaint, old-fashioned town
And his name became a legend—
The legend of Joe Brown.

> We've sung it once, we'll sing it twice
> He's the hardest man in the Rock and Ice
> He's marvellous—he's fabulous,
> He's a wonder man is Joe.

He first laid hand upon a crag
In the year of Forty-nine
He'd nowt but pluck, beginner's luck
And his mother's washing line.
He scaled the gritstone classics
With unprecedented skill—
His fame soon reached the Gwryd,
Likewise the Dungeon Ghyll.

> We've sung it once, . . . etc.

In the shadow of Dinas Cromlech
Where luckless leaders fall
The Corner it was towering high
And Joe uncommon small
But his heart was as big as the mountain,
And his nerves were made of steel—
It had to go, or so would Joe,
In a monumental peel.

We've sung it once, . . . etc.

He crossed the sea to Chamonix
And to show what he could do,
He knocked three days off the record time
For the west face of the Dru—
On the unclimbed face of the Blaitière,
The crux had tumbled down—
But he cracked the crux by the crucial crack
Now known as the fissure Brown.

We've sung it once, . . . etc.

When Evans raised his volunteers
For faraway Nepal
'Twas young Joe Brown that hurried down
To rally to the call
On Mighty Kangchenjunga
His country's banners blow
And the lad that raised the standard
Was known by the name of Joe.

We've sung it once, . . . etc.

In the cold, cold Karakoram
Where crags are five miles high,
The best in France had seen the chance
To pass us on the sly.
You may talk of Keller, Contamine,
Magnone, Paragot,
The man of the hour on the Mustagh Tower
Was known by the name of Joe.

We've sung it once, . . . etc.

With Colonel Hunt on the Russian Front
He paved the Paths of Peace
And helped to bridge the gulf that lay

Between the West and East
That Climbers all might Brothers be
In the Kingdom of the Snow
And the lad who led the Summit Talks
Was known as Comrade Joe.

     We've sung it once, . . . etc.

He's happy as an eagle
Soaring up the face
Swinging in his *étriers*
On a thousand feet of space
You should see him grin where the holds are thin
On an overhanging wall
He's known to every nig nog
As the Man who'll Never Fall.

     We've sung it once, . . . etc.

He's like a Human Spider
Clinging to the wall
Suction, Faith and Friction
And nothing else at all
But the secret of his success
Is his most amazing knack
Of hanging from a hand-jam
In an overhanging crack.

     We've sung it once, . . . etc.

But now Joe Brown has settled down
To raise a family
He's wedded to a local lass
By name of Valerie
But he sometimes takes his exercise
On Cloggy's gentle heights
When he isn't exercising
His matrimonial rights.

We've sung it once, . . . etc.

Some say Joe Brown is sinking down
To mediocrity
He even climbs with useless types
Like Dennis Gray and me
He's lost the pace to stay the race
And keep up with the van
And Baron Brown that tragic clown
Is now an also ran.

> They sung it once let that suffice
> For the Faded Flower of the Rock & Ice
> What's he doing? He's canoeing!
> Old Long gone Hand-Jam Joe.

Thus said Martin Boysen
And young Bas Ingle too
Ranting Allan Austen
And Peter "Motley" Crew.
When from the outer darkness
A voice like thunder spake
As Baron Brown, with troubled frown
From slumber did awake.

> He showed 'em once, he'll show 'em twice
> The Grand Old Man of the Rock and Ice
> He's marvellous, he's fabulous
> He's a Wonder man is Joe.

ONWARD, CHRISTIAN BONINGTON

Onward, Christian Bonington, of the A.C.G.
  Write another page of Alpine history
  He has climbed the Eigerwand, he has climbed the Dru—
  For a mere ten thousand francs, he will climb with you:
Onward, C. . . . B. . . . , of the A.C.G.
  If you name the mountain, he will name the fee.

Like a mighty army, faithfully we plod,
  Treading in the footsteps Bonington has trod.
From the Direttissima loud Hosannas! ring—
  Grave, where is thy victory, O death, where is thy sting?
Onward, C. . . . B. . . . , joyfully we sing,
  Down with McNaught-Davis, Bonington for King.

Live transmission will commence shortly after ten
  From the Kleine Scheidegg and the Alpi-Glen.
Do not miss this spectacle, you can watch for free:
  Bonington is on the wall, Tune in on B.B.C.
Onward, C. . . . B. . . . of the B.B.C.
  Fighting for survival, and a token fee.

When they climbed the Eigerwand, those two gallant men
  They received a message (sent) from Number Ten:
Well done chaps, Macmillan said, Victory was your due;
  Well done, C. . . . B. . . . the Führer's proud of you—
Onward, C. . . . B. . . . , hallowed be thy name,
  Digging out a belay in the halls of fame.

THE JOHN HARLIN SONG

It was on a winter's morning
High upon the Eigerwand
That John Harlin died in glory
Climbing for the Fatherland.

Cutting fiercely up the ice field
With his second close at hand
And his second was Bonatti
Second greatest in the land

Harlin's leepers, rurps and bong-bongs
Could not pierce the mighty face
So Bonatti cried "Finito"
He had failed to last the pace.

When he heard this sorry statement
From his comrade down below
With a voice that crashed like thunder
Big John Harlin answered "No".

All alone upon the Spider
With a skyhook in his hand
Big John Harlin climbed to glory
Martyred on the Murderwand.

Tightly lashed to his last bong-bong
(The) "Golden God" was near the end
So the Lord in all his wisdom
One death angel he did send.

Now he's on his last Blue Mountain
But his corpse is on the wall
From the shadows of the Eiger
You can hear his mocking call.

Another soul sent to Valhalla
Another murder for the Wall
On the Eigerwand in winter
Is the hardest climb of all.

So take heed Bergkameraden
Do not venture on the face
For the spectre of John Harlin
Waits for you to take his place.

THE MANCHESTER DELINQUENT'S SONG
Tune: I'm a rambler, I'm a rambler from Manchester Way

I'm a teenage delinquent from Manchester Way
I'm anti-social, I like it that way
I bask 'neath the high crags on Sunday
And skive at my work bench on Monday.

I throw stones at hikers and good motor bikers
And hide where the heather lies deep
I listen for moans, I chuck little stones
Down the grey rocks so rugged and steep
'Tis said that the screams of the dying
Would drive many men round the bend
But I pull the ropes, that hang down to the slopes
Just to see who's tied on to the end.

When I'm in the Gwryd my language is lurid
The landlord is pregnant with gloom
I've soiled his amenities and scribbled obscenities
All over the Everest Room.
There's some men who work for a living
They tell me its good for the soul
But I measure pleasure in man hours of leisure
My life's very sweet on the dole.

Oh climbing instruction and the art of seduction
Are closely allied you will find
For climbers have scruples, when choosing their pupils
They only take payment in kind.
There is one sure means of disposal
Its proof against any protest
We tie special bowlines round unwanted frauleins
And Nature takes care of the rest.

I once wooed a maid a meat grinder by trade
We had several theories to prove
And my little cutie said her course of duty
Was taking the rough with the smooth
They say that its time I was married
Or even just climbing instead
But if I must die on the mountains I loathe
I'd much rather perish in bed.

I'm a teenage delinquent, my lapses are frequent
They say that I'll never make good
But all my obsessions are merely repressions
Its just that I'm misunderstood
They say I should work for a living
They tell me its good for the soul
But I measure pleasure in man hours of leisure
Life is so sweet on the dole.

When I hear them calling that somebody's falling
I'm always the first to react
I shout to the man "Just hang on if you can
While I get my camera unpacked".
You've seen the wild hare in the gulleys
His antics are wholly absurd
Compared to the sight and the poetry in flight
Of man taking wing like a bird.

THE SQUIRRELS' SONG

She was poor but she was honest
Victim of a Squirrel's whim
First he loved her, then he left her
And she lost her honest name.

So she booked a room at ——
For to hide her grief and shame
There she met another Squirrel
And she lost her name again.

See her in the Squirrels' dosshouse
On a squalid heap of hay
Where the hard men and the hoboes
Come to pass the time of day.

In young Brian's arms she flutters
Like a bird with broken wing
She has got a karabiner
But she wants a wedding ring.

See him with another Tufty
Running gaily down the scree
While the victim of his passions
Brews a humble pot of tea.

Standing on the bridge at midnight
He remarked, with gentle touch
"There is Romance in the Mountains"
She replied "Too Bloody Much!"

It's the same the whole world over
It's the Tufties get the blame
It's the Squirrels get the pleasure
Ain't it all a bleeding shame?

THE PEOPLE'S CRAG
Tune: The Red Flag

The People's Crag is deepest Red
It's cushioned oft our falling dead
And broken ropes, upon the slopes
Are symbols of our shattered hopes
But raise the piton hammer high
Upon this crag we'll do or die
Though leaders fall and seconds peel
We'll raise the standard higher still!

British climbers are the best
Conquerors of Everest
British climbers never fall
In the Andes or Nepal
Raise your alpenstocks on high,
British Climbers never die,
Ever onwards, never rest
Climbing up Mount Everest

THE LAST OF THE GRAND OLD MASTERS

Tune: Carnival of Venice or My Hat, it Has Three Corners

As I strayed in the shade of the Buachaille
One cold and wintry day
I trod on a bod in a bog-hole
'Twas a climber old and grey.

"Now why do you lie 'neath the Buachaille?"
I asked that man of clay
With a curse and a mirthless chuckle
He to me these words did say:
"I'm the last of the Grand Old Masters
The Tigers of Yesterday
When the March of Progress passed us
We were left to Fade Away.

I was down with Joe Brown in Llanberis
When first he made his name;
With Brian, the Lion of Nevis
Set all Lochaber aflame.

Joe Brown lost his crown to another,
Though the legend lives on as before
And Brian the Lion is muzzled—
For him it's Lochaber, No More.

MacInnes has finished with pitons,
The Message won't ring any more;
Doug Haston has passed on his crampons
To Tiso's Alpine Store.

Now the Creag Dhu just make do with Moderates
Or maybe Curved Ridge in the Snow;
Jim Marshall's in partial retirement
And recording his hundredth Munro.

Lay me out on the pitiless Nordwand
Where the bivouac sites are few—
Alone—with a stone for a pillow
And an uninterrupted view.

I've had ale by the pail in the Kingshouse
Tried anything once for a laugh
I've played with a maid at Glenbrittle
And gambled in Lagangarbh.

Now the beer's far too dear in the Kingshouse
There's no one will stand me 'a half'
There's a shortage of maids in Glenbrittle
And the Police have closed down Lagangarbh.

Oh six stalwart climbers from Currie
Shall write me an epitaph drab
With a text from the works of Bill Murray
Writ in gold on a grey granite slab.

I'm the Last of the Grand Old Masters
But now I am old and grey
When the sweat on my neck turns to verglas
You will find I have passed away."

So passed on the Last of the Masters
To that far and distant shore
With two golden wings for a passport
He won't need his pegs any more.

On the pitiless slabs of the Nordwand
Where the bivouac sites are few
The Ghosts of the hosts of Old Masters
Are calling this warning to you:

Live it up, fill your cup, drown your sorrow
And sow your wild oats while ye may
For the toothless old tykes of tomorrow
Were the Tigers of Yesterday.

INDEX OF CLIMBERS AND CLUBS

INDEX OF CLIMBS